Practical ENGINE Airflow

John Baechtel

CarTech®

CarTech®

CarTech®, Inc.
838 Lake Street South
Forest Lake, MN 55025
Phone: 651-277-1200 or 800-551-4754
Fax: 651-277-1203
www.cartechbooks.com

© 2015 by John Baechtel

All rights reserved. No part of this publication may be reproduced or utilized in any form or by any means, electronic or mechanical, including photocopying, recording, or by any information storage and retrieval system, without prior permission from the Publisher. All text, photographs, and artwork are the property of the Author unless otherwise noted or credited.

The information in this work is true and complete to the best of our knowledge. However, all information is presented without any guarantee on the part of the Author or Publisher, who also disclaim any liability incurred in connection with the use of the information and any implied warranties of merchantability or fitness for a particular purpose. Readers are responsible for taking suitable and appropriate safety measures when performing any of the operations or activities described in this work.

All trademarks, trade names, model names and numbers, and other product designations referred to herein are the property of their respective owners and are used solely for identification purposes. This work is a publication of CarTech, Inc., and has not been licensed, approved, sponsored, or endorsed by any other person or entity. The Publisher is not associated with any product, service, or vendor mentioned in this book, and does not endorse the products or services of any vendor mentioned in this book.

Layout by Monica Seiberlich

ISBN 978-1-61325-524-7
Item No. SA308P

Library of Congress Cataloging-in-Publication Data
Names: Baechtel, John, author.
Title: Practical engine airflow: performance theory & application / John Baechtel.
Description: Forest Lake, MN: CarTech, [2015] |.
Identifiers: LCCN 2015017927 | ISBN 9781613251577
Subjects: LCSH: Automobiles--Motors--Design and construction. | Automobiles, Racing--Performance. | Internal combustion engines--Fluid dynamics. | Gas flow.
Classification: LCC TL210 .B285 2015 | DDC 629.25--dc23
LC record available at http://lccn.loc.gov/2015017927

Written, edited, and designed in the U.S.A.
Printed in U.S.A.
10 9 8 7 6 5 4 3 2

Title Page:
A similar choke point exists on the exhaust side. It also represents the minimum cross section and typically has a larger radius to encourage smooth exhaust flow, which exits under high pressure.

Back Cover Photos

Top Left:
The throat area immediately above the valveseat is the controlling factor in airflow efficiency. Maximum velocity across the valve should be generated here.

Top Right:
Cylinder heads are the most influential component of an internal combustion engine. They are the gatekeeper that regulates the amount and quality of the air/fuel mixture entering the engine.

Bottom Left:
Naturally aspirated applications typically require much more flow-bench work to extract maximum performance for each application. Experience pays off, but it still may require long hours of trial and error. (Photo Courtesy Smithberg Racing)

Bottom Right:
Modifying port entry angles via specific port matching produces power. The match between the runner exit and the intake port entry should be almost seamless with no sharp edges or area change. Epoxy filling is sometimes required to accomplish the smooth finish. (Photo Courtesy Wilson Manifolds)

OVERSEAS DISTRIBUTION BY:

PGUK
63 Hatton Garden
London EC1N 8LE, England
Phone: 020 7061 1980 • Fax: 020 7242 3725
www.pguk.co.uk

Renniks Publications Ltd.
3/37-39 Green Street
Banksmeadow, NSW 2109, Australia
Phone: 2 9695 7055 • Fax: 2 9695 7355
www.renniks.com

CONTENTS

Dedication 4
Acknowledgments 5
Introduction 5

Chapter 1: Airflow Basics 7
  Airflow Path 7
  The Seven Cycles to Max Power 9
  Torque and Horsepower 20
  Volumetric Efficiency 24
  Theoretical CFM 26
  Understanding BSFC 26
  Contributing Engine Systems 27

Chapter 2: Relevant Properties of Air 29
  Physical Composition of Air 30
  Mass and Weight 32
  Density 32
  Coping with Variables 33
  The Ideal Gas Laws 35
  Correction Factors 35
  The MSA and the Air Density Index 37
  Density Altitude 37
  Fuel Properties to Consider 39
  Octane Rating 40
  Gasoline Variables 41
  Conclusion 43

Chapter 3: Engine Airflow Components 44
  Fundamentals of Air Motion 45
  Cross Sections and Path Lengths 46
  Carburetors and Throttle Bodies 47
  Air Velocity and Boundary Layers 56
  Obstructions and Pressure Changes 57
  Wave Tuning 57
  Torque Peak RPM 59

Chapter 4: Intake Manifold 60
  Intake Manifold Types 61
  Plenum Characteristics 74
  Mixture Conditioning 76
  Surface Texturing 79
  Reversion 79
  Additional Intake Considerations 81
  Extrude Honing 83
  Flow Testing Intake Manifolds 83

Chapter 5: Cylinder Heads 89
  Component Compatibility 90
  Airflow Control Point 90
  Street versus Race Heads 91
  Where the Power Comes From 93
  Best Racing Combo 94
  Flow Factors 95
  Valves and Valve Sizes 95
  Evaluating Cylinder Head Potential 97
  Piston CFM Demand 100
  Critical Valve Transitions 102
  Bore Size 102
  Port Taper 103

Chapter 6: Combustion Chambers 104
  Cylinder Filling and Pressure Recovery 104
  Combustion Power and Efficiency 106
  Chamber Types 108
  Chamber Flow Concerns 110
  Chamber Texture 112
  Valve Shrouding 112

Chapter 7: Exhaust System 114
  Pressure Wave Tuning 114
  Flow Path Disruptions 116
  Exhaust Flow Tuning 116
  Power Adders 118
  Exhaust Port Surface Texture 120
  Valve Shape and Angle 121

Chapter 8: Flow-Bench Testing 122
  What Is a Flow Bench? 122
  Consider Application Differences 123
  Flow-Bench Information 124
  Flow-Bench Limitations 127
  Calculating Lift-to-Diameter Ratios 131
  Calculating Valve Curtain Area 132
  Flow-Bench Tools 134

Chapter 9: Practical Applications 139
  Begin with a Software Program 139
  Air Filters 143
  Carburetors and Throttle Bodies 143
  Intake Manifolds 144
  Cylinder Heads 145
  The Exhaust Side 146

Conclusion 158
Source Guide 160

DEDICATION

To Louie Hammel

My amazing friend Louie Hammel had a fondness for the impossible, frequently offering simple yet profound quips about engine performance that made you stop and think and, more important, imagine. Louie suffered for many years from the debilitating effects of leukemia and has since passed on, but I will always remember the day he looked at me and said, "You know, I'm an engine guy and when I die I want to be cremated and have one of you guys pour my ashes through the carburetor on a screaming high-RPM big-block on the dyno so I can watch all this stuff we talk about first hand."

Unfortunately Louie never achieved his goal, but I often wish he had because his reports from the other side would have been awesome and unquestionably accurate. He always wanted a personalized license plate that read TORQUE, and he had a million ideas about ways to generate it and improve engine performance. Although I was busy with a career at *Hot Rod* and *Car Craft* magazines, Louie honed his skills testing and developing parts in the dyno rooms at Edelbrock and later became a researcher and dyno technician at McFarland, Inc., evaluating and developing high-performance components for Jim McFarland.

Later, after Louie became sick, he used to come by my dyno shop in the afternoons and weekends and we would bench race engine tech and theory endlessly. Whenever something stumped us, we immediately thought to "ask Louie," whereupon he addressed our question with the thoughtful power of his amazing intellect. That made some people jealous, but he only sought to offer well-thought-out opinions, and he usually had a perfectly good explanation that solved our problem.

Louie was no poser. He never cared if he impressed anyone or what others thought of his ideas. He thought well beyond that and was truly immersed in the magic of engine performance and, in particular, the science of engine airflow. If I've learned anything over all these years, much of it came from Louie's remarkably thoughtful questions and subsequent discourse on said matters. Many of us miss Louie even to this day and can't forget the remarkable impression he left on us. And thus I dedicate this book to him, an exceptionally observant and knowledgeable man.

Somehow I think he still may have managed to find his way inside a running engine and he is still in there, taking notes and preparing reports for his old friends who still feel the need to "ask Louie." R.I.P., buddy.

This photo was shot at Jim McFarland's think tank R&D shop in Torrance, California, in the early 1990s before Louie was diagnosed with leukemia. That's an early GM ZZZ engine on the dyno. Left to right: Kevin McClelland, Rod Sokoloski, Louie Hammel, Keith Rudolph, and Jim McFarland.

ACKNOWLEDGMENTS

Resources are the lifeblood of any tech book. Without them an author could never pull together all the relevant information that applies to the subject of the book. Very few authors can write this stuff off the top of their head. It takes a concerted effort and the unfailing cooperation of numerous people who also have lives, jobs, and other things to do. Sometimes they forget or take longer than expected, but they come through in the end and their contributions lend substance to the book. Many people contributed to this book by necessity as I am far from an expert on the nuances of engine airflow. Each of them has my profound gratitude for the effort they expended.

Patrick Hale was my chief supporter and sounding board and, as I requested of him and everyone else, he pulled no punches when pointing out errors and inaccuracies. At the same time he contributed valuable input and commentary that was helpful beyond measure. The same can be said for Darin Morgan at Reher-Morrison Racing Engines whose intimate knowledge of internal engine passages seems virtually endless. Nick Smithberg at Smithberg Racing provided a wealth of photographic support, knowledgeable content, and the basis for a new and valuable relationship. Jack Kane at EPI, Inc. came through at the last minute with important artwork as did Dave Secunda at Wilson Manifolds, Jeff from Rottler Manufacturing, and Byron Wright at Thorpe Development. Mike Lefevers of Mitech Racing Engines contributed numerous photos and John Kyros of the GM Media Archives came through once again with critical historical photos.

I learned important philosophies from acknowledged experts such as Kenny Duttweiler, Jim McFarland, Larry Meaux, Chuck Jenckes, and many others. My admiration and heartfelt thanks to all of them.

Engine airflow is a complex subject. My intent is to provide a solid foundation of airflow characteristics that everyone can work from to advance their own projects. The fundamentals are pretty much set in stone, but their consistent application is crucial to making big power.

INTRODUCTION

This is a book about airflow through internal combustion (IC) engines, more specifically high-performance and racing engines. All the fundamentals of IC engine operation apply, but the chief concern is with the movement of air through an engine in the most efficient manner to produce optimal cylinder filling (volumetric efficiency) and maximum output in the form of tire-shredding power, or torque. It's not an engineering text, although engineering content and appropriate lingo are included where necessary along with input and commentary from recognized experts in the field. It's not a math book, although some mathematical equations are provided so you can learn how to calculate the values of various functions.

It *is* a book for performance enthusiasts eager to gain a fundamental knowledge of engine airflow and how it affects the operation and output of high-performance engines. My intent is to help build your general knowledge of core principles to help you select components that best suit the requirements of your specific application whether it is a hot street machine, bracket racer, road racer, or whatever.

Without discounting the necessary core physics of IC engines and the fundamentals of gas exchange that characterize engine performance, I begin with the assumption that performance-oriented readers already possess a basic understanding of four-cycle engine operation and the well-established reality that engine airflow is the key path to maximum power.

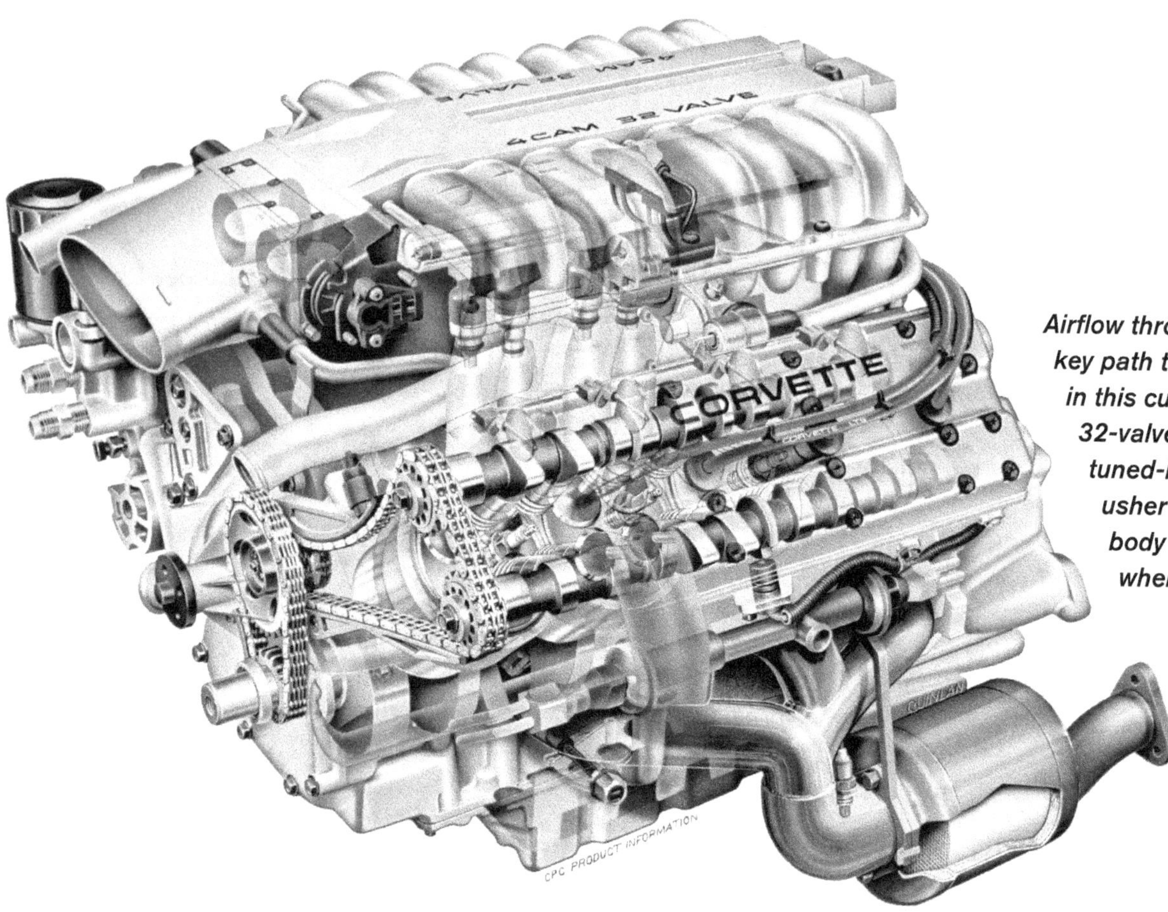

INTRODUCTION

Airflow through an engine is the key path to power. As illustrated in this cutaway of an earlier 32-valve Corvette LT1 V-8, tuned-length flow paths usher air from the throttle body inlet to the cylinder where it is burned with fuel and discharged via a tuned exhaust system. More air mixed with more fuel equals more power. (Photo Courtesy GM Media Archive)

A small-block hot rod with a single 4-barrel carb, or a small-displacement blower, and a good exhaust system is a great recipe for hot street performance. Beyond that, the bar continues to rise based on the fundamental requirement to put more and more air through the engine to increase output.

Tri-power carburetion featuring a trio of 2-barrel carburetors was a popular early induction choice for moving more air. Most muscle car versions used Holley 2-barrel carbs, but traditional hot rods are typically fed by 350-cfm Rochester carbs with progressive linkage (shown).

CHAPTER 1

AIRFLOW BASICS

Everyone has heard the traditional analogy that an engine is nothing more than a basic air pump, a very sophisticated air pump. In effect, a running engine provides continuously recurring spaces, or power volumes (cylinders), into which air flows due to atmospheric pressure or, in some cases, pressurizing sources such as superchargers and turbochargers. These spaces are essentially empty voids (vacuum) created by descending piston motion. They have negative pressure relative to atmospheric pressure and the atmosphere automatically seeks to fill them through the intake flow paths as each volume is created. The engine is not specifically pumping air, but rather mechanically providing an ongoing series of pressure differentials that encourage air movement through the engine's inlet flow paths. Air movement, or transfer, is similar to the pumping action; hence, it is referred to as intake pumping.

Airflow Path

Every time a piston descends on an intake stroke it creates a cylinder filling and fueling opportunity. This occurs on every other revolution of the crankshaft for each cylinder in the engine. The dynamics of this are extraordinarily complicated on a thermodynamic level and yet simple enough that even when things are pretty far out of whack, the engine still runs and drives comfortably in everyday vehicles. The descending piston creates a void, or space, that atmospheric pressure immediately attempts to fill when the intake valve opens because it is greater than the pressure in the empty cylinder.

The sucking sound you hear at the carburetor is the air rushing in to fill the void. It follows a torturous path through a venturi where it gains speed and mass because fuel is being added. Then it exits the carburetor throttle bores at high speed

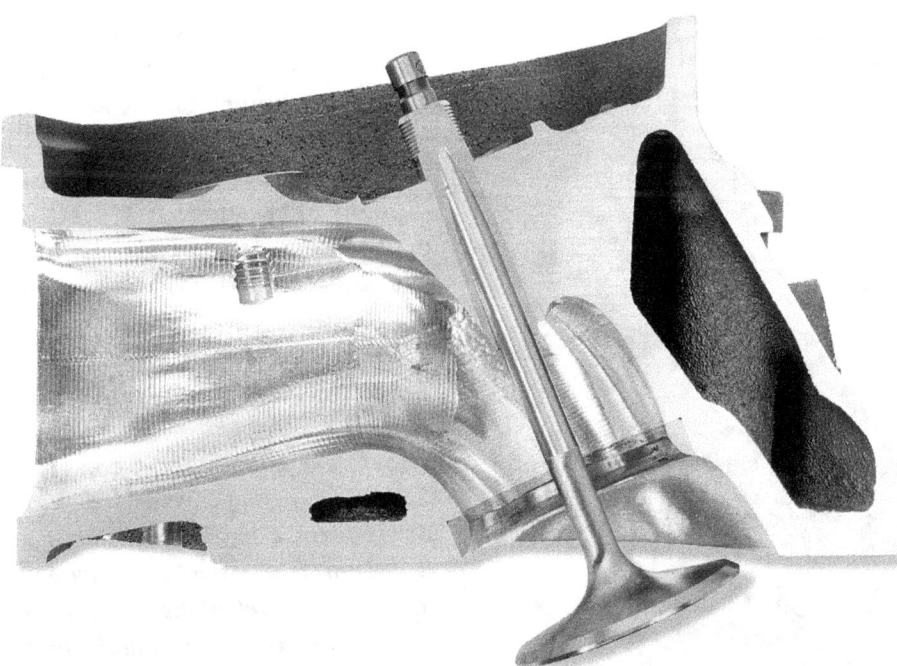

The intake valve in the cylinder head feeds fresh air to each cylinder for every new combustion event. The size, shape, and configuration of the intake port play a major role in how much air you can feed the engine to increase power.

CHAPTER 1

This factory cutaway of a 1950s Chevrolet 348-ci W-engine shows the inlet path from the carburetor to the cylinder on the driver's side and a portion of the exhaust path on the passenger's side. Not much has changed since then. The flow path starts at the air filter and can be traced all the way through the engine to the end of the exhaust pipe (not shown). (Photo Courtesy GM Media Archive)

into a larger staging area, or plenum. The dramatic change in area causes the air to lose velocity quickly, and the local pressure changes. This change presents the first opportunity for the atomized fuel to drop out of suspension.

The next cylinder in the firing order submits a filling request by exposing the empty cylinder via the opening intake valve. The mixture immediately seeks to fill the void in that cylinder by rushing into an intake runner where it picks up velocity and regains some pressure due to the smaller cross-sectional area of the runner. On its way to the intake valve, the mixture may experience a variety of obstacles and area changes that affect its speed and flow characteristics. Curved runners and intake ports that narrow around the pushrod area restrict flow. In a sense, runner taper (see Chapter 4) restricts the flow, but it builds

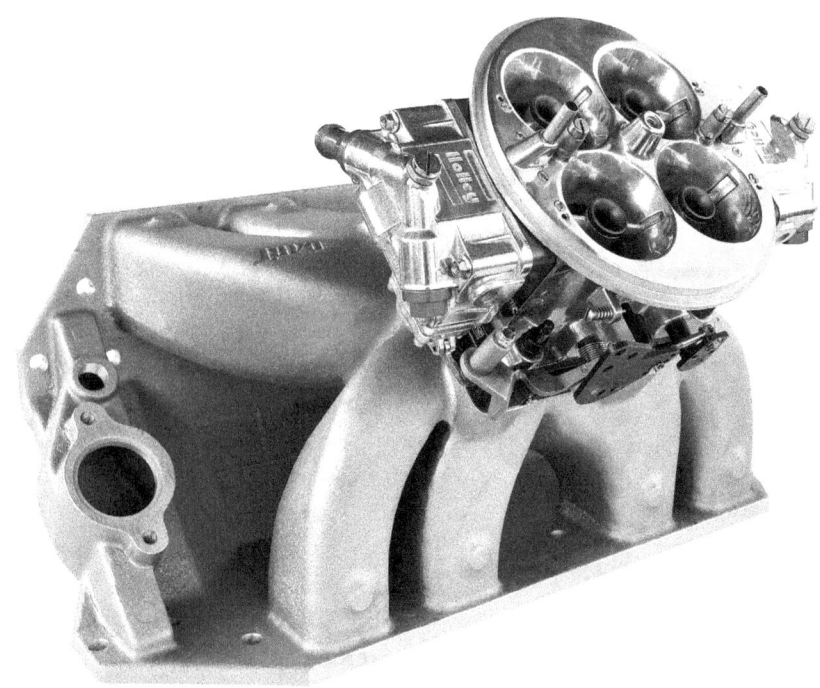

Most street engines and a great many Sportsman racing classes still rely on single-plane 4-barrel intake manifolds to support their induction requirements. Individual intake runners connect to a common central plenum. The intakes are typically outfitted with various-capacity Holley 4-barrel carburetors to suit their high-RPM operating range.

AIRFLOW BASICS

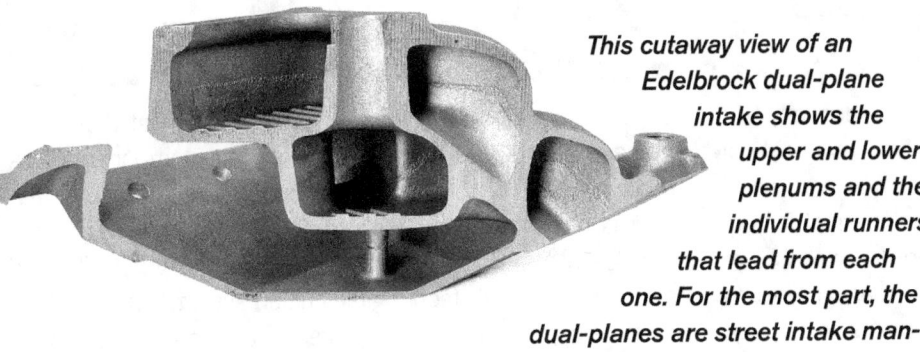

This cutaway view of an Edelbrock dual-plane intake shows the upper and lower plenums and the individual runners that lead from each one. For the most part, the dual-planes are street intake manifolds that build more low-end and mid-range torque than single-plane intakes because they help produce more efficient low-speed flow velocity. In some cases, the dual-plane intake can outperform single-plane intakes throughout the operating range while nearly matching them on the top end.

pressure and velocity, which encourages the intake ramming process.

After negotiating various curves in the manifold, the air may stumble at the gasket interface between the manifold and the cylinder head; this point is rarely an efficient transition unless steps are taken to ensure it. Then the air has to make a relatively sharp turn into the bowl area above the valve where it is interrupted by the valvestem and valveguide. Finally, it has to negotiate its way around the valve and into the cylinder, where it experiences a radical pressure change as it loses velocity. The throat area at the valve is typically the point of greatest restriction, which is why bowl porting is often so beneficial to stock heads.

During each of these phases, the air follows the path of least resistance, primarily influenced by the various shapes, sizes, area changes, obstructions, and surface textures it is exposed to along the way. In a fixed-configuration cylinder head (commercially available) you can take steps to influence the air. This is loosely referred to as porting, and it can make a considerable difference depending on the original layout of a particular cylinder head. Some heads respond better than others, primarily based on the shape and cross-sectional area of the port, configuration (raised or flat), relationship of the valve throat size to the valve size, and other things.

A combination of intake pumping, intake ramming, and wave tuning make up the cylinder filling process. Air rushes in because it is under pressure (atmospheric). The air can achieve considerable flow velocity because the intake path is very small relative to the larger source of air pressure (the atmosphere). This imparts inertia to the air. Fuel molecules rush to fill the void created by the descending piston. Depending on the stroke and the rod length, the piston reaches its maximum velocity somewhere around 75 to 76 degrees after top dead center (TDC). This point corresponds to the maximum velocity of the intake charge moving down the flow path. In a properly sized inlet path, the column of inlet air and fuel achieve enough momentum to continue filling the cylinder even though the piston has reached bottom dead center (BDC) and is beginning to rise.

At this point, the intake valve is still open, but starting to close. Resistance to flow begins to increase, but charge energy briefly overcomes it. This is the intake-ramming phenomenon that is largely controlled by piston motion and the length and cross section of the inlet flow path. It is the most important part of the cylinder filling process because it offers the potential for additional cylinder filling beyond the regular intake pumping process.

But it is only part of a broader seven-cycle process as described many years ago by Patrick Hale in his *Engine Pro: The Book*, a detailed tech manual that originally accompanied the Engine Pro simulation software he designed. (In 2007 Hale sold the copyright for Engine Pro, his other software programs, and the book to Don Terrell, the founder of speedtalk.com and racingsecrets.com.) The seven-cycle process (also called the horsepower chain) is now broadly recognized and largely adhered to within the performance community.

The Seven Cycles to Max Power

To reinforce the critical importance of engine airflow, note that top engine simulation programs such as Hale's original Engine Pro software focus heavily on calculating engine airflow and volumetric efficiency (VE). Sophisticated, modern electronic fuel injection (EFI) systems use similar input from the mass airflow (MAF) sensor to make the proper VE and tuning calculations for optimal performance relative to engine speed and load. EFI is so efficient because it knows the condition of the air mass as it moves through the engine and can provide the proper fueling calculations for maximum efficiency. It also monitors the air leaving the engine to help it determine the proper air/fuel ratio and the efficiency of the combustion event.

CHAPTER 1

Internal Combustion Fundamentals

The basic requirements of internal combustion (IC) engines are complex, particularly from the chemical and thermodynamic standpoints. From a less complicated perspective, we all understand the physical factors that characterize the process. Simply stated, the well-known breathe, squeeze, pop, and sneeze make the magic based on the available air/fuel supply and a throttling device to manage engine speed.

A basic understanding of the process requires that you recognize the following core contributors to the engine power equation:

- Airflow
- Fuel supply
- Flow paths
- Compression
- Ignition source
- Throttling device
- Containment device (cylinders)

Among these key factors airflow is the most difficult to manage. Thanks to modern performance components it is relatively easy to feed the engine enough fuel. And compression is easy to achieve with the advanced sealing characteristics of modern piston ring technology. Lighting it off is also easy with high-tech digital ignition systems while various carburetor and throttle body systems easily manage throttling concerns. Although complex thermodynamic and chemical processes govern the efficiency of all this, you don't necessarily require too keen a grasp of the deeper science to understand airflow through the engine and the various elements that tend to resist air motion and subsequent cylinder filling.

At this point, you are not yet concerned with air/fuel mixture quality, but simply the overall definition and efficiency of the flow path from the atmosphere above the air cleaner to the atmosphere behind the tailpipe. Pressure and velocity changes that occur along the entire flow path play a pivotal role in governing engine output. There are many ways to influence and alter an engine's air movement and the various forms of resistance that dictate its efficiency. ■

The carburetor is the traditional self-compensating fueling device that mixes air and fuel in the proper proportion and feeds the mix to the engine via the intake flow path, which consists of the intake runners and the intake ports.

Electronic fuel injectors come in various sizes to accommodate engine displacement and horsepower ratings. High-performance systems usually have the injectors in the intake runners.

High-performance electronic fuel-injected applications typically incorporate a large single throttle body or a four-hole unit that passes only air because the fuel injectors introduce the fuel.

AIRFLOW BASICS

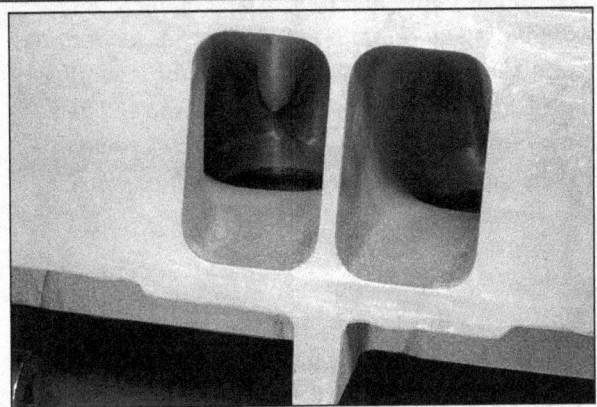

The intake port is the flow path that directs the air/fuel mixture into the engine. It is the primary influence on engine performance.

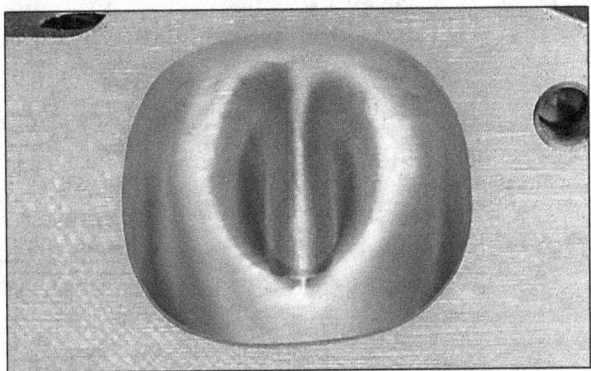

The exhaust port is always smaller so that the high cylinder pressure helps evacuate the cylinder after the combustion event.

Valve size and placement relative to the bore size, particularly the throat-diameter-to-valve-diameter ratio, determine the effectiveness of the port and its ability to turn the air into the cylinder with the smoothest possible flow.

The combustion space incorporates the combustion chamber, piston top (at TDC), intake and exhaust valves, spark plug, and a fuel injector if the engine incorporates direct injection.

The carburetor (or throttle body) is also the throttling device that regulates engine speed and power output via butterfly valves that vary air delivery to the engine. A throttle linkage connected to the gas pedal operates the butterflies.

PRACTICAL ENGINE AIRFLOW

CHAPTER 1

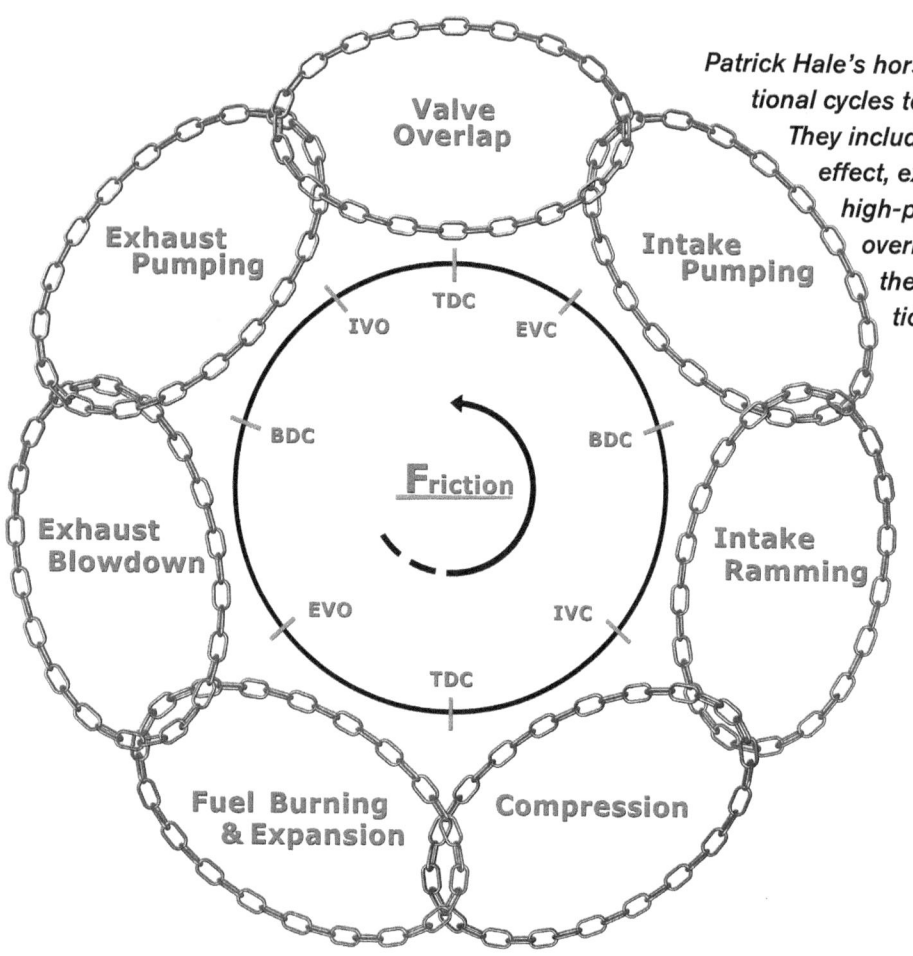

Patrick Hale's horsepower chain introduced three additional cycles to the traditional four-cycle engine model. They include intake ramming from the charge inertia effect, exhaust blowdown to account for the initial high-pressure exhaust evacuation, and the valve overlap period as a significant cycle affecting the intake and exhaust relationship. (Illustration Courtesy Scott Lozano)

Our task as engine builders is remarkably similar. We want to understand the air mass condition and the various influences that act on it so we can manipulate it to improve efficiency and power output in the power range most useful to our application.

Air moving through a running engine experiences a dramatic series of pressure changes before it finally exits the tailpipe and returns to atmospheric pressure. The seven cycles, or processes, identified by Hale define these pressure changes and how they combine to produce torque and horsepower. If you follow the air pump analogy and also think of the engine as an air processor, you can more accurately understand the major steps used to create power:

1. Intake pumping
2. Intake ramming
3. Compression
4. Fuel burning and expansion (power stroke)
5. Exhaust blowdown
6. Exhaust pumping
7. Valve overlap

The traditional four cycles are 1, 3, 4, and 6 on this list. These are what you have always had to work with, but as Hale points out, the major gains in engine output come from working with the three additional cycles that exert enormous influence on the overall process.

You must also consider the negative pumping effects that accompany these processes, including the cumulative consequences of friction, mixture compression, and airflow resistance (more commonly referred to as pumping losses). Resistance to the motion of the rotating assembly and the free movement of air through the engine are also primary culprits. The air does not specifically require pumping except in the case of supercharged applications designed to boost and improve the normal characteristics of atmospheric cylinder filling, or natural aspiration. Instead, it reacts to pressure changes to fill the cylinders.

One of the most important factors of the seven cycles is the close interrelationship among them. Each cycle represents a specific process inexorably linked and influenced by the cycle before it and the one following it. In Hale's words, "The output from one process defines the input for the next." They are inseparable. Each process affects the next in an unbroken circle or, as Hale calls them, links in the horsepower chain. It takes two revolutions of the crankshaft (720 degrees) of rotation to complete the seven processes for each cylinder. And then it begins again. Each process must be fully optimized to ensure maximum performance from the engine.

A fault, or less than optimal performance, from each process affects every subsequent cycle and degrades the power process. Hence the inputs and outputs and what you do with them within each process define how well your engine performs within its operating environment.

As Hale indicates, each of the processes adheres to a different set of physics. You can only manipulate their performance by changing the shapes, sizes, and various interactions of the components that make up the overall engine.

For example, commercial exhaust headers are by necessity a compromise based on a broad range of engine sizes and requirements. Header size and length are largely determined by what fits a specific engine and chassis combination. It's up to the engine builder to calculate and select the correct sizes. And to be honest, any full racing effort uses custom-built headers specifically tailored to that particular engine's requirements and operational characteristics. If the wrong headers are used many links of the chain become compromised and less than optimal performance occurs.

If residual exhaust gases remain in the combustion chamber through some failure of the exhaust blowdown or exhaust pumping process, they contaminate the fresh intake charge and seriously degrade the power potential. The contaminated charge then affects the entire process with a resultant power loss. That's why each process must recognize and complement the subsequent process to ensure optimal performance.

The individual seven cycles control the movement of air through the engine and ultimately influence the whole character of an engine's performance potential. It is very important to visualize their effect on the high-speed air column as it moves through the engine. These cycles influence the airflow resulting from pressure changes that lead to superior power output.

Intake Pumping

The intake pumping process begins when the exhaust valve closes (EVC). This event initiates during the valve overlap period and slightly

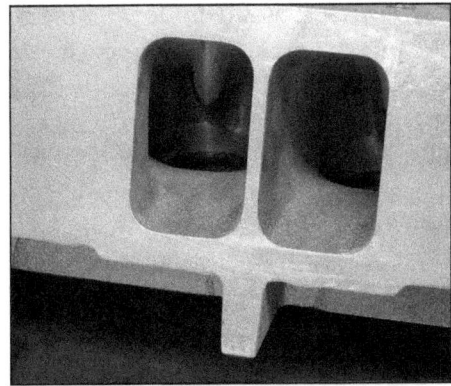

High-velocity air in the intake ports gains inertia to help ram-fill the cylinder above and beyond that achievable by normal pressure recovery. This creates the ramming effect that Hale calls "intake ramming." (Photo Courtesy Smithberg Racing)

after TDC. At this point the intake valve has also opened (IVO). The intake valve is accelerating toward its full-open position. The piston is descending at some given rate dictated by the stroke and rod length, typically faster with shorter rods and slower with longer rods. In either

In Hale's description, the descending piston (center) creates a depression (or low pressure) above the piston that tugs on the intake charge the hardest, somewhere in the neighborhood of 76 degrees after TDC. At this point air is rushing to fill the cylinder at maximum velocity. At BDC (left) the successful ramming process is still packing the cylinder to a density that exceeds the cylinder's physical capacity, and pressure begins to rise prior to any actual compression activity. When the exhaust valve opens the cylinder is still under high pressure and the initial blowdown is very rapid. Following that, the piston pushes the remaining charge out of the cylinder as it once again rises to TDC (right).

case, this exposes cylinder volume to the intake port at some particular rate and offers a filling opportunity. The highest demand (or draw) typically occurs about 75 to 76 degrees after TDC, where the piston achieves its highest velocity (speed), thus creating the lowest pressure in the cylinder.

The piston descends and the intake valve opens farther, the flow rate (velocity x area) increases until the valve reaches maximum lift at about 108 degrees after TDC. This is the intake pumping process, or the rapid transfer of the air/fuel mixture into the cylinder in pumping fashion. It ends when the piston reaches BDC at the bottom of the stroke and begins to reverse direction.

Thus begins the opening cycle of the traditional four-stroke internal combustion process. At this point, the intake valve is still open.

As Hale said, the output of each process affects the input of the next process. In this case excessive camshaft overlap (during the valve overlap process) can allow residual exhaust gases from the still open exhaust valve to contaminate the fresh incoming charge from the intake valve. This means that the exhaust blowdown and exhaust pumping cycle has inadequately evacuated the spent cylinder gases or that valve overlap needs to be lessened to accommodate the inadequate scavenging effect.

It is exceedingly difficult to manage the pressure changes: when they begin, when they end, and what happens as they change. In the presence of fixed piston motion, you can only alter valve timing or intake/exhaust flow characteristics to control each of the seven cycles.

An ideal intake pumping process begins at EVC and ends when the piston briefly stops at BDC. Assuming a 100-percent fresh-intake charge, no contamination can occur once the exhaust valve closes. Under ideal conditions, the intake pumping process ends with the piston at BDC, and the same 100-percent fresh charge occupies the specific swept volume of the cylinder at atmospheric pressure and temperature, give or take some heat contributed by the hot cylinder.

This cylinder filling scenario achieves a VE of more than 100 percent because the clearance volume (chamber) is also filled with 100-percent undiluted charge. The simplest description is an 11:1 compression ratio where the clearance volume is 10 percent of the swept volume. The ideal result is a VE of 110 percent.

Unfortunately, some conditions resist our efforts to fill the cylinder adequately, and these are the problems we address as engine builders. A few of the engine features that affect the intake pumping process include:

- Intake port flow capacity
- Carburetor and intake manifold runner steady-flow characteristics
- Degree of influence of restrictions
- Maximum piston velocity and camshaft timing
- Charge contamination during the overlap period

Intake port flow capacity must be measured on a flow bench at a high pressure drop and at the mid to high valve lifts that you intend to run, which might be established by modeling or consultation with your cam designer.

Carburetor and intake manifold runner steady-flow characteristics are best determined by the average plenum (manifold) pressure during intake pumping, although that's difficult to accomplish on the front end. Many builders often extrapolate by flowing the port with the manifold and carburetor attached to determine a more realistic approximation of the flow characteristics. They're simply determining the existing steady-state flow capacity and characteristics of the available flow path.

Finally, the maximum piston velocity and crank angle can be calculated via RPM and rod length-to-stroke ratio so it can be related to camshaft timing. This is done for you in most modeling programs.

With the goal of providing 100-percent VE at BDC plus the clearance volume VE, Hale's work describes VE as a strong predictor of engine speed at both peak torque and peak horsepower. The pumping process is not so much a function of the flow path cross section, but rather a result of the overall intake steady-flow capacity.

Flow-bench measurements are rightly viewed as trend indicators. A flow bench operating at 28 inches of water cannot emulate the same characteristics of a rapidly descending piston, which can easily induce a pressure drop more than double that of the flow-bench capacity. Under more dynamic conditions rapid piston motion results in a very strong tug or "yank" on the intake charge that the flow bench cannot replicate.

Intake Ramming

This cycle accounts for the considerable momentum (inertia) that the intake charge has accumulated during the initial pumping process. As the piston reverses direction at BDC, the intake valve is closing. But the momentum generated by a properly configured flow path continues

Capturing more air at speed via velocity ramming is the primary intent of most air scoops. The racy look is an attractive co-benefit. And, like air cleaners, scoops have evolved into some pretty bizarre shapes in an attempt to slow and direct the air to build even inlet pressure.

A storm is brewing between the air scoop and the header tips on this supercharged dragster engine. Air enters the engine at atmospheric pressure along with the ramming effect at speed. The supercharger compresses it and feeds it through the intake manifold and cylinder head ports to the cylinders where the magic happens. Supercharged drag engines generate a lot of exhaust volume and zoomie headers are the most effective way of passing it through without restriction.

to ram mixture past the valve and into the cylinder, even as the cylinder volume begins to decrease and cylinder pressure begins to increase.

Depending on the flow path characteristics and the strength of the intake column flow volume, it continues filling the cylinder well past BDC. At some point, equilibrium is achieved as rising cylinder pressure finally overcomes the intake charge momentum. Proper valve timing is essential here because the intake-ramming event ends when the intake valve closes (IVC), approximately 60 degrees after BDC.

Intake ramming is an essential component of true performance engines. You might call it VE augmentation. Recall that VE is the ratio of the actual trapped mass in the cylinder at the end of the intake valve event (and the ramming process) to the actual mass of the swept volume of the cylinder at ambient temperature and pressure. The ramming event accounts for VE percentages that often exceed 110 in racing engines. In very high-end engines the additional filling contribution of the ramming event can approach 18 percent with effective wave tuning offering another 2 percent of additional filling capacity. (See page 58 for more information about wave tuning.)

Again, the previous cycle can affect the current cycle. For example, extra-large ports and valves can initially help the intake pumping process, but they kill the subsequent ramming process because they can't build enough velocity to accomplish and sustain it. Port energy simply remains too weak except at very high engine speeds, which may be well out of your particular engine's operational range. It's why oval-port

CHAPTER 1

Influences on Intake Ramming

Engine features that play an important role in the intake ramming process include:

- Precise camshaft timing of IVC and RPM to prevent intake system reversion
- Overall intake runner length
- Intake runner cross section
- Total intake runner volume
- Intake system pressure waves (arriving at the intake valve before valve closing)
- Overall plenum volume
- Intake port flow capacity (as measured at lower pressure drops and low to moderate valve lifts)

Street supercharging has become a mainstream means of providing additional airflow to performance engines. Matt and Debbie Hay's award-winning 1988 Pro-Street Thunderbird sets the bar high with its radical fuel-injected twin-blower setup feeding a 351-ci small-block Ford V-8.

Engines with individual runner induction systems are tuned for a very specific operating range such as that found at Indianapolis. When Chevrolet returned to open-wheel Indy racing in 2002, it brought a 3.5-liter naturally aspirated methanol-burning engine that won 14 of 15 events and captured all three major titles: the driver's championship, manufacturer's championship, and team championship. (Photo Courtesy GM Media Archive)

AIRFLOW BASICS

Chevy big-blocks often outperform big-blocks with larger square-port heads.

Wave tuning can further aid the cylinder filling process. These finite amplitude pressure waves should be timed to arrive at the valve before BDC and again just before IVC to lend their energy to ramming even more intake charge past the valve to increase VE.

Pressure wave timing is largely a function of inlet tract length. Rapidly moving positive and negative pulses traveling back and forth between the valve and the inlet entry carry energy that can be harnessed to push more charge into the cylinder if timed correctly. Opening and closing valves generate a reflected pulse as does a large area change such as found at the inlet entry. When a pulse encounters an area change or closed valve, it reflects back in the opposite direction and changes its energy value, or tense.

For example, a negative pulse encountering a closed valve reflects a positive pressure pulse because of the stacking effect of the air against a closed valve. When that pulse travels back to the inlet entry, it loses energy because of the area change and reflects a weaker negative pulse traveling back to the valve.

The pulses swap phase, if you will, because sometimes they encounter a closed valve and reflect positively while others encounter an open valve and reflect negatively. So the inlet can reflect a positive pulse that can help fill the cylinder. These are very high-speed pulsations, but their timing can be calculated and manipulated according to the length of the flow path. Because they move at supersonic speed you generally have to take advantage of every third or fourth reflection to suit the packaging constraints of the inlet paths.

Inlet path length is typically calculated to take advantage of the third reflected wave for best power. The second wave works well for fuel-injected OEM applications, and most single 4-barrel race engines work best with the fourth wave. Builders no longer need to spend time calculating these lengths because it is done for them in a very affordable (less than 50 bucks) modeling program offered by Larry Meaux called PipeMax. Simply input your engine values and choose the recommended length from the calculated values. More on this later in Chapter 4.

It is important to time the IVC point correctly. We used to refer to it as late intake closing for the purpose of continued filling, but it was never adequately explained that the additional filling occurs because of intake charge inertia, or ramming. Because the piston is now rising and starting to initiate a pressure buildup, you must close the intake valve at the point where the pressure rise in the cylinder equals the pressure of the intake flow to ensure maximum ramming. This is the opposite end of the combined intake events (pumping and ramming).

At the beginning of the filling process, you have the potential for contamination because the intake valve opens before the exhaust valve closes (overlap). At the end of the filling process, you encounter a stalling effect to the flow if the valve is left open too long. Although minimal compression takes place in the early part of the compression stroke, it eventually reaches a point where it overcomes the strength of the incoming charge. This is the point at which you need to close the valve and count your blessings.

The intake ramming process provides the VE increase above 100 percent plus clearance volume. In very refined applications such as a Pro Stock engine, it can approach 130 percent. The momentum effect of the ramming process and the pressure waves that assist it are engine speed dependent and thus most effective at certain engine speeds. Chapter 4 includes a discussion of how the momentum effects of the fast-moving inlet air column affect the flow direction, mixture quality, and pressure recovery characteristics of any particular inlet and combustion chamber combination; this means they must be contemplated as a total system.

Compression

The compression cycle begins at IVC. Prior to this, the piston has already begun to rise, but the intake valve is still open, and there is no appreciable pressure change until the inertia of the intake charge is overcome. Even then it is minimal, but in some cases it's enough to dam up the intake process causing reversion, or the stacking up of the intake column to the point where a cloud of fuel vapor forms above the carburetor entry.

The actual compression event begins after the piston is well on its way up the bore. And it ends before the piston reaches TDC because the spark plug fires at about 35 to 30 degrees before TDC, ending the compression process and initiating the next cycle: the fuel burning and expansion process. Depending on the particular geometry of the slider crank relationship the piston may still be anywhere from 1/8 to 1/4 inch down the bore when the compression process (stroke) ends.

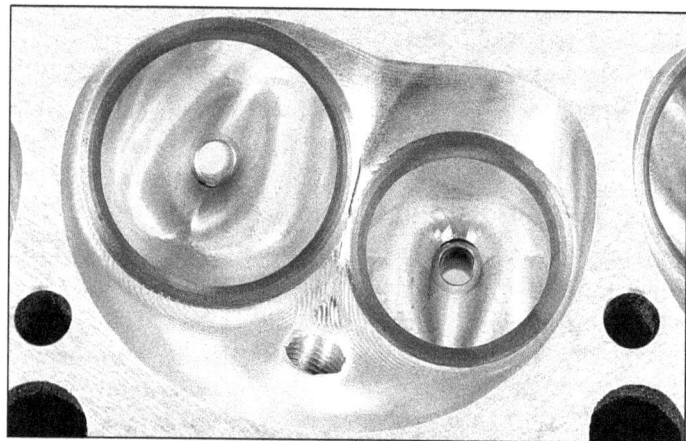
The bowl area below the valve serves as a conditioning space designed to help the flow transition as efficiently as possible around the entire circumference of the valve head. Valve throat diameter and the chamber wall and roof characteristics immediately around the valveseat largely determine the port's flow efficiency.

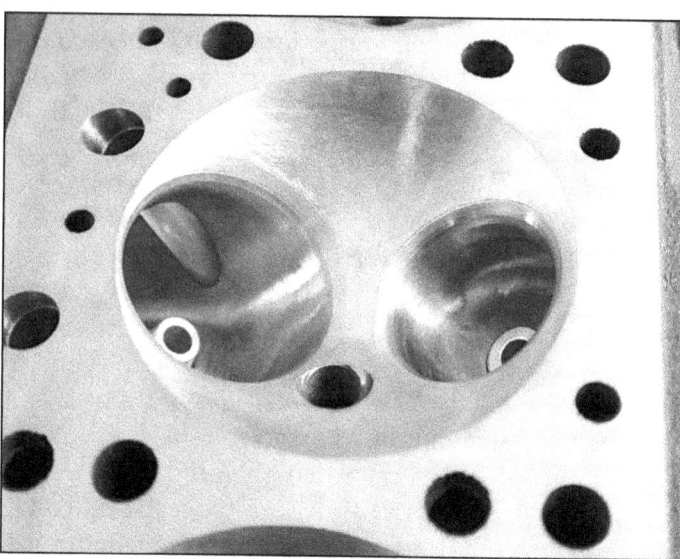
A Hemi head is less susceptible to shrouding because most of the valve circumference is not blocked by adjacent chambers walls as it is in a wedge-type chamber.

Here, the efficiency of the combustion chamber and fast-burn characteristics can affect pumping losses. The plug fires before TDC to give the combustion kernel time to grow and begin building pressure. The earlier the plug fires (more timing, as in 42 degrees before TDC instead of 35 degrees before TDC), the more pressure builds ahead of TDC. Early pressure rise resists piston motion and incurs a pumping loss to overcome the resistance. Modern fast-burn chambers require much less initial spark timing and thus reduce this parasitic characteristic.

The failure of the previous two processes to adequately fill the cylinder most often contributes to the faulty link that can occur in the compression process. Mixture density diminishes, and there is less trapped mass to compress before the firing sequence. It's a vicious circle. If any player on the team stumbles it defeats the whole process and power suffers accordingly.

The compression process is shorter than the actual physical stroke of the crankshaft. That's because it doesn't begin until IVC, and the piston is already part way up the cylinder. It ends when the plug fires, although the piston has not yet reached TDC. As an example, you might say that the compression portion of a 3-inch stroke only involves 2.2 inches of piston travel. These are arbitrary numbers, but you get the idea.

The ideal compression process gains no heat from the cylinder walls and fully stratifies the fuel vapor charge across the entire combustion chamber to achieve optimal combustion. The maximum unfired cylinder pressure (to prevent detonation or pre-ignition) for the fuel type and air/fuel ratio is achieved by piston motion just prior to the plug firing.

A higher static compression ratio translates to higher cylinder pressures depending on the IVC point. You can manipulate the rod-to-stroke ratio to alter piston speed and piston position at IVC. Plus, heat transfer can be partially controlled with thermal coatings, and you can select and modify piston domes and chambers to more favorable configurations to enhance the burn.

Compression Event Influences

Although ideal conditions are difficult to achieve, you can work with the following features to optimize the compression event:

- Static compression ratio
- IVC (determines the effective compression ratio)
- Rod/stroke ratio
- Initial temperature and pressure of the trapped air/fuel mass
- Heat transfer from the piston top, cylinder walls, and combustion chamber
- Piston dome and combustion chamber shapes and characteristics

Custom intakes with tapered runners are used to build pressure and velocity in the inlet flow path. This supports the intake ramming cycle, which relies on charge inertia to continue filling the cylinder. The radiused inlets encourage smooth airflow into each runner.

Fuel Burning and Expansion Cycle

The expansion cycle is the money cycle, as they say, although many argue that the ramming cycle is the most important. The combustion cycle is wholly dependent on the success of the preceding cycles. Its contribution is also influenced by ignition quality and consistency, fuel quality and mixture consistency, chamber efficiency, engine load, cooling, and other factors that combine to influence the quality of the burn and the power derived from it.

This cycle begins with the spark-induced ignition of the fuel mixture and subsequent burn and expansion of the gases. It is not an explosion, but pressure and temperature build rapidly, and the expanding gases push the piston downward. Combustion pressure multiplied by total piston area results in thousands of pounds of pressure exerted on the piston. Depending on the type of engine, pressure normally peaks about 12 degrees after TDC.

The bulk of the work occurs here and trails off over the next 100 degrees or so of crankshaft rotation. Pressure decays as the piston descends, until the exhaust valve opens (EVO) around 120 degrees after TDC. You get what you get at this point, and there is little you can do to influence it except provide complementary fuel to control detonation and regulate ignition timing to optimize the burn characteristics of the combustion chamber. Remember that the piston top forms the floor of the combustion space, and its shape and rate of approach can also influence combustion characteristics to some degree.

Exhaust Blowdown

The discharge process can be divided into two separate events characterized by different physics and thermodynamic processes. The first is exhaust blowdown, which initiates at EVO. Cylinder pressure is still relatively high, and some of the gases may still be burning. In some cases, a combination of poor cam timing and late ignition may even cause burning to continue into the header pipe. For the most part, high cylinder pressure attempts to exit the cylinder as soon as the valve cracks open. Exiting gases briefly achieve supersonic flow until the valve opens farther.

The blowdown cycle is the primary source of exhaust noise. The cylinder blows down rapidly because of the high-pressure gases escaping past the exhaust valve. Most of the exhaust exits the cylinder via its own high-pressure energy, and the event concludes when the piston reverses direction at approximately BDC. Depending on the timing, it's possible that the cylinder pressure could still be higher than atmospheric, and the piston is moving very slowly, so it's not precisely at BDC in every case.

Exhaust Pumping

This is the second discharge function, which begins when the piston begins to rise on what is traditionally called the exhaust stroke. Most of the cylinder has already blown down, but as the exhaust valve opens farther the rising piston pumps out residual gases. The valve reaches maximum lift at about 70 degrees after BDC and the piston achieves maximum velocity around 105 degrees after BDC.

On the exhaust stroke, the piston is chasing the exhaust valve, which is trying to close before the rising piston catches it. The piston pumps the remaining gases out of the cylinder, completing the exhaust pumping process when the intake valve just begins to open (IVO) as the piston approaches TDC.

The exhaust blowdown is a high-pressure self-induced evacuation

> **Exhaust Pumping Influences**
>
> Here are some of the factors that affect the exhaust pumping cycle:
>
> - Rod/stroke ratio (influences piston speed and acceleration)
> - Exhaust-port steady-flow capacity (at low to moderate depression and moderate to high valve lift)
> - Exhaust system pressure-wave tuning
> - Maximum piston speed
> - Cylinder displacement
> - Bore area–to–exhaust throat area ratio
> - Initial pressure and temperature

of the cylinder. The exhaust pumping cycle is the forced expulsion of the remaining low-pressure gases by the rising piston (the mirror image of intake pumping).

Important goals to accomplish during the exhaust-pumping event include minimizing the pumping effort and the residual mass of spent exhaust gases remaining in the cylinder at IVO. It's also important to reduce the cylinder pressure at IVO to less than intake port pressure to prevent spent gases from flowing back up the induction path and contaminating the next charge.

Valve Overlap

For a brief period around TDC, both valves are open at the same time, and various things can occur depending on the strength of the inlet flow and the remaining exhaust pressure. This event is called the valve overlap period. It begins just after IVO, and slightly before TDC. Valve overlap doesn't hit the piston because it is still up in the chamber at low lift. The exhaust valve is open but almost closed, and the piston does a drive-by of both valves at TDC. The overlap event ends when the exhaust valve finally closes and the intake pumping process is in full swing.

A proper overlap event ensures that all spent gases are expelled from the cylinder. The ideal condition is to have the exhaust scavenging process, assisted by pressure wave tuning, provide a slight tug on the intake charge just before EVC. The overlap event is necessary, complicated, and even quite valuable when properly timed.

Conclusion

As described by Hale, the seven cycles, or processes, are very much interrelated and overlap each other with their input and output influences. The illustration on page 12 is especially useful in visualizing the ongoing cyclical process and how each event influences the next. It is useful to pay close attention to the overlapping portions of each cycle relative to the various valve events and piston positions on the inner circle of the diagram.

For example, the compression cycle begins opposite the IVC point and ends at TDC. The fuel burning and expansion cycle overlaps compression to slightly before TDC to indicate the plug firing at whatever timing is set. Study these relationships closely to gain a solid perspective of how all these events interact. Then ponder the actual pressure changes and thermodynamic processes occurring within the chain every step of the way at mind-bending speed.

Torque and Horsepower

Engine power comes from the chemical oxidation of the fuel that the engine burns. Burning more fuel provides the potential to increase power if the essential requirements of internal combustion are served adequately. Burning fuel requires an oxidizer to support combustion. In a stroke of extraordinarily good

> **Overlap Influences**
>
> The following either directly or indirectly affect the overlap period to varying degrees:
>
> - Configuration and influence of the combustion space
> - Rod/stroke ratio (influences piston speed and acceleration)
> - Exhaust system pressure-wave activity
> - Initial pressure and temperature in the cylinder and the intake and exhaust ports
> - Inlet system pressure-wave activity
> - Instantaneous plenum pressure
> - Intake and exhaust port flow capacity (at low-pressure ratios and low valve lifts on the flow bench)

fortune, all IC engines enjoy a remarkably convenient and unlimited supply of oxidizer in the form of the earth's atmosphere. The 21-percent oxygen content that keeps us all breathing easy also makes engines run by providing the oxidizing component that sustains the combustion process. Hence engine airflow is effectively the controlling factor of high-performance engine output.

The goal of optimizing engine airflow is to produce performance and competition engines that deliver maximum torque and horsepower in an operational range most suited to the vehicle's specific application. This is characterized by high VE and effective management of engine airflow within the RPM range that constitutes the desired operational power band. Maximum torque across an application-specific range of engine speed is the objective. Torque is the twisting force representing the potential to perform work. Engine torque is the force potential, or turning moment, applied to the crankshaft flange, or flywheel, when combustion pressure is transferred to the crank throws via the connecting rods. When the flywheel turns, torque is measured by the resistance to rotation. Once the flywheel is turning, torque applies over a period of time, and horsepower is calculated via this formula:

$$HP = torque \times RPM \div 5{,}252$$

Where: 5,252 = mathematical constant

Torque is the measure of an engine's ability to perform work. It is characterized by high volumetric and combustion efficiency. Horsepower is the rate at which the work is performed. Torque accelerates the mass of a race car while horsepower, a derivative of torque, supports vehicle motion (speed) by maintaining the application of torque over time.

Engine builders strive to produce torque rapidly over a pre-determined range of engine speed (RPM) chosen to support the engine's final application. It is referred to as "transient torque," or the rate at which a loaded engine can accelerate through a specified range of engine speed. The greater the transient torque, the faster the engine is able to accelerate the vehicle under load.

All engines generate a variable torque curve that peaks at some point in the RPM range as determined by dimensional characteristics of the flow paths. This peak represents the

Pressure-Volume Diagram

Pressure-volume (PV) diagrams seem a little kooky to those not used to working with them, but they reveal a lot about the engine's airflow characteristics, and they help pinpoint abnormalities that need correcting. A PV diagram is a visual representation of the fluctuating pressure and volume changes in a running engine. These are the same pressure changes you seek to influence in your efforts to alter the engine's airflow characteristics to suit a particular application or purpose.

A PV diagram illustrates the same information displayed by a pressure crank angle diagram. A PV diagram consists of two primary loops that isolate work performed from work consumed, or wasted, in the process. Each loop is annotated by a plus sign (+) for positive work and a minus sign (−) for lost, or negative, work.

The area in the lower loop represents the pumping losses of the intake and exhaust strokes. It is commonly referred to as the pumping loop because it illustrates the intake and exhaust pumping cycles. The upper loop depicts work produced by compression, combustion, and the power stroke. Take note that the lower loop (−) follows a counter-clockwise direction and the upper loop (+) follows a clockwise direction.

This drawing is numbered to indicate the various points where the cycles begin and end. As you follow the sequence, bear in mind the cylinder pressure and piston displacement, as indicated on the X and Y axes at each point along the way.

The action begins at the same point as on the pressure crank angle drawing: point 1, IVO. Between point 1 and point 2 is the intake stroke. The pressure drops below atmospheric through this part, as indicated by the sag in the loop. As the loop rises from its lowest point, it indicates "pressure recovery" in the cylinder as the incoming charge exits the valve and fills the cylinder.

From point 2 to point 3 is typically the compression stroke, but the pressure spike you see between point 2 and the other loop indicates the intake ramming cycle, or inertia charging, as the charge velocity continues to fill the cylinder. A fatter loop at this point indicates rising VE due to ramming.

At point 3, you can observe the cylinder pressure increasing and the charge volume decreasing due to compression. When ignition occurs at point 3, cylinder pressure quickly

Pressure-Volume Diagram CONTINUED

spikes to peak based on charge density and combustion efficiency. It then begins to decrease as it pushes the piston down the bore. The volume remains relatively constant at the pressure peak and then increases as the burning gases expand down the cylinder bore against the piston top.

Points 4 through 6 represent the power stroke. Point 5 is the pressure peak that occurs approximately 10 to 12 degrees after TDC.

The piston reaches BDC at point 7 but the area from point 6 to point 7 represents the exhaust blowdown cycle where high cylinder pressure at EVO rapidly expels the bulk of the spent gases.

From point 7 to where the loops cross again is the exhaust pumping cycle. The crossover point represents the overlap period when the higher pressure determines what happens while both valves are open. If the exhaust pressure is still greater than the intake pressure, it tends to push residual exhaust back up the intake flow path. If the intake pressure is too great, some of it rushes through and out the exhaust before the door shuts. In a perfectly matched system, the last remaining residual exhaust exits the cylinder and invites the new intake charge to follow, which it does until the valve closes and cylinder filling begins again.

As engine speed increases, the PV loops tend to move upward on the pressure scale; very slightly on the pumping loop, but considerably on the exhaust loop. This is caused by insufficient time to blow down the cylinder because exhaust cycles become shorter as engine speed increases. Pumping work increases due to higher residual cylinder pressures, and horsepower begins to fade.

The PV diagram looks different in a supercharged application where positive pressure in the inlet tract eliminates the sag in pressure between points 1 and 2, and the whole loop tends to rise and become fatter because of the constant increase in inlet pressure.

All of this can also be related to crank angle in a pressure crank angle diagram.

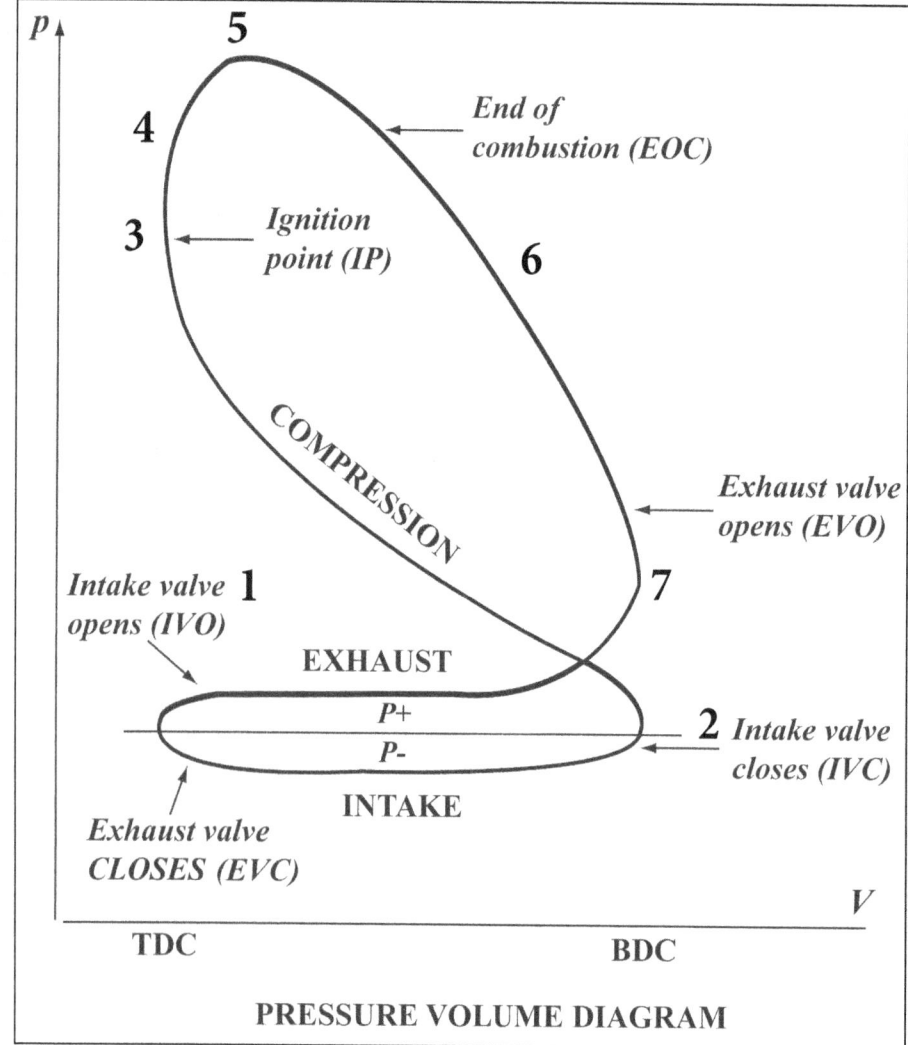

PRESSURE VOLUME DIAGRAM

The pressure volume diagram illustrates the pressure and volume changes that occur within the cylinder and combustion space during a typical cycle. The loop follows a clockwise direction as the air-fuel charge moves into and out of the cylinder and processes into power. The horizontal line on the lower loop shows how the pressure is negative as the piston descends while the valve opens. As the valve closes, pressure begins to rise during compression until the ignition point at which it spikes; expansion pushes the piston down the bore.

most efficient point in the engine's operating range and closely mimics the VE curve. The point of highest VE creates the torque peak. Various tuning and engine configuration techniques enable you to adjust the position of the torque peak to the most favorable spot in the power band and to reshape the curve around it for maximum performance benefit.

Power is governed by the overall efficiency of the specific component mix. It's relatively easy to supply enough fuel, but it is considerably more difficult to maximize airflow without the aid of a power adder. For any given collection of parts, an engine achieves a torque peak influenced predominantly by intake and exhaust tuning relative to its size (displacement) and engine speed. Stroke length, piston speed, and the valvetrain dictate the overall operating range while the intake cross section and ramming set the torque peak RPM. Within these parameters the engine's displacement (particularly with large bore and short stroke), intake flow capacity, and intake valve diameter provide the greatest influence on peak torque.

Through attentive manipulation of these and contributing component hardware, the torque curve can be shaped and positioned to suit the engine's final application. The trick lies in properly matching the math, and the component combination, to not just produce a torque peak at a desired RPM point, but also to fatten the curve below and above the peak by increasing VE. Hence, the major importance of the intake ramming process and supporting wave tuning is to pack the cylinders as full as possible throughout the effective RPM range.

This is the principal focus of all competent engine builders (designers), and it begins with the pursuit of VE relative to the engine's static air capacity. The air mass component depends largely on available air density and the VE that a specific component mix is capable of generating. It is primarily governed by inlet and exhaust flow-path dynamics, combustion chamber efficiency, valve timing, and elements of the bottom end and valvetrain that dictate final RPM capability.

The shape of the torque curve closely mimics the VE curve at peak torque. This is the point of maximum engine efficiency, and it typically

Taken to the extreme for a barely legal street car, Street Nationals champion Tim Arkebauer's PSI blown 1969 Camaro exhibits all the symptoms of street overkill in a radical Pro Street ride that's also capable of getting down the track at a pretty formidable clip. Although a bit impractical for the regular street driver, this setup moves all the air you could ask for at any throttle position.

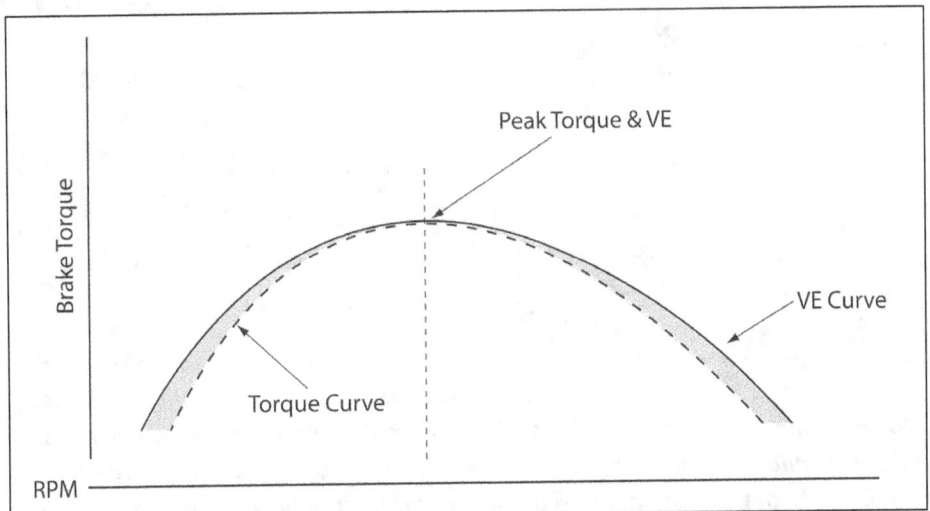

The engine generates a torque peak at its highest volumetric efficiency. Below this peak, torque trails VE because of insufficient intake velocity. Above the torque peak, torque falls off due to insufficient time to fill the cylinders.

reflects the lowest wide-open-throttle (WOT) brake specific fuel consumption (BSFC) numbers. Below the torque peak, torque trails the VE curve due to reduced combustion efficiency caused by inadequate intake flow velocity (ramming), air/fuel separation issues, and poor mixture quality. Above the torque peak, torque and VE decline due to insufficient time for cylinder filling caused by increasing engine speed (RPM).

Fortunately methods are available to address VE inefficiencies on either side of the torque peak and to inflate the overall torque curve. This refers to the "area under the curve" and seeks to expand the torque curve in all directions. Successful efforts to increase torque automatically improve horsepower. More important, a broader torque curve often produces greater acceleration even with a slight reduction in peak torque because it applies more torque over a broader range.

If the ideal mix of engine components targets an engine speed range most beneficial to the application, superior vehicle performance is ensured across the board. Complementing these performance gains with correctly matched gearing and tire combinations ultimately leads to faster cars and better racing through the effective production and utilization of torque. This works effectively even for engines operating well above the torque peak because the upper end of the torque curve expands accordingly, thus contributing more horsepower to the car's performance.

Volumetric Efficiency

The cornerstone of power building is volumetric efficiency. The more air an engine can process, the greater its power potential. VE is determined according to the engine's static air capacity, or displacement. A displacement of 400 ci represents 100-percent air capacity for an engine of that size. At any given engine speed, a percentage of that volume is being processed into torque depending on a host of variables that conspire to limit airflow. Without these pesky restrictions, atmospheric pressure can easily fill the cylinders completely (100 percent) every two crankshaft revolutions.

In practice this is difficult to achieve because airflow is restricted by a throttling device (carburetor, throttle body, or other), imperfect intake manifolds, intake ports, valves, and all the attending flow restrictions and pressure dynamics present in a running engine. Hence VE in a production engine rarely exceeds 80 to 85 percent. As previously mentioned, VE is reduced below the torque peak due mainly to insufficient airflow and poor mixture quality. And when operating at low RPM the piston pushes some of the charge back out after BDC so no ramming occurs.

Above the torque peak, VE is limited by inadequate time to fill the cylinder due to increasing RPM (typically two effects apply past peak VE, one for flow stagnation and

Hard-core racing applications such as NHRA Pro Stock still rely on highly specialized tunnel ram intake manifolds topped with twin Holley Dominator 4-barrels. Despite the precision drivability of electronic fuel injection (EFI), this combination actually makes identical or better power when finely tuned within its particular operating range.

Air filters are an important induction component because they are the first airflow restriction encountered by incoming air. Over time, racers and hot rodders paid greater attention to air filters and their utility for directing air into the carburetors or throttle bodies. This integral filter top is designed to provide greater flow capacity and is said to help straighten and smooth the airflow.

AIRFLOW BASICS

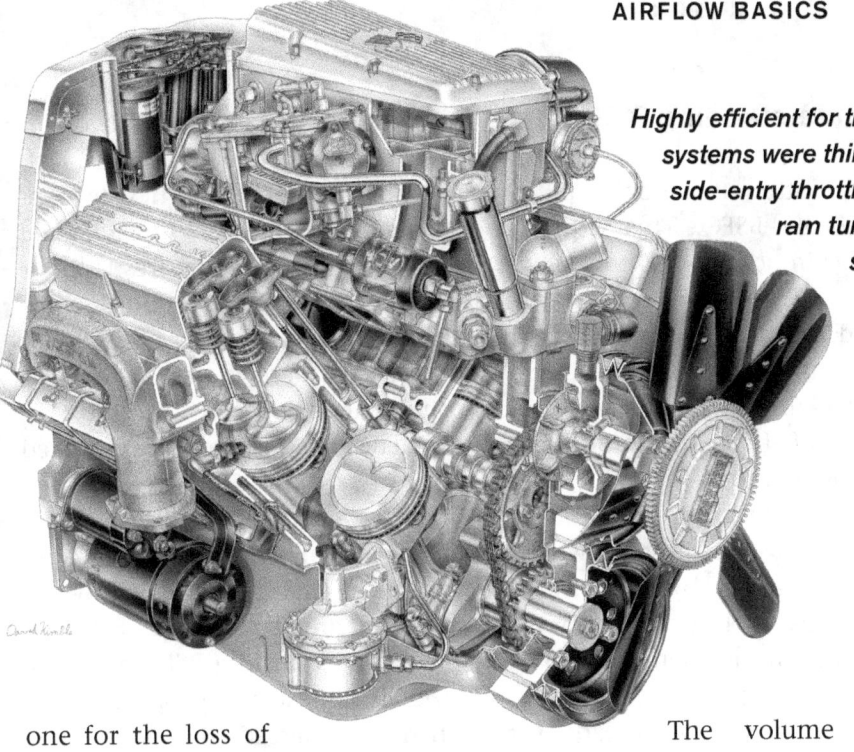

Highly efficient for their day, mid-1960s Corvette fuel injection systems were thinly disguised tunnel rams with sealed tops and side-entry throttle bodies. It was quite a tidy setup with a bit of ram tuning. Air capacity was more than adequate on this small-displacement 375-hp 327-ci small-block. (Photo Courtesy GM Media Archive)

one for the loss of intake/exhaust wave tuning). One of the engine builder's primary goals is to exceed the static air capacity of the engine and optimize combustion efficiency once fuel is introduced to the process. Savvy engine builders skillfully manipulate the component composition to accomplish this, broadening the torque curve and positioning it to best suit the intended application.

All engines generate their torque signature based on displacement, engine speed, VE, flow-path dynamics, and not surprisingly, specific architecture (I-4, I-6, V-6, V-8, V-10, V-12, etc.), each of which applies different attributes to cylinder filling, mean net torque, and overall engine smoothness. Every combination generates a torque peak, or "sweet spot," where its operational dynamics achieve maximum VE.

With competition engines, this often exceeds 100-percent VE, sometimes by a considerable margin. At 100 percent a cylinder contains a volume equal to the same space at atmospheric pressure above the inlet.

The volume within the cylinder also contains a fuel mixture that reduces the amount of air (and oxygen content) by the specified air/fuel ratio. So the two volumes are similar but different. More correctly you might argue that 100-percent VE means that the cylinder has achieved pressure equilibrium with the atmosphere. When a cylinder exceeds 100-percent it effectively becomes naturally supercharged. This occurs by the ramming effect of proper inlet sizing and valve timing to mildly pressurize the cylinder at IVC.

By specifying components to meet VE requirements builders target intake ports, dimensional qualities of intake manifolds and exhaust headers, carburetor size, rod-to-stroke ratios, valve timing, and static compression ratio. The specific component matrix is adjusted to suit the application's operational requirements.

Oval track and road racing engines typically call for a component mix that produces a broad torque curve over a wide range of RPM. This affords the engine builder an opportunity to tune the intake and exhaust systems separately to effectively broaden the power band. Conversely, drag racing applications seek a higher and narrower power band in which intake and exhaust tuning are more closely aligned. Identifying and targeting the required power band is one of the engine builder's first steps.

Although VE and engine speed are closely aligned, it is critical to target VE modifications to the desired engine speed. If a drag racing engine leaves the starting line at 7,000 rpm and cycles to 9,000 rpm through the gears, its VE at 5,000 rpm is largely irrelevant. And, of course, an engine delivering power between 4,500 and 7,200 rpm needs a broader tuning efficiency because of its parts combination. Hence airflow management within the targeted engine speed range becomes a central challenge in matching or exceeding an engine's potential VE capacity.

Trapped Mass and VE

When all is said and done, all you've got to work with is the effectively trapped mass you are able to contain and compress within the combustion space (clearance volume) at the point of ignition. That is the effective VE. Larry Meaux uses the following formula in his broadly popular PipeMax Header Design software program. It incorporates parameters that you may fail to consider:

Trapped VE = measured CFM − ring-blowby CFM − CFM lost during overlap

Theoretical CFM

In a properly configured engine, the ring blowby and CFM (cubic feet per minute) lost to overlap should be minimal, but must be considered for accurate modeling. And thus they are integral to modeling programs such as Meaux's PipeMax, Hale's Engine Pro, and most other high-quality simulation programs. For the purpose of airflow improvement, you are largely limited to static or steady-state flow measurements of individual flow path components or some combination thereof (where, for example, you might flow a head port with the manifold and carburetor attached).

Many street-strip types of high-performance engines still do not achieve 100-percent VE largely because they are a mixture of economic and manufacturing compromises. Cylinder heads are designed to have broad application on various engine sizes, and the camshafts are typically catalog grinds with the same prerequisites. The intake manifolds and headers cannot be properly sized for optimal performance, and the carburetors are often improperly sized. So these engines, with higher performance than most, may still only achieve a VE somewhere in the 90- to 96-percent range.

Your efforts to improve engine airflow and thus VE center on removing those compromises and substituting optimal flow efficiency across the engine; not just in the intake path, but also in the exhaust path, and most important, past the valves. Unless restricted by rules, you are free to employ any means possible, including some pretty formidable technologies that make racing engines breathe better than ever.

Understanding BSFC

Combustion efficiency is typically indicated by BSFC. This expresses fuel usage in pounds per horsepower per hour. BSFC is frequently misunderstood. Many people mistakenly believe that it is an indicator of rich or lean fuel mixtures, but it actually is a measure of efficiency that indicates how well the engine uses the fuel it burns. More specifically, it is the rate in pounds of fuel per horsepower per hour that a given engine consumes to make power. Most engines have a range of optimal efficiency, and BSFC defines that range.

As you may have already surmised, the term "brake" is the first word because BSFC is usually measured with the engine running on a dyno. BSFC figures are typically quoted for WOT conditions, but it is also a measurable quantity that relates to fuel economy at part-throttle operation. In the performance world, it is used to judge the efficiency contribution of various engine combinations and to predict certain requirements such as fuel-injector flow rate.

A particular cylinder head may make more power with less fuel, and that's an indicator of higher efficiency, most likely because of improved cylinder filling and a more efficient combustion chamber that extracts more energy from a given fuel mass. Guidelines for evaluating BSFC are well established and are frequently used to predict engine performance. One-half pound of fuel per horsepower per hour (0.50 BSFC) is the default norm for most calculations, but you can adjust this for competition engines.

Herein lies part of the problem if you think of BSFC numbers as indicators of mixture ratios. At 0.37 BSFC, a Pro Stock engine may be thought to be running too lean when, in fact, it is operating at the highest level of efficiency. In contrast, supercharged engines run richer mixtures to complement boost pressure and discourage detonation. They run richer; not because they are inefficient, but to complement specific combustion characteristics inherent to boosted applications, not the least of which is charge cooling and the need for more fuel to augment the greater volume of air being supplied by the supercharging device.

When evaluating BSFC numbers, lower is almost always better (even when supercharged); 0.60 is still more efficient than 0.65, as long as the combination supports safe combustion without detonation or overheating. Any engine still needs to run at the air/fuel ratio that produces the best power. That's usually about 13:1 in naturally aspirated engines and 11.6 to 12:1 in supercharged applications. One engine with poor efficiency may generate a BSFC of 0.55 while another may run at 0.40, and yet both may have the same air/fuel ratio. You can't just run the engine lean and expect to get a low BSFC number.

Remember that there is no magic BSFC number that guarantees max horsepower. However, there is a BSFC number that your particular engine generates when performing at its best. The lower the number (within reason), the more efficient your engine is at converting fuel into power. Tune for maximum torque and let the BSFC indicate how efficiently you generate that torque. For example, at an indicated BSFC of 0.50, the engine burns 0.5 pound of fuel per horsepower per hour (lb/hr). If the engine makes 500 hp, that's 250 lbs/hr. If you're building a racing engine, your BSFC should be way better; something on the order of 0.38 to 0.42.

These figures are for gasoline only; they differ considerably for methanol applications. With methanol the engine uses much more fuel, something on the order of 1.0 to 1.3 BSFC at the minimum and in some cases as high as 1.7 or more depending on the application. It's very much dependent on the application and the efficiency of the particular combustion chamber. In drag racing, most applications are supercharged so the BSFC trends higher in, say, an injected car or an injected circle-track car. Short-track cars typically run around 1.0; sometimes even less.

Read your plugs and tune accordingly. Whatever BSFC your engine generates is what you get when you have your best tune onboard. Don't worry about it for track purposes. And if you don't think it's good enough go back to the drawing board and figure out what part of your combination is causing the inefficiency. Determine where that falls in the horsepower chain and take appropriate steps to remedy it.

Remember that BSFC is affected tremendously by the burn characteristics of a particular combustion chamber and the filling and emptying abilities of the flow components. You can chase that free lunch all over the engine, but the horsepower gods have dictated that you have to pay for it somewhere. That's where optimizing each of the processes in Hale's horsepower chain becomes so important. Optimization and efficiency go hand in hand.

Contributing Engine Systems

The induction and exhaust systems are the primary contributors to the total engine airflow equation. The camshaft plays the role of traffic cop, determining when and where air flows and the specific timing of air movement during the power production process. The induction system is the most important, but exhaust system efficiency plays a critical role in the efficiency of overall air movement, and the camshaft still pretty much runs the show.

The induction system comprises everything upstream of the intake valve including the valve, intake port, intake manifold including plenum and distribution runners, and any associated spacers that may be employed. It also incorporates the air and fuel metering device (carburetor or throttle body), air filter, and air scoop or in some cases various types of cold-air packages that redirect cooler air to the induction system via underhood passages and strategically located air inlet openings. In the absence of a supercharging device air moves through the engine based on the creation of pressure differentials or voids (empty cylinders) into which it naturally flows (naturally aspirated) because of atmospheric pressure.

When contemplating engine systems that contribute to maximum VE we typically think of only the induction system. But as Hale's horsepower chain of processes demonstrates, every link in the chain contributes to or influences the overall VE equation. The induction system is the most familiar player. But it goes nowhere without the exhaust system and all the subtle and less recognized contributions made by the correct combination of short-block components to gain the optimal rod-stroke ratio, effective ring seal, and proper valve and ignition timing. To be sure, most of the important VE actions occur in the cylinder heads where the air/fuel

---

BSFC Comparisons

Here are a couple of handy equations you can use to calculate BSFC for comparison purposes:

$$BSFC = \text{lbs/hour of fuel consumed} \div \text{uncorrected HP}$$
$$BSFC = (BSAC \div \text{A/F ratio})$$

Where:
BSAC = brake specific air consumption
A/F = air/fuel ratio (typically at peak torque)

When checking dyno results, BSFC is always calculated from the uncorrected, or raw, power figures. If you divide the fuel usage by corrected power numbers, the calculation will be incorrect, and it will throw you off.

Larry Meaux at Meaux Racing Heads provided the following handy equation for making ballpark estimates of fuel consumption when planning a fuel system:

$$\text{Fuel Consumed} = ci \times rpm \times 0.0001$$

Where:
0.0001 = mathematical constant
For example, a 565-ci engine running at 7,500 rpm would consume 423.75 lbs/hr (565 x 7,500 x 0.0001).

charge is introduced, processed, and discharged with the short-block providing convenient means of transferring the power generated into a rotational force at the flywheel.

In this book I spend a great deal of time on cylinder heads and intake manifolds, but not to the exclusion of any other factors in the horsepower chain. The system has three basic elements: induction system, exhaust system, and short-block. Within the induction system you have air scoops, air cleaners, carburetors, throttle bodies, carb spacers, intake manifolds, and cylinder heads with intake and exhaust valves and the all-important combustion space. The exhaust system also incorporates the cylinder heads and valves plus the headers, collectors, and in some cases full exhaust systems with mufflers or shaped discharge orifices such as collectors. The short-block contributes to VE by providing cylinders or displacement volume. The rotating assembly influences airflow via the rod-stroke ratio and its ongoing rotation. The reciprocating activity provides piston motion to achieve cylinder filling, compression, power transfer, and exhaust pumping.

These elements are inseparable and although the physics and thermodynamics that govern them are extraordinarily complex you only have to grasp a portion of it to gain a working knowledge of how you can influence and manipulate engine airflow to suit your power demands. To that end, I define and examine the engine airflow paths and discuss the appropriate processes that need to occur in each of them. But first I discuss some of the basic properties of air and fuel and how they affect your decisions about how you mix and process them into power.

Despite all of the modern technology and power adders, a single 4-barrel carburetor with conservatively sized intake passages in a light car still makes a remarkably fast hot rod.

Although turbocharging is quickly becoming the go-to power adder, traditional supercharging is still the darling of the hot rod set.

CHAPTER 2

RELEVANT PROPERTIES OF AIR

One of the goals of this book is to provide racers and engine builders with basic engine airflow information and some simple ways of looking at it without drowning them in mathematical theory and equations. My intent is to build a foundation from which to make intelligent airflow decisions based on known facts and fundamentals. The most important thing is to understand the characteristics of air movement through an engine and the various forces that influence it.

First and foremost, air is its own master. You can trick it and manipulate it to some degree, but it pretty much does what it wants: seeking to fill any void of equal or lesser pressure via the path of least resistance. You can predict its behavior according to known principles and values, but you remain subject to its whims. For most applications, air is a uniform gas of constant composition with average values comprised of all its constituents. The relationship of these components at any given time is the "state" of the gas and is defined by the Ideal Gas Law, which says that any change in air density is directly related to a deviation in temperature and pressure.

The state of the gas also comprises its chemical composition, mass, volume, density, temperature, and pressure. Most testing and design work is performed to these industry standards (actual aerospace standards), or average values.

In the absence of a supercharging device, the earth's atmosphere conveniently fills an engine's cylinders for free, with the annoying exception of various penalties for airflow restrictions that interfere on the way to the valve. Restrictions prevent atmospheric pressure from completely filling the cylinders, so engine builders must take steps to assist it. Improving the volume and quality of airflow through the engine is a challenging task. It cannot be fully appreciated or easily accomplished without a reasonable understanding of the physical properties of air and the different fuels you mix with it.

The whole atmosphere is available to power engines, but only about 14.7 psi of air pressure is accessible at any given sea-level location. This illustration shows altitude (in kilometers) and temperature variations within the earth's atmosphere. As a familiar point of reference, a dragstrip is almost exactly .4 kilometer long.

PRACTICAL ENGINE AIRFLOW

CHAPTER 2

Physical Composition of Air

A veritable ocean of air surrounds us. We move through it and breathe it comfortably as if it were not there, but it has significant and measurable properties such as mass, density, pressure, temperature, specific volume, and viscosity. The values, or dimensions, of these properties are variable and change in a predictable fashion as each one varies according to another. In its simplest form air is defined as a gaseous mixture containing 78-percent nitrogen and 21-percent oxygen with traces of carbon dioxide, argon, water vapor, and other components in minute amounts.

With the exception of water vapor, these percentages remain relatively fixed. However, volume, density, and viscosity vary with temperature and pressure, and these characteristics affect the movement of air through the engine. Contaminants such as dust and smog may also contribute to air quality in varying degrees depending on the amount of pre-induction filtering, leakage, and reversion in the intake tract.

The component of air that interests us most is its oxygen content, the part that supports combustion when ignited with various fuels in appropriate ratios. Fuel, whether gasoline, alcohol, or some exotic blend, is the fundamental source of power in an IC engine, but it does not burn without oxygen. Because air is only 21-percent oxygen, only one-fifth of its total content is used to burn the fuel. Therefore, only 21 percent of

Superchargers and turbochargers increase the air density in engines beyond that provided naturally by the atmosphere. Packing the cylinders with a denser air/fuel charge extracts more power from the engines.

A 1-inch-square column of air reaching from sea level to the edge of space distributes 14.7 psi of pressure on whatever it touches. Wherever a lower pressure is presented (as in a cylinder), the atmosphere attempts to fill it. Pressure and air density decrease with altitude, as does engine performance.

The green portion of this pie chart depicts the amount of atmospheric oxygen available to power the engine. The airflow through the engine must be dramatically increased because only 21 percent of it is oxygen available for combustion with the fuel.

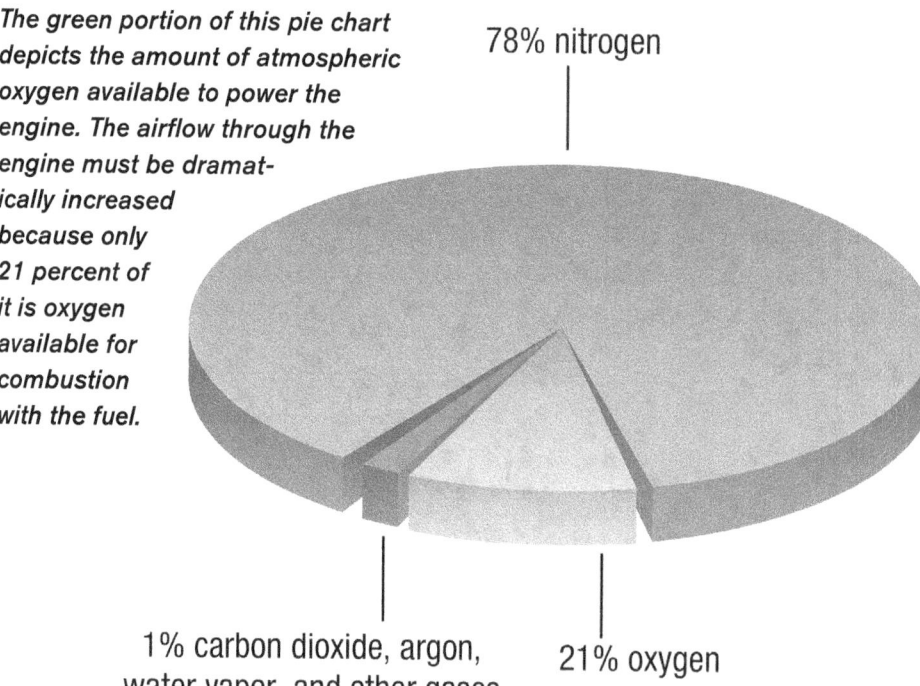

the total airflow is used to achieve proper combustion within the cylinders. That is why airflow is the key to engine power.

Nitrogen is inert and contributes nothing to the power equation. However, it does take up space along with the rest of the trace constituents, leaving less room for power-producing fuel. They are pretty much along for the ride with minimal effect on power, but often have quite specific effects on emissions.

Adding more oxygen lets you burn more fuel and make more power if you can effectively contain it within the cylinders. The primary means of adding more oxygen is by adding more air via supercharging. This increases the oxygen content by packing the cylinders with a denser mixture of air and fuel.

Another way to add more oxygen is to use oxygen-releasing compounds such as nitromethane and nitrous oxide (see sidebar "Oxidizers and Oxygen-Releasing Compounds" on page 31). This requires additional fuel to accommodate the extra oxygen. It is a key path to power, one that largely overcomes more traditional methods of coaxing more air into the engine via manipulation of the flow path dimensions through ram tuning, head porting, and valve work.

For the most part, I concentrate on examining and understanding airflow in the naturally aspirated sense. Moreover, it is a fortunate coincidence that most airflow enhancements are pretty much complementary to any type of supercharging.

Next, you need to quantify some basic properties of air and think about how you can influence or

Oxidizers and Oxygen-Releasing Compounds

Atmospheric oxygen is the most plentiful oxidizer available for IC engines. It offers the considerable advantage of an unlimited supply that does not require onboard storage. There is no weight penalty and the power-to-weight ratio is favorably increased for free.

Although my focus here is on engine airflow and the techniques that can be employed to improve it, you should note that in addition to mechanical supercharging (and turbos) more oxygen can also be supplied to enhance IC engine performance in two primary forms: nitromethane racing fuel and nitrous oxide injection. Both release extra oxygen during the combustion process and thus require more fuel to ensure the proper air/fuel ratio for best power. This is often referred to as chemical supercharging because the added oxygen is artificially introduced via a tube and not directly supplied by atmospheric pressure.

A secondary means of supplying the additional fuel to support the increased oxygen content is required. Kits to support this are plentiful and easy to apply. Numerous other oxygen-releasing compounds are available, but most are too toxic, corrosive, or difficult to store and handle. This makes nitromethane and nitrous oxide the most popular secondary sources of oxygen. ∎

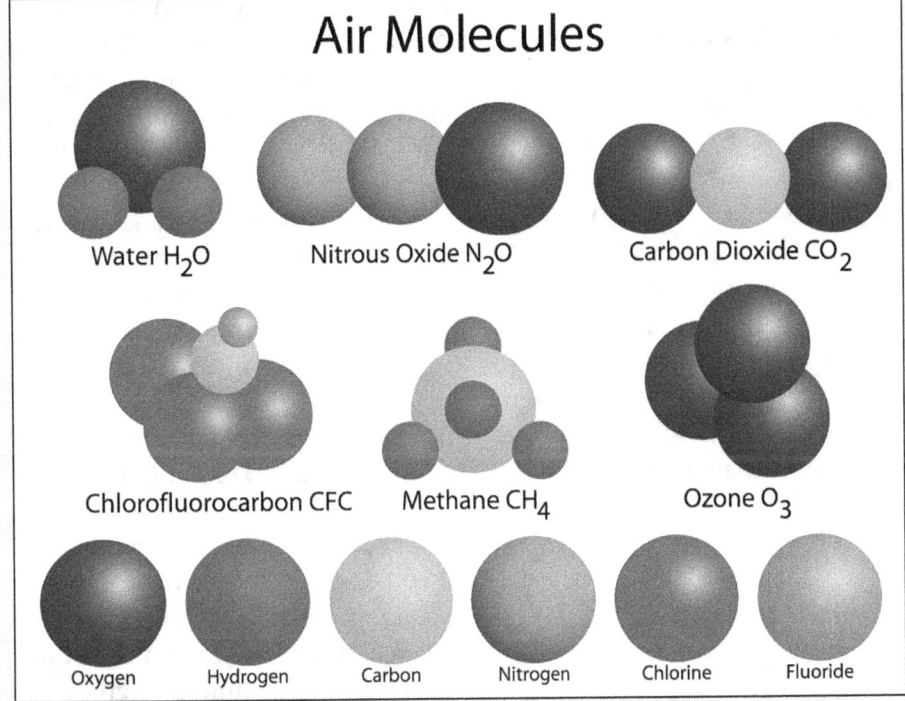

This color-coded chart illustrates common combinations of molecules. For the purpose of this engine discussion, only oxygen and nitrous oxide are useful. In a nitrous oxide–injected engine, the oxygen separates at 565 to 575 degrees F, thus providing additional oxygen that must be supplemented by additional fuel for more power.

employ them to fill your engine's cylinders more effectively. As shown in the chart (at right), the basic properties of air are characterized by mass, volume, density, specific volume, pressure, temperature, and viscosity. Their relationships seem complicated for something as seemingly intangible as ordinary air, but they are pretty well defined according to scientific principles.

Most of this has a much greater effect on tuning issues than airflow, but it's important to understand the fundamentals. Maximizing airflow is your goal, but some properties of air can impede this to some slight degree.

Basic Properties of Air

Property	Symbol	Dimensions	Value/Sea Level Static (standard day)
Density	r	mass/volume	1.229 kg/m^3 (0.00237 slug/ft^3)
Specific Volume	v	volume/mass	0.814 m^3/kg (422 ft^3/slug)
Pressure	p	force/area	101.3 kN/m^2 (14.7 lbs/in^2)
Temperature	T	degrees	15 C (59 F)
Viscosity	mu	force-times/area	1.73 x 10-5 N-s/m^2 (3.62 x 10-7 ft-lbs^2)

Mass and Weight

Mass is generally represented by air density, which is a function of temperature and pressure. Cooler air is heavier and denser; hotter air is lighter and less dense. When discussing these properties it is advantageous to recognize the distinction between mass and weight. Scientifically, mass is defined as the amount of matter contained within an object. It does not change. Weight is the force of gravity acting upon a given mass. It is represented as:

$$W = mass \times g$$

Where:
W = weight (force)
g = gravity (acceleration)

The mass of an object times the acceleration equals the active force or weight with acceleration or gravity equal to 1 g.

Weight is a force. Gravity causes the upper levels of the atmosphere to press down on the air underneath it, creating pressure relative to the particular elevation point in the vertical air column. Air surrounding an object presses against all sides of the object with equal force. The specific weight of air varies with elevation, temperature, pressure (elevation determines pressure), and the amount of water vapor and/or fuel contained within a given air mass (volume of air). Standard air at sea level weighs 0.0763 ft-lbs^3.

Dry air at 15 degrees C (59 degrees F) and minimal or dry moisture content is the standard (ideal) reference. Dry air contains little or no moisture so there is more room for fuel vapor in a given volume. Cooler air also promotes greater density (oxygen content), which requires the addition of more fuel to burn completely.

These terms are frequently misused because the mass of an object is commonly (incorrectly) referred to as its weight. For example, the volume of an air/fuel mixture in a given cylinder is referred to as the "trapped mass" when the valves are closed. The greater the trapped mass, the higher the theoretical power. That mass has a specific weight and volume according to its density, which varies according to temperature and pressure.

The weight of air depends on where the air is located within the local column of air that extends from sea level to the edge of space. Air on a mountaintop is less dense and lighter because there is less air above it pressing down on it; the temperature is also lower. So you have a temperature and pressure reduction and a lessening of water vapor pressure as well.

Pressure, temperature, and water vapor content are important components of engine performance from a tuning standpoint. Higher pressure (density) improves performance; higher temperature lessens performance. And water vapor is the joker that spoils everything by displacing oxygen. Your charge as an engine builder is to achieve optimal airflow despite the influence of these components, which are generally identified as weather conditions.

Density

Density is the mass (weight, in a sense) per unit of volume, or the specific amount of matter contained within a specified volume (density = mass ÷ volume). Density increases with pressure; high density increases the mass-per-unit volume. Higher density equals greater trapped mass and, thus, more power from the increased amount of oxygen, provided you can supply the correct amount of fuel to encourage effective combustion.

RELEVANT PROPERTIES OF AIR

Water with a density of 1 is the common reference, or 1.000 g/cm³ by definition.

Air density is a huge factor in operating high-performance engines. Denser air contains more oxygen molecules unless it is saturated with water vapor. Density is primarily influenced by elevation, temperature, and humidity, but not pressure. A given volume of colder air contains more air molecules than the same volume of warmer air, thus more oxygen is available to burn more fuel. Your car feels peppier on a cool, dry day as opposed to a blisteringly hot day with lots of humidity displacing what few oxygen molecules are available.

To a lesser degree, high humidity also affects air density by displacing oxygen molecules. Air saturated with water vapor is less dense than dry air and because it contains water vapor and fewer oxygen molecules, it doesn't support greater power output. Cool, dry air is the most desirable. It is denser, thus providing ample room for additional oxygen molecules.

Relative Density

Substance	Relative Density	Substance	Relative Density
Dry air	0.0013	Nitrogen	0.00125
Alcohol	0.82	Oxygen	0.00143
Aluminum	2.72	Petrol	0.685 to 0.725
Carbon dioxide	0.00198	Rubber	0.96
Carbon monoxide	0.00126	Steel	7.82
Cast iron	7.20	Water (4 degrees C at sea level)	1.00
Hydrogen	0.00009		
Lead	11.35		
Mercury	13.59		

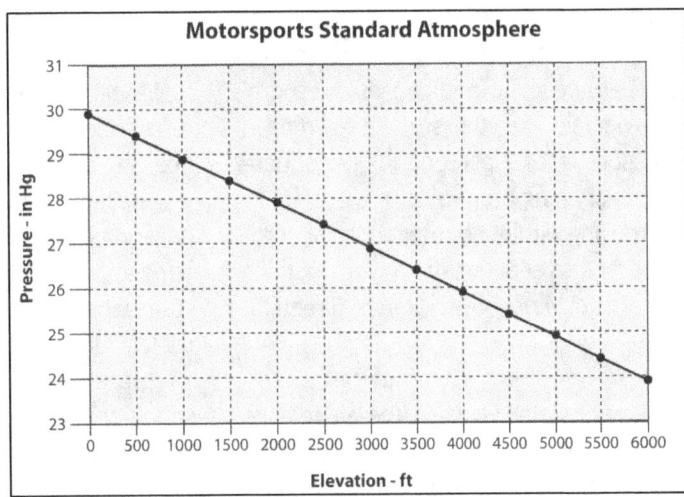

The MSA uses 29.92 inches Hg for standard sea-level pressure. As elevation rises, pressure decreases in almost linear fashion. As shown here, it drops to 24 inches Hg at 6,000 feet. (Photo Courtesy Patrick Hale)

Coping with Variables

If you look at a cubic foot of air at any given location, you are required to contemplate its density based on its temperature, pressure, and amount of water vapor. When any of these variables changes, the density varies. So a hotter cube of air is less dense than a cooler cube. Oxygen content changes with these variables. Vapor pressure is also a factor by displacing some amount of oxygen molecules within the given volume.

Dealing with these atmospheric variables makes it difficult to accurately judge air density. In the absence of an "oxygen meter" you have to rely on density standards for tuning purposes. Air density gauges that display density as a percentage based on the measured air temperature and barometric pressure are essentially "ballpark" devices. Racers have learned how to work with them to improve performance, but they can't measure or factor in humidity to account for how the vapor pressure influences oxygen content independently of pressure and temperature.

The motorsports industry relies on a standard temperature of 60 degrees F and 29.92 inches Hg (mercury) barometric pressure with dry air (no humidity). These conditions correspond to the standard atmospheric pressure of 14.696 psi, commonly expressed as 14.7. (You may also see 14.68 psi, which is calculated by using the aviation standard temperature of 59 degrees F.) This is zero density altitude without the influence of vapor pressure. Any drop in pressure or increase in temperature or vapor pressure raises the density altitude with a corresponding reduction in indicated air density.

All of this affects the oxygen content of the air, which is a big factor in fuel combustion. And as previously mentioned, engines perform their best under conditions of high barometric pressure, low temperature, and minimal water-vapor pressure (low humidity).

CHAPTER 2

Important Terms

The following terms are useful in understanding the various qualities attributed to air. They are variable and influenced by changes in each of them.

Dry Bulb Temperature

Regular "air temperature" measured with a thermometer.

Dew Point

The temperature at which water vapor condenses and separates from air.

Pressure

Air applies pressure to any surface it touches. Pressure is measured as force per specified area. Gravity pulls air toward the earth because air has weight. That causes pressure, resulting in denser, heavier air near the surface exerting a normal sea-level air pressure of 14.7 psi (pounds per square inch, or 1,013 mbar) on everything around it.

The pressure of air moving within a runner varies according to the port velocity, port cross section, and any restrictions where it may encounter abrupt variations in area or direction.

Relative Humidity

This is the percentage of water vapor in the air relative to the maximum amount the air could hold under those temperature and pressure conditions. Relative humidity is 100 percent at the dew point.

We generally discuss relative humidity as it relates to human comfort, with the average person feeling most comfortable at about 50-percent relative humidity. Perspiration increases above that point; lower percentages are often too dry for many people, causing headaches and dry throat, skin, and nasal passages.

Specific Volume

The specific volume of a substance is the ratio of its air volume to its mass. As described in Boyles Law, the given volume of a gas varies depending on its temperature and pressure. For any given temperature, the gas occupies a specific volume. Remember that (mathematically) specific volume is the inverse of density (specific volume = 1 ÷ density).

Temperature

Temperature is usually expressed in degrees Fahrenheit unless conversion to Centigrade, Celsius, or Kelvin is specified. A gas (air) at any given temperature or pressure occupies a specific volume according to its mass, temperature, and pressure.

An absolute temperature scale (Rankine) is used for engineering and thermodynamic calculations. The Rankine scale has the same number of increments as the Fahrenheit scale, but the absolute zero point is equal to –459.67 degrees F (absolute zero is recognized as the coldest temperature in the universe). Outside the fields of meteorology and petroleum engineering, Rankine is used rarely and you will likely not encounter it for the purpose of understanding and working with engine airflow.

Viscosity

Air also has fluid qualities that affect its movement through a passage or port. Air viscosity is a measure of friction and the resistance to efficient flow. It is based on differing velocities near the center of the port and near the port walls (drag).

Because air is compressible, it can gain or lose pressure depending on airspeed and flow area, and the drag varies depending on viscosity. Shear, or stress, determines air pressure depending on viscosity, which varies depending on fuel content, droplet size, and the severity of area and direction change.

Because air is compressible, it can also emulate basic spring characteristics when subjected to sudden starts, stops, and abrupt direction changes along with various shear properties depending on how heavily it is laden with fuel or water vapor.

Water Vapor

Water vapor is the most variable component of the engine's intake air, and it exerts considerable influence on the combustion process. It constantly changes according to temperature, time of day, weather conditions, and the proximity of water sources, such as lakes, rivers, or clouds. Although water vapor provides a cooling effect it also displaces fuel molecules, thus requiring a leaner mixture to obtain optimal fuel ratios. This is primarily noted as the weather effect for tuning purposes, but it is also experienced when using water injection for charge cooling.

The presence of water vapor actually decreases density and essentially makes the air lighter. That's because the molecular weight of water is less than the combined molecular weight of the oxygen and nitrogen that make up the bulk of the atmosphere. This is difficult to grasp at first until you recognize that you're not talking about liquid water, but rather water vapor, which itself is a gas that is lighter than the

RELEVANT PROPERTIES OF AIR

combined weight of oxygen and nitrogen.

Although temperature and pressure exert the greatest influence on air density, humidity has a lesser but potentially harmful effect. In addition to being lighter, it occupies space that could otherwise be occupied by fuel, thus reducing the oxygen content and the energy content (fuel) available to produce power.

Wet Bulb Temperature

This is equal to dry bulb temperature when air reaches its saturation temperature (dew point), or the lowest temperature water can reach via evaporative cooling. The difference between wet bulb and dry bulb temperatures is a measure of the humidity. ■

Engine performance is fully dependent on the airflow through the engine. Because there are so many variables and factors that influence airflow and air quality, correction factors were conceived to help engineers make more accurate comparisons. They use the correction factors during product development and dyno testing, whether on an engine dyno or in a running vehicle on a chassis dyno.

The Ideal Gas Laws

The following three laws relate air density to pressure and temperature. They combine to define gas behavior based on a hypothetical ideal gas. They are named for the three men who postulated them and they apply perfectly to the gas you know as air.

- Avogadro's Law states that at constant pressure and temperature, the volume of a gas is directly proportional to the amount of gas. (Volume is relative to temperature and pressure.)
- Boyle's Law states that the volume of a gas is inversely proportional to its pressure. (Volume increases as pressure decreases.)
- Charles' Law says that the volume of a gas is directly proportional to its temperature. (The gas expands with temperature.)

This equation represents the ideal gas law:

$$PV = nRT$$

Where:
P = Absolute air pressure
V = The given volume of air
n = The actual amount of air measured in moles
R = The Ideal Gas constant
T = The absolute air temperature (this is where degrees Rankine fits in: you don't use degrees F)

The volume, pressure, and temperature of air are easier to measure than its specific mass. Your primary concern is the behavior of air (a gas) as it undergoes changes in temperature and pressure, which are the parameters that affect engine power output. You want to understand the behavior of air as it moves through the engine negotiating restrictions (area and velocity changes) and reacts to the influence of fuel droplets present in the airstream. The ideal gas laws allow you to predict air movement based on known constants.

Correction Factors

Correction factors are established to support accurate comparisons of data recorded under different conditions such as location, elevation, time of day, and basic weather data. Although useful in testing, they require careful application and very accurate data to ensure meaningful comparisons. They also invite abuse and the potential for misleading information based on improper input or, in rare cases, attempts to fool the sensors. Although most dyno testing is comparative, both observed and corrected data can serve your needs.

For that matter, observed numbers are often more instructive as long as you maintain consistent comparisons. Observed numbers tell you what is really going on, right then and there. The important thing is to choose a standard and stick with it during all your testing. There are two basic dyno correction factors: the SAE (Society of Automotive Engineers) and the STP (Standard Temperature and Pressure). SAE numbers are used by OEMs for all their testing and they are generally the standard for most chassis dynos as well. These are automotive standards.

Most dyno shops and "magazine" testers stress STP numbers because they are roughly 4 percent higher than SAE numbers. STP numbers are recognized as the "motorsports" standard and are described as such by motorsports authority and author Patrick Hale in his book, *Motorsports Standard Atmosphere and Weather Correction Methods*.

Hale is the founder of Racing Systems Analysis (RSA) and the author of the popular Quarter and Quarter Jr.

dragstrip computer simulation software and the Engine Pro engine simulation program. He eventually sold off the RSA software business and now operates Drag Racing Pro (DRPro), a motorsports consulting firm. Hale's book defined the Motorsports Standard Atmosphere and how it applies to weather for tuning purposes.

Engine dynos collect only raw uncorrected data. Whatever correction factor is applied is merely a percentage calculation based on contributing factors input by the operator or recorded by sensors. Your dyno printout can be set to list observed (raw or as-recorded), SAE, and STP numbers plus the actual numerical multiplier so you can determine the "validity" of the correction factor for yourself. Serious tuners use uncorrected numbers and raw recorded data and recognize that the larger the correction factor, the more likely the numbers are to skew incorrectly.

Correction Factor SAE J607

This factor is common to the performance industry, particularly for engine dyno testing. It corrects observed data to standard temperature and pressure (STP), or 60 degrees F at a barometric pressure of 29.92 inches Hg and dry air (zero humidity). It also subtracts corrected vapor pressure from observed barometric pressure to correct for water vapor in the air. Numbers according to this correction factor used to be referred to as STP corrections, but are now commonly referred to as Hale's Motorsports Standard Atmosphere (MSA) corrections.

$$\text{SAE J607} = (29.92 - \text{corrected barometric pressure}) 1.2 \times [(\text{observed inlet Fahrenheit temperature} + 460) \div (520)0.6]$$

Where:
29.92 = standard barometric pressure
460 = Rankine conversion

The resulting factor is multiplied by observed torque and horsepower to obtain figures corrected to the common standard. This most often results in a higher reading than the observed numbers. Note that temperature in this formula is converted to degrees Rankine (by adding 460 to the Fahrenheit number), and that it yields power numbers approximately 4 percent higher than SAE 1349.

Correction Factor SAE 1349

This is the auto industry standard and is the normal correction for chassis dyno work, although most engine and chassis dyno software automatically calculates both. The software converts raw data to 77 degrees F air temperature, 29.31 barometric pressure (990 millibars), dry air, and includes a factor for an agreed standard of 84.7-percent mechanical efficiency. Numbers according to this correction factor are commonly referred to as SAE corrections.

$$\text{SAE 1349} = 1.18 \times [(29.31 \div Pd) \times \{(Tc + 460) \div 537)0.5\} - 0.18$$

Where:
29.31 = barometric pressure
Pd = pressure of dry air in hPa (990 hPa = 99kPa)
Tc = air temperature in degrees Celsius
460 = Rankine conversion

Why Use Corrected Numbers?

Uncorrected test figures are your benchmark; they permit accurate analysis of fuel and air usage, and BSFC numbers. If you're seeking or selling dyno numbers, you need to know the correction factor. If you're an engine builder validating your combination, uncorrected numbers tell you everything you need to know. The chances that your engine will ever run with the same conditions as the correction factor are slim to none, so what's the point?

Magazine testers use corrected numbers because they are higher and editorially expedient. Engine builders glean most of what they need to know from the raw data, particularly with regard to BSFC, VE, air consumption, fuel flow, air/fuel ratios, airflow, brake mean effective pressure (BMEP), and the shape of the torque and power curves.

If you think about it, the engine makes what it makes and the data recorded tells how and why it performed the way it did. The numbers change wherever you go. Correcting them to some pie-in-the sky number serves only your ego and can lead to considerable confusion.

For example, if you were in San Diego the engine would make more power. Well, yeah! If the air were colder it would make more power and on and on. If you're testing and tuning in Denver, the numbers are different than if you go to the beach. But it doesn't matter if you only race in Denver.

Bonneville racers routinely see big numbers on the dyno and then go to the salt flats and experience density altitude numbers anywhere from 4,000 to 8,000 feet and the corresponding loss of power they have come to expect. Either way the tune-up is different.

The correction factor's real value is not in predicting power based on an arbitrary correction; rather, it provides the direction for tuning adjustment to compensate for actual weather conditions. Either way, your engine is still going to make less power in Denver, but standardized corrections can help you optimize its performance for existing conditions. That doesn't impact actual engine airflow from a physical standpoint to any huge degree. But it does influence the weight and content of air, which has some effect on air movement through the inlet tract.

The MSA and the Air Density Index

The motorsports industry has universally adopted the MSA as described by Patrick Hale. That reference is for 60 degreees F, 29.92 inches Hg (sea level), and dry air (the absence of water vapor). These conditions constitute an Air Density Index of 100 percent. Any elevation above sea level or temperature above 60 degrees F has an Air Density Index of less than 100 percent.

At the MSA standard, the actual density of air calculates to 0.07633 lbm/ft³. Based on this, a pound of air at sea level has a volume of 13.1 cubic feet. Confusion is introduced with regard to atmospheric pressure, which decreases with increasing elevation, ranging from 29.92 inches Hg at sea level to 23 inches Hg at 7,100 feet. Hale's description is clear: "Whenever the 'actual' ambient pressure equals the corresponding 'standard atmosphere' pressure for the 'actual' elevation, the 'corrected' barometric pressure will always be 29.92 inches Hg."

Density Altitude

Density altitude is a great tool for making sure your plane is able to fly in given weather conditions. And it does a great job of helping you jet a carburetor, but it's not really ideal for motorsports corrections from an engine-tuning standpoint. Hale points out that engine power is not directly related to density altitude. He also states flat out that density altitude is not even necessary for proper engine tuning. Instead he recommends the HP Correction Factor, citing the importance of the type of fuel being burned and whether or not the engine is naturally aspirated.

According to Hale, engine torque and, thus, power varies with the inverse square root of absolute temperature. He points out that tuners have incorrectly assumed that the VE percentage of a given engine is not affected by changing weather conditions. This assumption suggests that a given inlet path flows the same regardless of pressure, temperature, or water vapor content; and that, of course, relates to your airflow concerns because you select and adjust airflow components based on calculations to achieve maximum VE. The VE percentage increases with

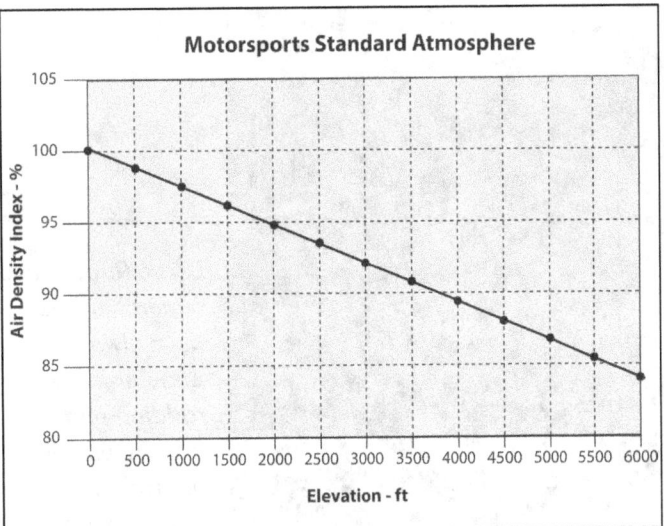

The Air Density Index based on the MSA equals 100 percent at sea level with 60-degree dry air and 29.92 inches Hg pressure. It also decreases almost linearly (hold a straightedge next to the line), dropping to about 84 percent at 6,000 feet. (Photo Courtesy Patrick Hale)

Naturally aspirated engines take considerably more finesse to pack the cylinders with air. Each application requires its own optimized package of intake and exhaust components to maximize efficiency.

CHAPTER 2

Large Roots-style superchargers have always been popular in hot rodding and racing circles. Every hot rodder keenly understands the imposing look of a big blower.

rising temperature because the speed of sound increases with the square root of absolute temperature. Hale reminds us that peak mach numbers within the intake runners remain constant for any given RPM. This affects the timing of pressure waves within the inlet tract.

For a detailed explanation of how this works refer to Hale's handbook, *Motorsports Standard Atmosphere and Weather Correction Methods*, available at DragRacingPro.com. It is the most comprehensive description available on weather corrections for motorsports. It is primarily a tuning guide for drag racing, but it discusses how atmospheric conditions affect engine performance. It provides a solid foundation for tuning and makes you aware of the behavior of air from a tuning standpoint.

For example, racers at Bonneville routinely face density altitude conditions equivalent to 5,000, 6,000, 7,000 feet or more based on the base elevation of 4,200 feet with temperatures approaching 90 to 100 degrees F and moderate humidity. Density altitude provides a benchmark so you can approximate a general tune if you have good records from previous races.

Yet it is still an approximation because there is nothing to tell you the oxygen content of the air and how it is affected by temperature, elevation pressure, and the presence of water vapor in the air. With the exception of Bonneville, Pikes Peak, and a few other high-elevation venues, most motorsports activity takes place somewhere within the first mile or so of the atmospheric air column.

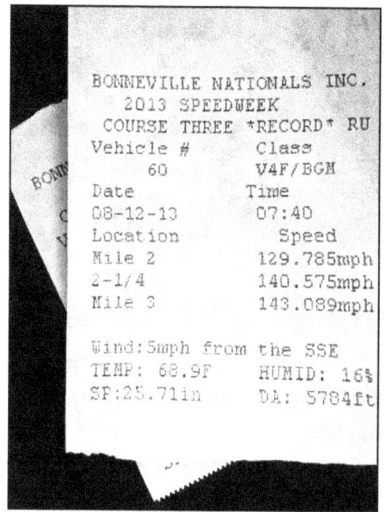

Temperature and Humidity

The accompanying time slip from Bonneville illustrates the primary air conditions affecting engine performance. It tells the racer the conditions that existed during his run through the measured mile. They include the ambient temperature, humidity, station pressure, and the density altitude.

Taken individually temperature and humidity provide an indication of the current air quality. Moderate temperature and relatively low humidity indicate generally good air quality for that elevation. Higher temperatures lower the air density and reduce power. Higher humidity indicates water vapor in the air, which displaces fuel in approximately the same percentage. Recall that 60-degree dry air is the motorsports standard.

Station pressure is the actual, measured, on-site pressure (inches Hg). It is the mercury barometer reading at that location under those conditions. By way of comparison, the motorsports standard pressure is 29.92 inches Hg, which is the barometer reading at sea level with dry air at 60 degrees F. Mercury reacts automatically to small changes in pressure caused by air temperature and water vapor, but its greatest change comes from a pressure drop due to elevation. As a rule air pressure drops

Here's a time slip from a lower-class roadster at Bonneville. It provides important weather data including temperature, humidity, station pressure (local barometer reading), and the density altitude (DA) for those conditions. Bonneville is at 4,200 feet, but the DA is 5,784 feet due to the local weather conditions. Note the barometer reading compared to the sea level standard of 29.92 inches Hg (mercury).

RELEVANT PROPERTIES OF AIR

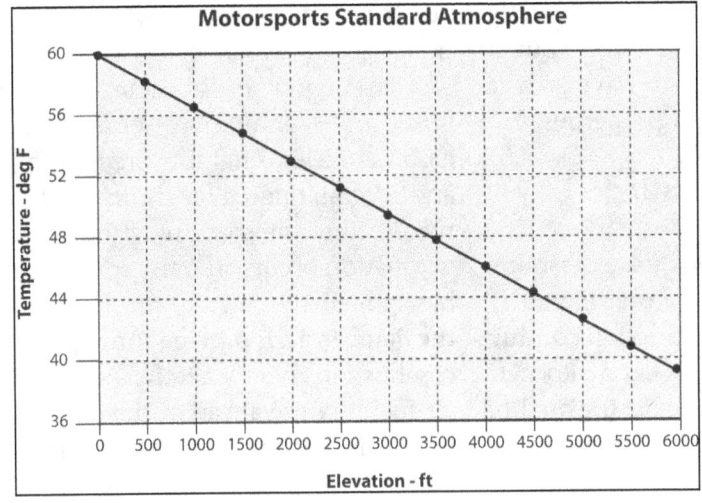

The MSA standard temperature is 60 degrees F with dry air. It decreases linearly with elevation, falling to about 38 degrees at 6,000 feet. (Photo Courtesy Patrick Hale)

about 1 inch of mercury for each 1,000 feet of elevation.

The station pressure shown in the example converts to about 12.63 psi, in contrast to the standard of 14.7 at sea level. The altitude at Bonneville is roughly 4,200 feet. The pressure reduction due to elevation along with the temperature increase above the standard (60 degrees F) and the presence of water vapor combine to yield the density altitude of 5,784 feet. This is the altitude the engine sees in terms of pressure or actual oxygen content relative to the standard. So although the physical elevation is 4,200 feet, the engine is ingesting an air density equivalent to an altitude of 5,784 feet above sea level.

Fuel Properties to Consider

From an airflow perspective the relevant properties of fuels differ significantly from those of combustion requirements. Optimal combustion requires consideration of octane rating, energy value, burn rate, evaporative cooling effect, and the specific mix of hydrocarbons that best suits the burn characteristics of a particular cylinder head and the operating condition of the application. In terms of airflow, you're seeking to maximize cylinder filling and, in particular, mixture quality entering the combustion chamber; not just maximum fuel and air in ideal proportions, but a highly conditioned mixture optimized to provide the best possible burn. Steps you can take to accomplish this include the following:

- Maintain optimal air speed
- Minimize fuel separation
- Enhance ram effect through wave tuning
- Optimize flow path cross section and length
- Minimize restrictions and direction changes
- Minimize cross-sectional area variations except for taper
- Optimize quench and encourage mixture turbulence
- Optimize pressure recovery exiting the valve

Fuels exhibit their best performance (energy release) when they are very finely atomized, almost to a vapor state. The greater surface area of many very fine fuel droplets burns more evenly and with fewer combustion anomalies created by vastly differing sizes burning at different rates and sometimes not burning at all. From an airflow perspective, you're trying to be conscious of the effect that droplets of varying size have on airflow, especially around turns, past obstacles, through the valve, and across the chamber.

Fuel puddling and wet spots along the way increase drag on the airflow column with detrimental impact on airflow mixture quality and quantity.

Fuel droplet size can also impede airflow by interrupting smooth flow at the boundary layer next to the port wall. Fat, heavy droplets tumbling against the walls tend to attract and "trip" finer droplets, upsetting their path to the valve.

As with air, fuels possess physical and chemical properties that influence their activity. These include chemical makeup, density, specific gravity, vapor pressure, caloric value, latent heat, etc. Different fuel blends exhibit a range of variations depending on the requirements of the application and the specifications of the fuel vendor. Most of these characteristics exert their influence on the combustion process itself with minimal effect on airflow within an inlet flow path.

From an airflow standpoint the most influential characteristic of any fuel is how well it atomizes and how well it remains in suspension during its torturous journey to the combustion chamber. Air is the medium by which fuel is transported to the combustion chamber. The quality of that mixture has a profound influence, not only on the transportation process, but also on how well the mixture burns once it arrives. Hence, the ability to adequately atomize the fuel and maintain its homogeneous state all the way to the combustion chamber is a paramount concern in the development of any high-performance inlet path.

Gasoline is the primary fuel used in street and high-performance engines. Many types of street and racing gas are available, generally distinguished by the octane rating as denoted on the pump at your local gas station. Premium gasoline is usually rated at 91 or 92 octane with a mid-range version at 89 octane and straight regular unleaded at 87 octane. In some parts of the country you may also see lower ratings such as 85 octane, but they are pretty rare.

Gasoline quality as it relates strictly to airflow plays a lesser role, but it is nonetheless useful to have a basic understanding of fuel properties.

Octane Rating

Most applications using gasoline refer to the particular fuel blend by citing its octane rating. According to fuels expert Tim Wusz at Rockett Brand Racing Fuel, the octane quality of a gasoline is essentially its ability to resist an abnormal combustion condition called detonation. Detonation is an explosive event that occurs when the air/fuel mixture in the combustion space reaches a temperature and/or pressure where it can no longer avoid self-ignition.

Two types of abnormal combustion commonly occur in gasoline-fueled engines: pre-ignition and detonation. Pre-ignition takes place before the spark plug fires, and detonation occurs after the spark plug has ignited the air/fuel mixture and the flame front is moving through the combustion chamber. If the unburned air/fuel mixture ahead of the advancing flame front reaches a temperature and/or pressure at which it no longer remains stable, it burns very rapidly. This initiates a new flame front that collides with the one that originated at the spark plug.

Gasoline Glossary

The following descriptions give you a general understanding of properties common to all fuels.

Aromatic

Chemical compound referred to as a cyclic organic due to its circular molecular structure. All gasolines contain aromatics, typically as toluene. Xylene is less common, and benzene is restricted to very low levels due to its toxicity.

Distillation

A gasoline is made of various hydrocarbons that boil at different temperatures. The boiling range can extend from 80 to 437 degrees F, in contrast to water, which boils at 212 at sea level.

Octane Numbers

A research octane number (RON) is measured under mild load conditions and is important in controlling part-throttle knock.

A motor octane number (MON) is measured under severe conditions and is most important for octane performance at WOT.

An anti-knock index (AKI) is the average of the RON and the MON. This is the number posted on retail gasoline pumps typically indicating 87, 89, 91, or 92 octane. Racing gasolines have AKIs between 100 and 118.

Oxygenated Compounds

Required in street gasolines in most of the United States to help reduce exhaust emissions. The two most common oxygenated compounds are methyl tert-butyl ether (MTBE) and ethanol (an alcohol).

Reid Vapor Pressure

Typically measured in PSI, Reid vapor pressure (RVP) is a measure of the front-end volatility of a gasoline. It is important for getting a carbureted car to start in cold weather. Summer RVP is 7 psi, and winter RVP is 13.5 psi.

Specific Gravity

Measures the density of gasoline compared to water. A specific gravity of 0.72 means that the gasoline weighs 0.72 times as much as water, or it is 72 percent of the weight of water. Most gasolines weigh about 6.2 pounds per gallon.

Volatility

Defines the ease with which a gasoline turns from a liquid to a vapor. Low volatility refers to low RVP, indicating fewer light hydrocarbons in the gasoline's front end. Summer-grade gasolines in Southern California (for example) have low volatility. Winter-grade gasolines in Michigan (for example) have high volatility, or high RVP, to make the engine easier to start in sub-zero temperatures. ■

Under these conditions maximum cylinder pressure occurs before the piston reaches TDC and tries to push the piston down before it is physically able to reverse direction. That causes an instant drop in power and is the primary cause of pounding out rod bearings, rattling the rings and landings, and destroying combustion chambers.

Pre-ignition usually starts from a local hot spot in the combustion chamber, which causes the mixture to ignite before the plug fires. Pre-ignition at WOT destroys pistons in seconds.

Research Octane Number (RON)

This number is scientifically determined in a single-cylinder, variable compression ratio engine operating at 600 rpm with a 125 degree F inlet air temperature at standard barometric pressure. Spark advance is fixed at 13 degrees before TDC. In a real-world OEM engine, RON is necessary to satisfy part-throttle knock problems.

A good-quality racing gasoline has a RON in the range of 110 to 115. A high-quality racing gasoline can have a RON in excess of 120, which is the top of the octane scale. The range of RON, however, is not very important to racing engines.

Motor Octane Number (MON)

This number is also determined in a single-cylinder engine but with a few changes that make operating conditions more severe, and thus these octane numbers are lower. A MON engine runs at 900 rpm with a 300 degree F mixture temperature. The spark advance varies according to the compression ratio. In a real-world engine, MON is necessary to satisfy the octane demand at WOT.

This number is particularly important for racing engines because they spend a higher percentage of time under high-speed and high-load conditions. Octane quality is critical to a racing engine because detonation or pre-ignition quickly destroys pistons, rings, rods, bearings, and in severe cases complete engines.

The MON appetite of an engine with a 13:1 compression ratio and a 4-inch bore varies with operating conditions but is commonly around 101. Good-quality racing gasolines have a MON ranging from 100 to 110. High-quality racing gasolines have a MON in excess of 110.

It is important to note that if your engine requires a 101 MON, it is of no value to use a gasoline that has a 115 MON. To cover yourself for extreme conditions, it is wise to have an octane cushion, but there is no advantage to using a very high-octane product if you do not need it.

Anti-Knock Index (AKI)

This number is the average of RON and MON. AKI must be posted on the dispensing pump at retail outlets in most states. It is the most commonly used octane reference today. It came into use in the early 1970s as a compromise between RON and MON for advertising purposes, and to avoid confusing the consumer with too many different terms. It is often erroneously referred to as the road octane number (RdON).

Observed Road Octane Number (RdON)

This number is determined by testing a gasoline in real-world multi-cylinder engines, typically at WOT. It was first developed in the 1920s and remains a reliable number today. The original testing was performed with cars driving on the road, but as technology advanced, testing was moved to chassis dynamometers to eliminate the many variables of road operation. Some companies have even built elaborate chassis dynamometers with tight environmental controls to improve consistency.

Some companies have modified this test to use it with racing engines on engine dynamometers. This provided the opportunity to develop racing blends from fuels that have a good RON and MON, but that did not respond well in a racing engine under a full-throttle excursion through the entire RPM range. According to Tim Wusz, these conditions were the true indicators of how the fuel could be best developed. In an intense development program, testers found that the gasoline blending components and their ratios are far more important to the racing engine response than a high RON and MON. RON and MON can only be used as a guide; the final work must come from the RdON.

Gasoline Variables

Many racers spend whatever it takes on new heads, manifolds, carburetors, etc., before trying a different fuel that might significantly increase performance by more closely matching the combustion characteristics favorable to their particular engine and operational environment. But just pouring in a different gasoline may not provide an improvement without fine-tuning. It's just like putting on a new carburetor without making any adjustments. If it works perfectly right out of the box, you probably got lucky.

When you finally decide to seek out the best gasoline for your application (assuming you are not saddled with a spec fuel) it is important to make the proper tuning adjustments to get the most out of your "test" gasoline so you do not prematurely abandon something that may be a performance improvement. Two main variables must be considered when trying a new gasoline. The first and most obvious is carburetor jetting; the second is spark timing. You also need to consider flame speed.

Carburetor Jetting

To determine whether the current carburetor calibration is suitable for the new fuel, you need to know the specific gravity (SG) of the gasoline. Most racing gasoline suppliers include this information in their literature. SG is a measure of how heavy the gasoline is compared to water. A gasoline with an SG of 0.72 is only 72 percent of the weight of water. The higher the specific gravity, the higher the float sits in the gasoline. This shuts off the fuel flow earlier at the needle and seat thereby lowering the liquid level in the float bowl.

A lower liquid level reduces the pressure from the "head" of the gasoline to help move the fuel through the jets at a given airflow compared to a carburetor with a higher liquid level. The height of the liquid level is important and should be the same for each fuel used. That is the purpose of the sight hole in the float bowl. When switching to a different gasoline, always reset the float level.

If you are moving from a high-SG gasoline to a low-SG gasoline, the rule is to richen the mixture with larger jets. On the other hand, if you are moving from a low-SG gasoline to a high-SG gasoline, you need to lean the mixture by using smaller jets.

If the new fuel is lighter (lower SG) than the old fuel, you should richen the mixture by one jet size for every 0.010 difference in SG. If the new fuel is heavier (higher SG) than the old fuel, lean the mixture by one jet size for every 0.010 change in SG. This only works if the carburetor was correctly jetted for the old gas. You're programming the carburetor, and like a computer it responds accordingly in terms of performance.

Example 1: The old gasoline has an SG of 0.718, and the new gasoline has an SG of 0.728. Although the new gasoline is heavier, the mixture needs to be leaner by about one jet size. If the new gasoline had a specific gravity of 0.738, the mixture should be leaned by about two jet sizes.

Example 2: The old gasoline has an SG of 0.724, and the new gasoline has an SG of 0.704. The new gasoline is lighter by 0.020, so the mixture needs to be richer by two jet sizes.

The above suggestions are most accurate with a Holley 4-barrel carburetor and racing gasoline. They may not be accurate with street gasoline that contains oxygen compounds, such as MTBE and ethanol. They also do not apply unless you adjust the carburetor float level to provide the correct liquid level.

Spark Timing

A new fuel may have burn characteristics that are entirely different from the original, and they must be optimized to make certain you extract the maximum possible energy. A timing variation of 1 degree can make a difference, so don't move the spark timing more than 1 degree at a time. Try going both ways from where the previous gasoline was optimized to see what combination works best. If the new fuel has faster burn characteristics it likely requires less initial timing and that helps reduce pumping resistance on the compression stroke.

Flame Speed

Different gasoline blends burn at different rates. This is called the flame speed. For maximum torque, maximum cylinder pressure should occur at about 12 degrees after TDC. If there is too much spark timing, the peak pressure occurs too soon, power is lost, and detonation is possible. If the timing is not enough, the pressure occurs too late in the power stroke, and power is lost. Without a fully instrumented engine and dyno, optimal spark timing (and therefore maximum horsepower) can be found by watching lap times in circle-track racing, and watching speed in drag racing.

How to Choose

The ever-increasing use of pump gas for performance engines requires some thought. If the new gasoline is heavier (higher SG) than the old one, reduce the jet size and thus lean the mixture. If the new gasoline is lighter than the old one, richen the mixture. If you don't have a clue to the specific gravity of either fuel, follow the rule I learned when I was about 17 years old: "When in doubt, go richer." This puts you in a safe position. If the mixture is too rich, you can lean it cautiously without damaging your engine. How this relates to engine airflow is relatively subtle, but knowledge is a powerful tool when it prompts you to examine the not so obvious alternatives.

For example, does the specific gravity of a heavier gasoline cause it

RELEVANT PROPERTIES OF AIR

to drop out of suspension more easily when navigating abrupt changes in direction or exposure to insufficient velocity? It just might; and how would you know that if you do not have good information about the wet-flow characteristics of your induction system? Stains on the plenum floor and runners are often a good sign and can also offer good clues about the efficiency of your setup and how well the air hangs onto the fuel during its joyride to the valve.

Conclusion

I can now assert some basic facts about the behavior of air and fuel based on their physical properties and how they interact within an IC engine. Air seeks to fill any void of lesser pressure and it determines its own best path to accomplish that task. In that sense, you could say that all engines are atmospherically supercharged with air pressure based on elevation and, to some degree, prevailing conditions. Air content and motion are affected in varying degrees by atmospheric conditions. Air has weight and as such it follows the laws of inertia regarding its movement. Air is compressible and thus to some degree elastic, particularly when it compresses behind a closed valve.

Air travels at a certain velocity according to the cross-sectional area of a confined passage and the amount of pressure (differential across the passage) behind it, whether atmospheric or artificial (boosted). Various restrictions provide resistance along the way and the science of engine airflow is devoted to dealing with them and exploiting them where possible.

High-velocity air is also a cooling medium. The cooling comes from evaporation of some portion of the fuel and is a sort of density multiplier based on air speed, temperature reduction, and the ramming effect. These are all plus factors for naturally aspirated applications.

These physical properties of air and its behavior in the atmosphere affect the way it behaves in your engine. Although their influence relates more to tuning issues than optimal airflow, the combined effect helps you improve engine power. (These effects and how to tune for them are discussed in detail in Chapter 6 and Chapter 15 of the MSA Handbook.)

To take full advantage of the air passing through your engine, you must recognize the source: atmospheric pressure and its many nuances. Once you fully understand where it's coming from, you are better equipped to hasten and improve its journey, so you can utilize it for your stated purpose, which is making lots of horsepower.

Altitude Pressure

Pressure decreases with altitude. The chart below shows the pressure change percentage based on miles above sea level. Since you rarely operate an engine at more than 2 miles above sea level the percentage of change is much smaller. This is seen in declining barometric pressure as altitude increases.

Miles above Sea Level	Sea Level Pressure (percent)
3.5	50.00
10.0	10.00
19.4	1.00
29.9	0.10
40.4	0.01
49.2	0.00

Useful Conversions

To Convert	Multiply By
Atmosphere to inches of mercury	29.921253
Atmosphere to psi	14.69595
Atmosphere to kilopascals, Kpa	101.325
Inches of mercury to atmospheres	0.0333211
Inches of mercury to kilopascals	3.37685
Kilopascals to atmospheres	0.0098692
Kilopascals to inches of mercury	0.296134
Kilopascals to psi	0.1450377
Pascal to psi	0.000145
Psi to atmospheres	0.068046
Psi to inches of mercury	2.036021
Psi to kilopascals	6.894757

CHAPTER 3

ENGINE AIRFLOW COMPONENTS

This investigation of airflow requires an examination of the entire airflow path through the engine, as it exits from the atmosphere above the carburetor to the atmosphere behind the tailpipe. This chapter introduces all of the various components and categorizes some of the problems, demands, and influences that affect each contributor's function. The airflow path very much follows Patrick Hale's seven cycles and adheres to the principles he describes. Here I call out each path individually and describe its function and relationship with the others.

The engine airflow path through the engine is a tortuous journey and one that would certainly pop your eardrums if you were riding along.

Air pressure and velocity vary all along the way, and everything happens at blinding speed.

In most cases, air enters the engine through an air filter, which can be the first point of restriction. Then it enters the carburetor or perhaps a long inlet tube as found on late-model electronic fuel injection systems. The air must make a turn into the carburetor venturis and boosters or into a throttle body and then into a plenum (serving chamber). Here it must navigate a veritable hurricane of air pressure pulses and air motion to find its way to a runner.

Then the air moves pretty briskly toward the intake valve, which is rapidly opening and closing the door as the air squeezes past it into the cylinder. The valve is either a hindrance or an aid depending on its configuration and timing. Air expanding into the bowl area of the runner is set up for the turn into the valve, but it must first negotiate the valve throat, or choke point, which is the primary vena contracta in the engine. Cam timing and residual pressure in the cylinder can mess this up and so can the valveseat, the shape of the valve, and the combustion chamber because they all attempt to recover

The air filter is the gatekeeper between the engine and atmospheric pressure; thus it is the first point of airflow resistance. Manufacturers try to provide as much filter area as possible to ensure adequate flow capacity and minimize restriction. The shape, height, and configuration of the filter all contribute to its flow capacity and its ability to support the engine's air demand at all engine speeds.

ENGINE AIRFLOW COMPONENTS

Smaller filters are often used on street hot rod applications, which is generally okay because the street engine's air demand rarely exceeds capacity. Drag race engines often forgo filter use, but most other applications use as much filter as possible to ensure minimal pressure loss.

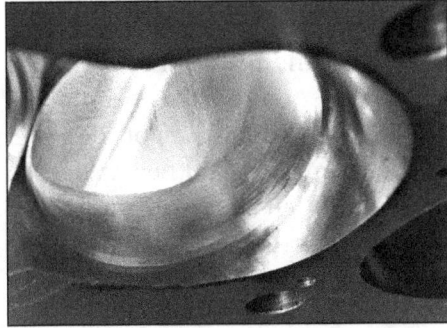

The throat area immediately above the valveseat is the controlling factor in airflow efficiency. Maximum velocity across the valve should be generated here.

atmospheric pressure in the cylinder and do it in such an efficient manner that the entire path is able to provide a sort of supercharging effect called inlet ramming.

Fundamentals of Air Motion

Air moves through an engine because of pressure changes. When the engine is off, air creeps in and maintains equal pressure inside and out just as it does in, say, your house. When the engine starts and combustion occurs, you suddenly have a small world of pressure changes. Air seeks equilibrium, to press against everything equally from all sides. But now when the piston descends it creates a new unfilled space; and air, due to the pressure and weight of the atmosphere above it, rushes in to fill the void.

When the space is filled, the air has fulfilled its function, but you can trick it to impart greater momentum than it can generate on its own. For the most part, you do this by speeding up the air's own energy through carefully sized passages. And of course, every 720 degrees of crank rotation you have to take time for a combustion event, and then everything can start flowing again.

Pressure and velocity are the primary factors governing air movement. You continually seek to master it via proper management and timing of the cycles in the horsepower chain, and via physical manipulation of the volumes and service passages the air uses from the air cleaner to the tailpipe.

If you study this view you can draw a line depicting the complete flow path through the engine. Air enters at the filter, passes through the carburetor and plenum chamber, into the manifold runners and intake ports, across the combustion chamber, then out the exhaust port and the headers. Pressure changes affect the air's behavior every step of the way.

If engines ran on water at the bottom of the ocean, they would be seriously supercharged because of the weight and pressure of the water above them. Instead, they operate in an ocean of air that, by comparison, has very little density. Therefore, you have to cajole and encourage the air to come in, so you can blow it up. This is managed by manipulating pressure and velocity in the intake system.

Because air is relatively thin and light, it can change speed and velocity quickly, and you can further encourage it by restricting its flow area. That makes it speed up and temporarily lose pressure; hence you have created a control circuit. So, on the way from the air cleaner to the cylinder, you speed up and lose pressure, then slow down and gain pressure (recovery). This is done multiple times as you introduce fuel and navigate through the carburetor and into the plenum, then into the runners and ports, and finally into the valve.

Although the air is pretty cooperative about where it's headed you ask it to carry some baggage on its journey and load it up with fuel. This affects its performance and you have to make allowances.

Cross Sections and Path Lengths

Cross section is the size of an opening or a passage through which intake air or exhaust flows. It controls the flow volume and velocity. It is a major contributor to where the torque curve falls in the RPM range. Cross sections are found in the diameter of a throttle bore, venturi, or booster; a manifold runner; a port section; and a valve-throat choke point. Like the vena contracta, a cross section creates a specified restriction that governs air velocity for any given feed pressure.

The small peanut ports on a big-block truck cylinder head are pretty energetic about feeding the engine at low speeds, and thus, they generate stronger torque. Likewise, the big rectangular high-performance ports are pretty lazy and unresponsive until you increase engine speed to initiate better flow velocity. It works because higher engine speeds create a lot more cylinder filling opportunities, so the air has to speed up to meet the increasing demand.

The path length influences tuning characteristics by controlling the timing of finite amplitude waves, which lends energy to the charge movement if the waves arrive at the correct time to add momentum to the charge. Although the cross section sets the position of the torque

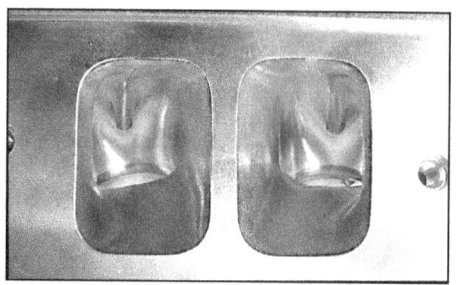

"Cross section" refers to the overall area of a flow path opening if you take a slice across it at any given point. The opening can be round, oval, square, or rectangular with rounded corners. The minimum effective cross section is usually the throat area directly above the valve, but in some cases it occurs closer to the port entrance because of the pushrod hump. You can also measure it at both locations and calculate the average cross section. Multiply the height by the width; or, at the valve, calculate the area of a circle: $A = \pi r^2$.

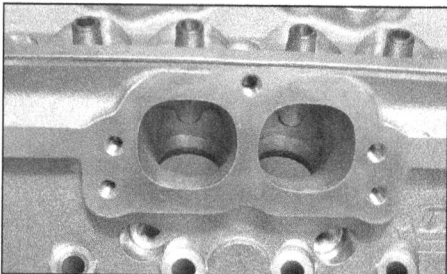

The valveguide temporarily disrupts the cross section, but you can generally ignore it for overall cross-section calculations. The cross section influences torque peak efficiency because it affects velocity and flow quality according to area consistency and the path to the valve.

An oval or peanut port of a big-block Chevy head is a perfect example. The smaller cross section keeps mixture velocity high for low-speed efficiency and area-generated intake ramming. The improved cylinder filling at low engine speeds enhances low-speed torque.

Large rectangular ports become more effective at high engine speeds as RPM increases port velocity. However, these ports are typically lazy and ineffective at street engine speeds due to insufficient velocity.

ENGINE AIRFLOW COMPONENTS

peak, the path length can shift torque above or below the peak to varying degrees depending on the tuned length.

The pressure pulses in the path reverse direction (reflect) whenever they encounter a large area change or blockage such as a closed valve. The path length influences the timing of these reflections, and to some degree the cross sections influence their strength.

Carburetors and Throttle Bodies

Because engines breathe air, I have to begin with a discussion of the air supply (atmosphere). You have an unlimited supply of air with its 21-percent oxygen content all around you. The first order of business is to get this air into the engine. If not for the various obstructions required to package an engine's contents in some usable fashion, the atmosphere would easily fill every cylinder instantly over and over. Because that's not literally possible, you need a way of admitting air to the engine in measured quantities so you can control it and make the engine run at varying speeds depending on your operating requirements.

The means to do that is a throttling device that limits airflow and, thus, VE according to throttle opening, so the engine can idle and run smoothly at different speeds according to the amount of air (throttle opening) you allow it to breathe. Either a carburetor or a throttle body,

The carburetor is the first point of significant flow restriction. It throttles the engine by regulating air and fuel delivery in the required proportions for the performance demand. Airflow through the carburetor venturis creates a pressure differential that pulls fuel into the airstream where it is atomized in the proper ratio for optimum combustion.

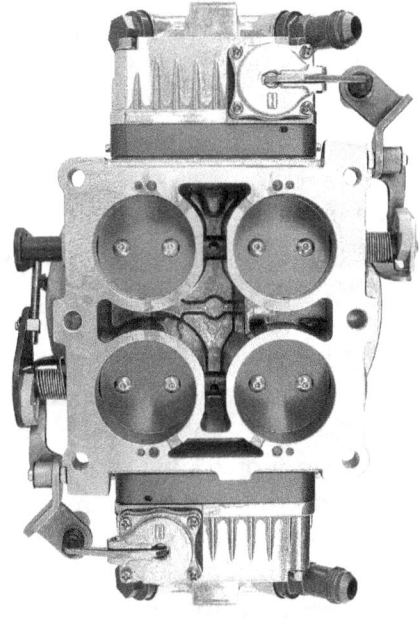

Air scoops are employed to capture airflow and direct it into the engine. Depending on their size, shape, and vehicle speed, they can often create a mild pressure rise within the inlet tract.

This view of a Holley Dominator shows the larger throttle plates; they are set farther apart to accommodate placement that is more in line with the port runners. Newer models use rounded button-head throttle-plate screws to reduce flow restriction.

PRACTICAL ENGINE AIRFLOW

CHAPTER 3

The view from the top with the throttle blades open shows the massive airflow capacity available from the 4500-series Holley carburetors. Out-of-the-box versions now flow up to and beyond 1,400 cfm.

both of which incorporate one or more butterfly valves to control the amount of air entering the engine, most often accomplishes the throttling function.

Carburetors and some throttle bodies meter fuel based on demand as determined by load and vacuum or electronic sensors. If fuel is metered via direct port injection, the throttle body becomes an air-only device.

Carburetors and some throttle bodies not only accomplish the engine throttling requirement, but also satisfy the fueling demands by introducing fuel to the airstream in the correct quantity to meet the desired air/fuel ratio for best power. Carburetors are very well developed, and in some cases they are much more efficient at making power than many electronic fuel injection proponents would have you believe. In terms of starting, drivability, fuel economy, and emissions, carburetors struggle to compete with EFI. For all-out power, however, carburetors equal and often out-power EFI applications in similar builds.

That's because the proper air/fuel ratio for best power is essentially the same for either of them; on a case-by-case basis, some carburetor applications can actually atomize fuel better. The primary difference lies in the manifold configuration, and for OEM cars it is generally compromised by requirements to properly package the system under a stock hoodline. Racing applications typically do not have that problem so they are more likely to be able to apply the best manifold configuration possible.

Because carburetors are pressure-sensitive devices, they perform their primary function based on the air flowing through them. For the most part, pressure-actuated control circuits within the carburetor provide relatively accurate adjustments (calibration) for proper fueling regardless of carburetor size, flow capacity, or the amount of air you actually move through it at any given time. Here, you are concerned with how carburetors (and throttle bodies) affect airflow through an engine.

You can obtain carburetors and throttle bodies in pretty much any size you want to match your engine's air capacity and VE potential. Most of that selection process is mathematically determined by the following equation:

Air Capacity = (displacement x RPM) ÷ 3,456

Where:
3,456 = mathematical constant

As an example, the theoretical requirement for a 565-ci big-block Chevy at 7,500 rpm might be 1,226 cfm (565 x 7,500 ÷ 3,456). The closest applicable size would be a 1,250-cfm Holley Dominator.

In practice, this formula should be used only as an approximation. It does not specifically accommodate an engine's actual VE or its ability to ingest more air than its volumetric capacity at different operating speeds. That's based on components of the horsepower chain being able to force-feed the engine to achieve increased VE with properly sized flow path dimensions and appropriately matched valve events. Even if you are able to verify VE on a dyno, a carburetor can still be too small for some applications, depending on the engine's dynamic range and transient response characteristics, which are affected by inlet and exhaust tuning, camshaft profile, and external influences such as gearing, tire size, and vehicle weight.

It is important to remember that a carburetor must always have at least 1 inch of pressure difference between the intake manifold below the throttle bores and atmospheric pressure above the carburetor. This minimum differential is necessary to maintain adequate airflow velocity through the carburetor at WOT.

A common trick is to multiply the result of the above formula by 1.1 to anticipate the increased VE that a racing engine is expected to achieve. Using the same example as above, CFM adjusts to almost 1,350

ENGINE AIRFLOW COMPONENTS

(1,250 x 1.1 = 1,348.6) and probably works pretty well on a very efficient high-speed engine unless run at higher altitude where the air is thinner and atmospheric pressure is lower. And yet most 565-ci engines offered by professional race shops are equipped with 1,150-cfm Holley carburetors. Why?

It's most likely because they are intended for Sportsman drag racing applications that have a broader operating range than, say, a Pro Stock engine. They need to maintain strong velocity through the carburetor for optimal transient response across their operating range, which may typically encompass 5,500 to 6,000 rpm through 7,500 to 8,500 or more.

An engine's ability to make power is determined primarily by engine speed, camshaft timing, and the cylinder head's capacity to flow air. In selecting a carburetor or throttle body to service that capacity, you have to closely tailor the flow rating and dimensional features to suit the specific requirements of the intended application and RPM operating range.

As a rule, engines with narrower power bands, such as in Pro Stock drag racing, call for more airflow capacity than the formula indicates because they have a minimal range of operation between gear changes and spend all of their time at WOT and max RPM. For lower-class circle-track and road racing applications with more frequent throttling and a broader dynamic range, the formula can more closely predict a proper carburetor size. A notable example of appropriate carburetor sizing is found in Reher-Morrison Racing Engines' recommendations for basic Sportsman and professional-class drag racing.

There are many instances of unintended over- or under-carburetion for the application. Race engine performance is typically optimized with the smallest possible induction components that do not cause a reduction in horsepower. When you over-carb an engine, air velocity through the venturis is reduced, and the venturi/booster combination cannot pull enough fuel to support the engine. A lean condition ensues and the engine falters due to lack of fuel. This condition cannot be corrected by installing larger jets because the engine runs too rich at higher engine speeds when air velocity finally catches up. You can never fully balance the mixture delivery across the entire operating range of the engine and performance suffers across the board.

Carburetor Airflow Evaluation

When evaluating race carburetors tuners are primarily concerned with the maximum amount of airflow (CFM) moving through the carburetor and the pressure drop, or vacuum, that occurs below the carburetor. In technical parlance this is called a pressure differential and is typically referred to as the delta P (or ΔP). The standard for a 4-barrel carburetor is 1.5 inches Hg and 3 inches for 2-barrel carburetors.

In a running engine, the delta P is essentially the manifold vacuum in the plenum under the carburetor. On a flow bench, it is typically registered by a probe in the bench, but carburetor tuners have found that air velocity and turbulence often skew the reading making it difficult to perform accurate carburetor testing. Why is this important?

Well, because it affects the pressure recovery characteristics of the air exiting the carburetor. In simplified terms, air enters the carburetor at local atmospheric pressure and loses pressure through the carburetor bores and venturis as it gains velocity. It must recover that pressure exiting the throttle bores in order to maintain airflow pressure and feed the runners.

Carb tuners are very concerned with how the airflow characteristics of their carburetors, combined with various carb spacers and manifold types, affect this pressure recovery. Good pressure recovery creates minimal turbulence and encourages smooth, efficient entry into the manifold runners with minimal fuel separation. The same is true with a throttle body (except for the fuel separation), where you are again trying to smooth the transition from the air entry device through the plenum and into the runners with minimal turbulence.

All of this is influenced in varying degrees by pressure effects initiated by the overlap period, the rate (and volume) of delta P exposure created

Reher-Morrison Recommended Carburetor Sizes

Engine Size	Carburetor CFM	Total CFM
327 to 366 Sportsman	(1) 650 to 800	650 to 800
400 to 460 Sportsman	(1) 780 to 850	780 to 850
500+ Sportsman	(1) 1,050 to 1,150	1,050 to 1,150
350 to 366 Pro	(2) 850 to 1,050	1,700 to 2,100
500+ Pro	(2) 1,150 to 1,300	2,300 to 2,600

CHAPTER 3

The Vena Contracta

A functioning engine is all about the manipulation and management of pressure. A fluid (including air) moving through an orifice or restriction achieves a particular point in the fluid stream at which the diameter of the stream is the smallest, the flow velocity is highest, and the static pressure is low. Engineers call this point the vena contracta. Engines have multiple vena contractas, each serving a specific purpose. Within the overall airflow path, a throttle bore in a carburetor and the booster inside the throttle bore are vena contractas. Each represents a restriction created by its orifice size and provides a flow path with fixed resistance, forcing the air to gain velocity due to the constant air pressure behind it.

In a carburetor this point is near the bottom of the booster and provides the strongest pull on the fuel supply through the jets. The divergent or expansion region is the fuel cone that forms below the booster as the high-speed air/fuel mixture immediately begins to decelerate and regain pressure. If you could see the fuel cone at full throttle, it would appear almost solid exiting the booster and pretty much disappearing about an inch or two down the throttle bore as it loses speed, regains pressure, and disperses into the plenum.

Hence there are two distinct divergent regions: One is below the booster and the other exits the actual throttle bore. Each represents a velocity and pressure gradient carefully tailored to help optimize and maintain fuel atomization.

The cross section of the airstream at the vena contracta is the smallest point. You might be surprised to learn that the

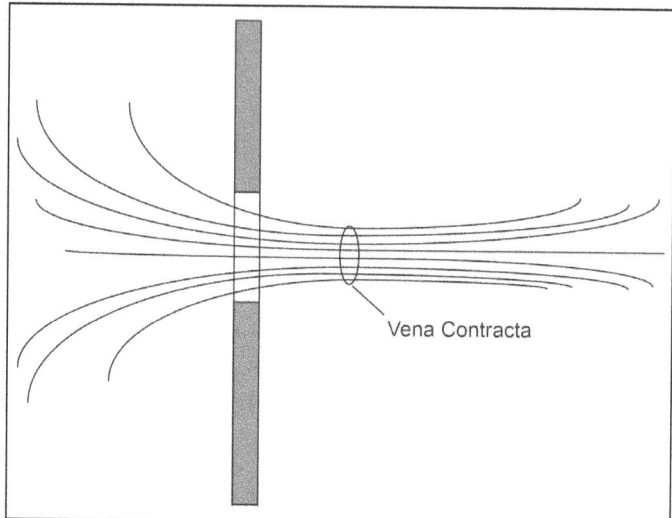

This illustration of the vena contracta shows how air flowing through an orifice is pinched to a smaller flow path after the orifice to create a discharge coefficient based on the pressure gradient and the orifice size.

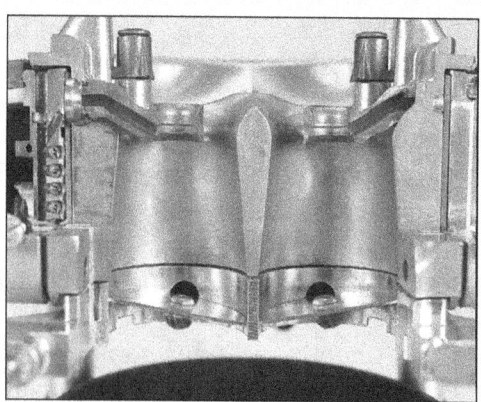

This cutaway shows a pair of venturis with the discharge port of the booster venturis located right at the point of maximum depression within the main venturis. That is the smallest-diameter flow path where the airspeed is highest and the pressure is lowest. Then, the venturis expand to meet the throttle plates, which control airflow. The red passages show the fuel path from the main well into the boosters.

This view shows a Demon carburetor at maximum flow. You can see fuel exiting the discharge port in the upper boosters and observe how it disperses off the booster discharge nozzle to form the fuel cone beneath each booster. This is the point of maximum atomization. Part of the overall airflow-sizing requirement must allow for the partial blockage created by the emerging fuel cones at peak demand.

vena contracta is not located at the orifice itself but rather at some point downstream. High-speed air rushing through an orifice seeks a convergence point where it begins to expand, losing velocity and gaining pressure. Convergent flow results in a narrowing and smoothing of the airstream before it expands in the divergent region after the vena contracta. The distance from the orifice to the vena contracta is largely controlled by the pressure differential (delta P) across the orifice, the momentum imparted by the pressure behind it, and the area of the restriction itself.

The pinching effect of the orifice forces the high-velocity air (forming a jet effect) to remain pinched briefly and form the narrowest area of flow at some arbitrary distance past the orifice. That is the convergence point, or the vena contracta. The area of the vena contracta is thus smaller than the area of the orifice, forming a ratio called the coefficient of contraction. ∎

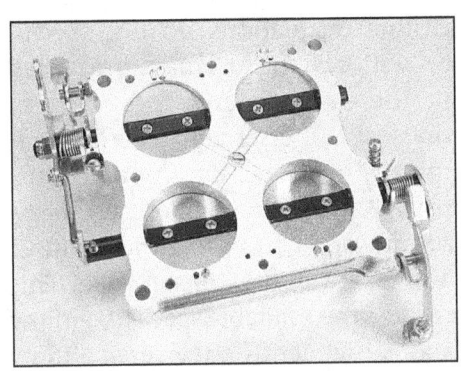

The throttle plate on the bottom of the carburetor controls the air's exit to the plenum space. On certain carburetor bodies, some carburetor specialists switch to larger-capacity throttle plates to gain flow if the particular body accepts the larger bores.

by the descending piston, and, of course, the unseen finite amplitude waves racing back and forth through the runners. For the purpose of this discussion, the best result of effective pressure recovery is higher airflow with minimal disturbance, which is what you need to pack the cylinders full to make more power.

Pressure Recovery

Pressure recovery is the term applied to regaining atmospheric pressure anywhere in the inlet tract after the air has been pinched down, accelerated, and subjected to a loss of pressure as occurs in a carburetor venturi or a valve throat area. In a typically aspirated application, you have two ways to fill the cylinder: intake pumping and intake ramming. Both depend on having the full available weight of atmospheric (head) pressure to push air into the cylinders. Air passing through any restriction gains velocity and loses pressure. That's the operating principle of a carburetor venturi.

The reduction in atmospheric pressure in the venturi allows normal atmospheric pressure above the fuel in the float bowl to push fuel through a nozzle and add it to the high-speed airstream. If it were possible for the air to maintain equal velocity through the venturi, pressure would be equalized and fuel would not flow. The slightest change in pressure affects fuel flow, which is further controlled by jetting and internal fuel circuit restrictions.

A similar effect occurs wherever air experiences a pressure change caused by a change in area or velocity. It happens at the valveseat as air enters the cylinder. It happens below the carburetor as high-speed air loses velocity exiting the throttle bores. In many cases, it also occurs at the pinch point in the port around the pushrod. Carb tuners, manifold designers, and head porters are very much concerned with recovering the full effect of atmospheric pressure once the air loses velocity. If you can't recover the pressure, you're not applying the full weight of the atmosphere to the task of filling the cylinders.

Selective manipulation of flow path shapes, dimensions, and even wave tuning also takes advantage of this critical pressure recovery to aid in the intake ramming cycle where you do your best to pack the cylinders beyond their physical capacity. Part of the trick in this whole process is to maintain the best possible fuel atomization as the mixture changes velocity passing through the plenum and into the individual runners.

If you have less than atmospheric pressure in the cylinder at IVC, you don't have much to compress. Air entering the cylinder is chasing the piston down the bore. The rapidly accelerating piston is creating a larger and larger void for the air to fill, making it difficult to recover the pressure, particularly in the first half of the stroke. This is the intake's pumping phase as air is drawn into the cylinder.

The intake ramming process is based largely on the established momentum of the moving air column to not only recover atmospheric pressure, but also add to it before IVC. It is an extraordinarily subtle balance controlled primarily

CHAPTER 3

by engine speed, flow path dimensions, and certainly pressure recovery. These conditions also occur in the manifold plenum before the air enters the manifold runners, where it achieves a mean flow velocity. The runner shape and size, as well as the influence of any other restrictions, such as sharp turns, transitions, or abrupt changes in area, have an impact on this balance.

Pressure recovery in the plenum is accomplished with the desired 7-degree angle exiting the carburetor and by adjusting plenum volume (if possible) to suit the capacity of the engine according to operational conditions. These include throttle response versus high-RPM power and the air requirements that best suit the engine's purpose. (See Chapter 4 for more details.) To adequately meet the engine's air demand at any given engine speed it is desirable to achieve the maximum possible pressure recovery in the plenum so that the airflow demand from each runner is serviced by as close to atmospheric pressure as possible.

Pressure recovery in a naturally aspirated engine, whether it is in the manifold plenum or the cylinder and combustion chamber, is a major contributor to engine performance as related to the intake pumping and intake ramming processes.

Over time, carburetor manufacturers and tuners have made valuable revisions to accommodate clearly identified anomalies and/or airflow gains based on improved air entry shapes, booster modifications, and other "tweaks" intended to facilitate smoother air entry into the engine. One frequently unrecognized consequence of carburetor airflow is the proximity of the throttle bores to one another and how each bore affects another in the struggle to pull air. Although they are equal in size, they may be individually influenced by peculiarities in the nearest runner inlets, some of which may transmit stronger or weaker air demand signals depending on their shape, size, and proximity to the individual throttle bore and others around it.

Despite your best efforts to equalize flow, the configuration of the manifold and the cylinder head runners does not always complement the neatly arranged throttle opening at the bottom of the carburetor. Consequently, some runners may tend to rob some flow from the throttle openings closest to them. And the intensity of this may also change with RPM.

Hot rod applications are generally a compromise between appearance, flow capacity, and street functionality. If properly sized, these setups often provide surprisingly good performance.

Carburetor entry revisions have improved this, but they can't entirely compensate for unusual conditions above and below the carburetor, including air scoops, air filters, and other influences that can affect equal flow into each throttle bore. These problems affect carburetors and multi-bore throttle bodies as well, and they can be difficult to troubleshoot and correct.

Equally frustrating, the standard airflow calculations do not specifically address the fuel mass introduced in the boosters and the effect of the fuel disbursement cone in each throttle bore. Fuel mass not only displaces air, the fuel cone itself forms a semi-solid barrier to airflow almost as resistant as the booster itself. This reduces the available space for airflow and consequently the overall airflow capacity of each throttle bore. Once fuel has been introduced, its mass also reduces airflow velocity.

Carburetor tuners study these things and lose sleep while contemplating ways to compensate for them. They usually use large-capacity carburetors and booster modifications to remedy the problem. But they still have to flow the required amount of fuel, and there's no easy path around or through that fuel cone. On average, a carb flows 10 to 14 percent less with a fuel cone than it does when dry on the flow bench. This is particularly true of alcohol carburetors in which the fuel mass is almost doubled, and flow is further restricted.

These are legitimate problems that tuners ponder so they can figure out how to tweak the fuel cone to minimize its disturbance of the airflow column without affecting its ability to atomize the fuel consistently. The problem is further compounded with alcohol carbs because

ENGINE AIRFLOW COMPONENTS

they have nearly twice as much fuel flowing as with gasoline.

Butterfly Challenges

Back in the day, we all used to grind down the screws securing the butterflies on the throttle shafts to improve airflow. Although this helped, it was just not possible to overcome the real flaw associated with airflow and butterflies. Theoretically, as the butterfly opens it exposes the same flow area on the high side as on the low side, but physics interferes and disrupts the process.

The high side of the butterfly (the side that's rising) tends to introduce more turbulence because of the shearing effect of the blade against the oncoming flow. The lower side is less turbulent and all throttle openings tend to speed up flow across its open area because the flow moves smoothly across the lower opening blade. It also tends to dominate the mixture flow.

Each bore has turbulent flow that hinders pressure recovery entering the plenum and uneven fuel distribution at part throttle because the partially open butterfly distributes fuel unevenly before it exits the throttle bore. The low side distributes rich; the high side is lean and it is variable depending on the degree of throttle opening.

Because the mixture exits immediately after the throttle blades into the plenum, some cylinders have the opportunity to pull more or less mixture independent of the pressure recovery that is also required upon carburetor exit. Therefore, you have multiple problems all conspiring to upset the smooth movement of air through the system.

Some carb tuners have introduced modifications to direct additional fuel to the lean (high) side of the butterfly and saw improved part-throttle performance, but air still hates any disruption that causes turbulence. The problem primarily affects part-throttle operation and is less severe in applications with full-time throttle opening, such as drag racing. It can, however, cause a lot of head-scratching for road racers and circle-track racers that have more frequent part-throttle operation and the need for instant throttle response.

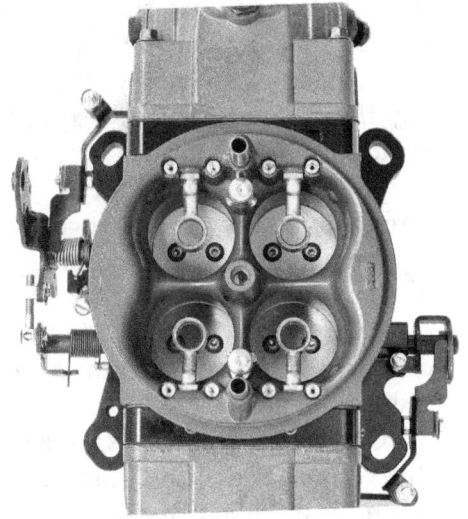

The carburetor air entry is critical to optimal flow. Performance carburetors have a smooth radius inlet to the throttle bores to minimize flow loss. Each primary venturi has its own booster venturi to deliver atomized fuel to the engine according to the fueling demand created by the pressure drop across the carburetor.

Carb Sizing

Most carburetor sizing charts and the commonly applied sizing equation are really intended to provide general guidelines for street engines that rarely achieve high engine speeds and typically reside in a relatively narrow operating range that

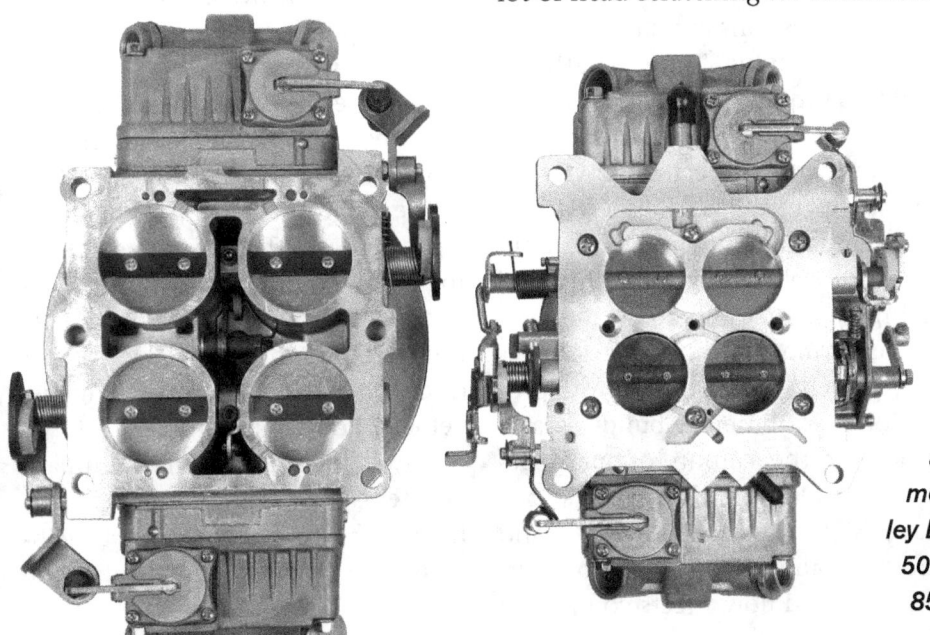

Carburetors are sized to suit the calculated air requirements of each application. Larger or smaller throttle bores provide the ideal velocity for good fuel atomization and the maximum air requirement at WOT. For example, a 1,050-cfm Holley Dominator (left) might be used on a larger 500-ci performance engine while the smaller 850-cfm 4150 model (right) accommodates smaller-displacement engines.

PRACTICAL ENGINE AIRFLOW

CHAPTER 3

is easily serviced by standard carburetor sizes. In a high-RPM racing environment, particularly drag racing, the engine is typically expected to achieve 1½ inches Hg (vacuum) at WOT, but it can't get there if the carburetor is too small. A larger carburetor almost always provides superior performance, particularly when carefully matched to a specific range of engine speed for a given engine displacement.

Carburetor specialists suggest that road racing and circle-track engines requiring a broader effective operating range work best when generating about 0.8 to 1 inch Hg (vacuum). Heavier drag cars tend to want a carb that delivers about 0.6 to 1 inch Hg. High-speed drag racing and Pro Stock engines often incorporate much larger carburetors generating only 0.1 to 0.2 inch Hg in the narrow high-RPM power band where they thrive. With proper gear spacing and minimal RPM changes on each shift, these engines function in a very narrow range that allows the carburetor tuner to pinpoint the ideal carburetor size and appropriate metering signal for best performance. In racing at least, the general trend is toward larger carburetors for almost any application.

The carb technicians at C&S Specialties also point out other inconsistencies for racing carburetors operating in extreme environments outside normal test parameters. As an example, they cite a 390-cfm NASCAR 4-barrel that might generate more than three times the standard 1½ inches Hg for a standard street 4-barrel. Or, a very large 2-barrel carb that may generate only 1½ inches Hg instead of the commonly cited 3 inches. All of this, of course, is very much dependent on the carburetor size, the operational engine speed, and the air demand the engine generates.

Flow Testing Carburetors

Carburetor flow testing can open the proverbial can of worms because there are no particular standards that apply across the board. Real-world performance dynamics suggest that all airflow components should be tested with the greatest possible pressure drop to simulate actual conditions. This is not possible with most flow benches and the most common standards are the original Holley numbers adopted back in the day: 4-barrels rated at 1.5 inches Hg and 2-barrels rated at 3.0 inches Hg.

Flow-bench test pressure ratings are indicated in inches of water so the equivalent 4-barrel test pressure equals 20.4 inches of water, and the 2-barrel rating is 40.8 inches of water. These figures are "wet rated" based on a typical air/fuel ratio of 12.5:1, but this is conditional because there is no specific standard for the effects of the fuel disbursement cone at different depressions as would occur in a running engine. The wet rating is said to be equivalent to an 8-percent reduction in CFM, but there is no accounting for specific gravity so the opportunity for data skew arises. The standard value more than doubles for alcohol; it reduces the CFM rating by up to 18 to 20 percent.

As a rule, this sort of testing is pretty well accomplished by professional carburetor builders and tuners or the carburetor manufacturer. Calibration specifications have significantly improved, and most carburetor suppliers now furnish detailed flow sheets comparing throttle-bore flow figures. In terms of airflow capacity, you are not specifically contemplating carburetor calibration as much as you are examining the airflow capacity of the carburetor and flow-related influences that tend to reduce airflow. Unless you flow carburetors for a living, it is pretty easy to get lost and trick yourself on the flow bench.

Booster Effects

Higher airspeed through the venturi is a desired effect to improve fuel metering. Venturi boosters are responsible for increasing the local pressure drop through the venturi and introducing emulsified fuel to the airstream. They vary in design and degree of effectiveness according to the application. The booster type affects how much fuel can be drawn through it, and also influences the amount of air the carburetor can flow.

A "straight-leg" Holley type of booster works fine on a street application, but the fuel disbursement bar across the center of the booster disrupts and limits airflow through the booster. "Downleg" boosters are easy to spot because of their angled booster leg. They distribute fuel to the airstream via a bleed hole on the inboard side of the booster. The downfall of the dogleg booster is this single fuel disbursement hole that is typically less effective at fuel shearing and atomization. However, its open design flows more air and its downleg design places the booster directly in the path of the highest velocity air through the venturi.

By comparison, an "annular" booster is the most effective. There is no center bar, and the fuel is distributed via a series of holes around the inner circumference of the booster. It too eliminates the booster crossbar

ENGINE AIRFLOW COMPONENTS

to improve airflow, and it improves fuel atomization because of the multiple fuel-discharge holes around the inner annular channel. All of this combines to achieve higher airflow velocity, a stronger signal, and better mixture quality. The chief advantage of higher air speed is better fuel atomization. This contributes smaller fuel droplets that burn faster and more completely than larger droplets and, thus, contribute to more efficient combustion.

Many carb tuners have experimented with their own booster designs to improve atomization. They were drilling steps in the bottom of boosters more than 25 years ago in an attempt to improve the shearing effect exiting the booster. This has proved to be an effective measure, and others have carried it further, designing their own boosters for various applications. C&S Specialties, for example, has incorporated a unique parabolic-curve entry designed to reduce turbulence at booster entry. In effect they created their own vena contracta with the most desirable location for the fuel feed.

In an age when electronic fuel injection and air-only intake manifolds have begun to make serious inroads, carburetors are still holding their own. The primary concern for any engine lies in increasing the airflow and maintaining mixture quality. At WOT carburetors still do a great job.

Backward Airflow

Can air flow through a carburetor backward? The answer is yes, it most certainly can. During the overlap period when both valves are off the seat at the same time, improper cam timing can cause the air to stack up due to higher remaining cylinder pressure because the exhaust has not finished blowing down at IVO. If the pressure is still greater in the cylinder, it can resist and even push the incoming charge back up through the carburetor briefly until the overall pressure equalizes when the exhaust event finishes.

This is a cam problem. The exhaust event must initiate and complete a strong blowdown of the cylinder so that cylinder pressure is reduced to atmospheric or less due to the scavenging effect of the departing gases. The strength of the blowdown event depends largely on the amount of residual cylinder pressure at the end of the combustion cycle and the timing of the exhaust valve, which initiates supersonic flow as soon as the valve cracks open.

It's a delicate balance to create an exhaust event that adequately empties the cylinder and provides a little tug on the intake charge as a bonus. That tug is a pressure differential when the incoming charge achieves pressure dominance, and strong exhaust pressure waves encourage the intake charge to follow. At this point, a well-designed cam slams the door on the exhaust valve, so none of the incoming charge is allowed to escape out the exhaust unburned.

This phenomenon is called reversion because it encourages the backward flow of residual exhaust and contaminated intake mixture. Reversion can be slight, or it can be so severe that you observe a fog of rejected fuel above the carburetor at full throttle. The higher the cylinder pressure at IVO, the more severe the reversion. That fog of fuel above the carburetor can't enter because the pressure in the inlet tract is too great. It is likely that the air/fuel mixture has been driven back through the booster, creating a localized pressure drop that pulls more fuel. Due to similar, strong pulses from other cylinders, the mixture may be blasted through the booster and back multiple times, pulling more fuel each time, and the engine goes dead rich.

Some pretty serious math describes these events, but you don't need to know it to understand the cause and effect. Mixture contamination and fuel enrichment are real and valid concerns, but the overriding problem is that you have all but stopped flowing air through the engine. It may still rev, but it only makes enough power to run itself and not the race car too. Suffice it to say that detailed discussions with your cam grinder are necessary to pinpoint the optimal timing to suit your application. All too often people expect to read a book and come away with a magic formula that changes everything. A "step-by-step do this, do that" report works pretty well when you're describing how to install an intake manifold or time a distributor. But the dynamics of a high-speed racing engine are such that you can't assign strict values to things such as cam timing so people can use them. In this book I provide you with insight to understand the process so you can ask good questions and understand the answers when spec'ing a cam or talking with a head porter.

In general, wider lobe separation angles (LSA) of 112 degrees or more are less prone to reversion because they reduce the overlap period. A narrower LSA invites reversion if you get the specs wrong. You have to be sure the cylinder has blown down sufficiently before you crack open the intake valve. You also don't want the rising piston to help push residual exhaust gases into the intake.

To give the inlet system a head start, the intake valve opens a specified number of degrees before TDC on the exhaust stroke (based on the assumption that efficient exhaust timing has sufficiently evacuated the cylinder). The exhaust valve can remain open for as much as 50 degrees after TDC. So as the piston begins the intake stroke it can pull from the open intake valve and the open exhaust valve, contaminating the mixture and resisting or overcoming initial intake flow if the exhaust pressure is still high.

Also keep in mind that the intake valve remains open on the early portion of the compression stroke to aid filling. If this is not timed correctly the pressure rise from initiating compression may overcome the intake ramming effect and push back into the inlet system. To some degree reversion can also be compounded by connecting-rod length. Although many consider the effect small, shorter rods in an engine tend to accelerate the piston down the bore more quickly, producing a stronger depression that pulls in contaminating exhaust. With a slight increase in dwell time and a slower departure rate from TDC, longer rods may resist reversion more easily.

Reversion is a severe power robber that causes major disruption in the smooth flow of air through an engine. Remember that you are always talking about pressure changes, and this is one of them. Higher pressure almost always wins, so you have to open and close the valves accordingly to make pressure work *for* you and not *against* you.

Air Velocity and Boundary Layers

Top head porters tell you that high air speed is everything. It moves more air, maintains mixture quality in carbureted applications, and very much supports the intake ramming link in the horsepower chain. As briefly discussed in Chapter 2, air does not like interruptions, excessive restrictions, or area changes. Interruptions create turbulence, which affects air speed; excessive restrictions limit the quantity of air you can flow; and area changes cause disturbing fluctuations in airspeed. The overriding goal of engine airflow is to establish the smoothest possible movement of air everywhere in the engine with minimal turbulence.

If 100 runners tried to rush through your front door all at once, chaos would ensue, and only a handful would make it through. If each one represented 100 cfm, you wouldn't have much to work with. If the same 100 people established a smooth, orderly line with no interruptions, they could all run through that door single file in less than a minute bringing with them 1,000 cfm of potential. Put a sprinkler orifice over the door, and you've just added fuel.

Friction and turbulence are enemies of good airflow. Using the door analogy again, let's say it's an Oscar party, and there's a long line of media hacks on both sides wanting to shake hands, say a few words, and get a photo or a sound bite. That's the friction preventing the runners from hauling through that door as fast as possible. Any activity between the press and the runners, such as stopping to talk or shake hands, is the boundary layer.

In terms of air and fuel molecules, some get stuck and remain

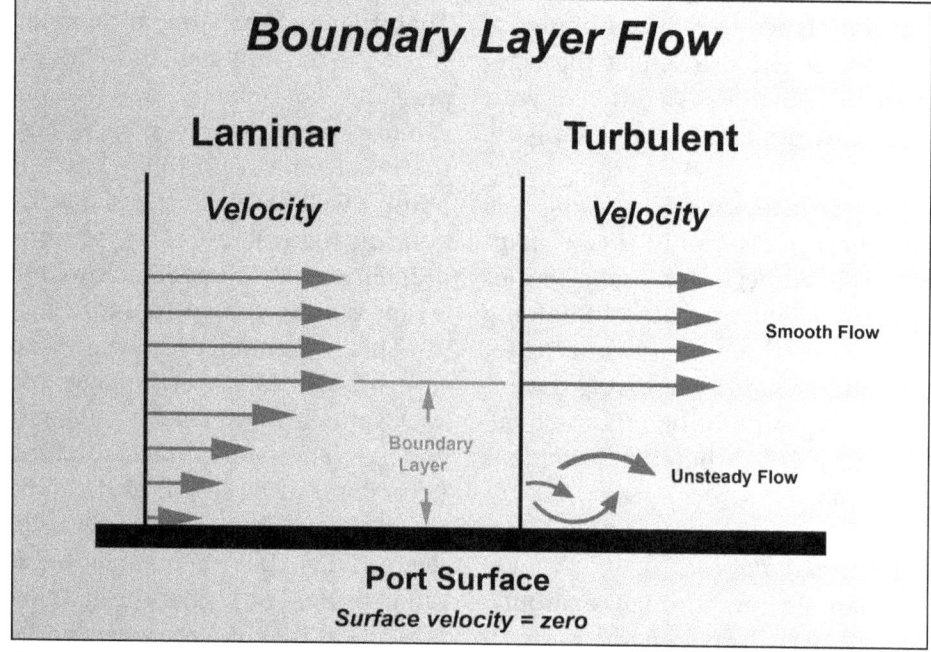

Smooth laminar flow remains attached to the port surface with zero surface velocity and a gradual velocity gradient as you move farther away from the surface. Turbulent flow may be smoother in the center of the flow path but it incorporates drag due to unsteady, detached flow closer to the surface.

ENGINE AIRFLOW COMPONENTS

Street carburetors have additional airflow restrictions such as the choke housing and choke plate that help provide fuel enrichment on startup. Carb specialists often machine material off the choke housing to improve airflow on carbs slated for performance duty.

attached, others stumble over them and create turbulence and more drag on the airstream. The degree to which this occurs depends largely on the viscosity of the moving fluid (air) and its compressibility, or ability to stumble or take a hit and keep on moving. When fuel droplets are added, the air becomes stickier and viscosity increases. As you move farther away from the surface the effect lessens. The highest velocity is in the center of the flow, but that's not necessarily in the center of the physical flow path because the air defines its own center.

Boundary layers come in two types: laminar and turbulent. Laminar flow tends to remain smooth with reduced velocity near the surface and increased velocity away from the surface. It is the smoothest and most desirable type of flow. You might say that laminar flow resembles the runners racing past, but maybe slapping hands as they pass. They keep moving, and the activity doesn't slow them down much. In contrast, turbulent flow is more chaotic and more closely resembles the analogy of the runners stopping to talk and party on their way to the door.

The thickness of the boundary layer is defined by its Reynolds number, which is the ratio of inertial resistance to viscosity, or the tendency to create drag via stickiness. Within the engine's airflow path, flow can be laminar in some portions and turbulent in others. The goal is to achieve the smoothest possible uninterrupted flow everywhere possible. It's a tall order because of the influence of area and velocity changes, pressure recovery, and even thermodynamic effects.

Obstructions and Pressure Changes

Your attempts to achieve smooth, efficient flow encounter many obstructions that disrupt the airstream. Air stumbles and becomes turbulent more easily when it encounters obstacles. These obstructions include abrupt changes in direction or area. Sharp edges or objects in the airstream (such as valvestems, gasket edges, and a severe mismatch where the manifold runner meets the intake port) also cause problems. In the overall scheme of things, you do your best to straighten and smooth the airflow path as much as possible. And you employ tricks, such as runner taper to accelerate the air as it approaches the valve.

All along the way you attempt to recover and maintain as much atmospheric pressure as possible because that is all you have to work with outside of physical manipulations to increase the ramming effect. The same is true even in boosted applications where you have more initial pressure. You still want to take advantage of it all the way to the cylinder.

Turbulence anywhere in the path has a negative effect. So you make sure you don't have the bottom of rocker studs protruding into the intake ports or mismatched ports at the manifold-to-cylinder head interface. It's why you smooth and taper the valveguides and round the runner entry points in the manifold. The goal is increased airspeed and the ability to pack the cylinder with every last molecule the atmosphere has to offer. It can be a pretty tough chore, but you have many tools at your disposal. The challenge is to use them effectively and not lose anything along the way.

Wave Tuning

The practice of improving VE by increasing the pressure in the intake port just before the point of IVC is referred to as wave (or ram) tuning. It is a method that seeks to take advantage of finite amplitude waves, or pressure pulses, in the intake and exhaust system to add energy to ramming the incoming charge or extracting outgoing exhaust gases. This section elaborates on the use and effects of wave tuning in the intake system.

Here is the Runner Length Formula:

$$L = [(k \times c) \div N] + 3$$

Where:
L = length of the inlet path in inches
k = mathematical constant (Chrysler chose 72,000)
c = 1,100 fps
N = engine speed (rpm)
+ 3 = recommendation to encourage experimentation to determine the actual "weet spot"

You can find simplified optimum runner length constants (k) by dividing the selected constant by the RPM:

2nd pulse = 108,000 ÷ RPM
3rd pulse = 97,000 ÷ RPM
4th pulse = 74,000 ÷ RPM
5th pulse = 54,000 ÷ RPM

Chrysler Ramcharger Research

Sharp-eyed readers note differences in the equations presented below and those above. They are not erroneous. The ones offered below are taken from work performed by Chrysler Ramcharger engineers more than 60 years ago. They are still correct in that they represent a range of possibilities.

The Chrysler recommendations fall almost directly between the third- and fourth-wave equations provided in modern engine simulations. Hence they split recommendations that encompass a broader range based on 60 additional years of testing and evaluation. In the absence of very tightly controlled dyno testing, these calculations are meant to get you in the ballpark, particularly if you are already stuck with fixed-dimension hardware.

The calculations may suggest that your combination has more to offer with modified dimensions. You can model it in a simulation program (which is also a generalization) to see if it predicts a favorable outcome, or you may choose to bite the bullet and reconfigure your dimensions with new components and then test. It's important that you gain a better understanding of your engine's potential. Given enough data, any engine's performance can be reduced to the mathematic principles that define it. Discovering those pesky variables is why you calculate, why you model, and most important, why you test.

Harmonic Cycle

Although much is made of the activity in the combustion chamber, an extraordinary world of tuning potential exists in the captured column of air between the back of the intake valve and the opening of the intake flow path, either at the plenum entrance to the intake runner or the opening of an individual runner ram tube. A similar environment also exists between the exhaust valve and the opening of individual header primaries to the collector.

On either side, a harmonic cycle defines this unique phenomenon. Here, I examine the intake side. A harmonic cycle occurs in sets of four events, and each initiates a pressure and velocity change within the intake runners at supersonic speed. Each event starts at one end or the other of the flow path between the valve and the plenum or ram tube opening.

The first event occurs when the relatively fast moving air/fuel charge slams into the back of the closed intake valve causing a pressure spike relevant to the air density of the charge, its velocity, and the local sonic speed depending on temperature. As more charge slams into the stalled mass, it creates a secondary pressure spike that separates and reflects back up the runner at sonic speed. The piled-up air/fuel charge remains in place, but the pressure pulse reverses and moves through the charge mixture as if it didn't exist.

When the leading edge of the pulse reaches the plenum, the larger area causes local air molecules to disperse away from the opening. A phase change occurs, and negative pulse is reflected back down the runner at sonic velocity (with the air in the runner at zero pressure and negative flow). When the pulse reaches the valve again, the air experiences a negative pressure equal in magnitude to the initial positive pressure. This causes another reversal and another pulse to travel back up the runner to the plenum. It arrives at negative pressure, and plenum air begins to flow into the runner again, but there is minimal pressure with positive velocity. This constitutes one harmonic cycle. When the pulse reaches the valve another cycle initiates immediately.

Research by the Chrysler Ramchargers racing team in the 1950s determined that the best time to open the intake valve was after the third harmonic cycle, which means that the pulse traversal between the valve and the plenum has occurred 12 times. When timed properly the pressure peak arrives at just the right moment to add energy to sweep more charge into the cylinder than typically occurs. These pulses reflecting back and forth in the system, and their arrival at the valve, can be calculated and controlled by the length of the inlet passage.

Additional research determined that the first reflection is very strong

ENGINE AIRFLOW COMPONENTS

and arrives too quickly to do much good. Chrysler engineers in the 1950s initially felt that the second reflection called for excessively long runners and too large of an air/fuel mass to accelerate successfully. Fuel-injected engines that add fuel near the valve don't suffer that problem, so the second reflection is often applied to modern sprint engines and fuel-injected high-torque OEM engines.

The second and third reflections typically generate the most torque. The third and fourth reflections are generally used to apply useful intake tuning to race and performance engines. The third wave is most useful on Pro Stock and Comp Eliminator drag engines to produce maximum horsepower.

In most applications the fourth reflected wave is the most effective with single-plane intakes, delivering less peak torque, but still good horsepower. And, it is typically useful for packaging induction systems under stock hoodlines.

The Chrysler Equation

Calculated values for tuned lengths vary depending on the length of the flow path and the RPM for which you're tuning. The Chrysler equation has proven to be very effective and is still in use today:

$$N \times L = 84{,}000$$

Where:
N = the desired tuning RPM
L = the tuned length of the flow path
84,000 = mathematical constant

To achieve ram tuning at any given engine speed, simply divide the constant by the desired engine speed. For example, adjusting the formula to tune for 6,500 rpm, you get 12.92 inches (84,000 ÷ 6,500). This means that you should make your total flow path from plenum to valve as close to 12.9 inches as possible.

In many cases, you're likely to be working with fixed-length ports and runners, and you must adjust the formula to find the RPM at which your engine tunes with existing hardware.

To calculate RPM, bolt the intake to the head with the appropriate gasket and measure the flow path centerline. You can use a piece of welding rod or a length of string. As an example, for a flow path centerline measurement of 10.4 inches you get 8,077 rpm (84,000 ÷ 10.4). Some anomalies have emerged in subsequent testing. In a 1999 *Hot Rod* magazine test conducted by Steve Magnante and me with on-site support by one of the original Ramcharger engineers, Bill Shope, Chrysler's initial equation was more aligned with short-duration camshafts. After a few thoughtful moments with a calculator, Shope offered that longer camshafts with faster ramps tune slightly different. He suggested revising the equation to compensate for longer-duration cams:

$$N \times L = 80{,}300$$

In this case the ideal tuned length is 12.35 inches (80,300 ÷ 6,500). It is reduced by approximately 0.6 inch, which follows logically given the increased overlap periods and longer seat-to-seat times.

Torque Peak RPM

Keep in mind that the most important mathematical induction system parameter is still the cross-sectional flow area versus the cylinder displacement that it serves. You can also use the McFarland cross-section equation (Chapter 4 page 53) to pinpoint the torque peak RPM and use the Chrysler equation (on this page) to calculate the desired length that supports optimal wave tuning at that engine speed.

The cross section generates an optimal flow velocity that dictates the torque peak RPM. Below the torque peak, cylinder filling trails off due to insufficient velocity in ports large enough to support top-end air demand. Above the torque peak, VE suffers due to less available time for filling and the increased pressure drop. Torque values above and below the peak can be shifted slightly with runner length, and the system can also resonate at more than one speed. It may go in and out of resonance at different speeds above and below the peak speed where it resonates the strongest.

Some tuners like to calculate the effective resonance points. That may be effective in some cases, such as smaller engines in sports cars and circle-track applications in which a fatter, but slightly lower, torque curve with multiple peaks serves the engine's purpose better. Some builders also deliberately use different dimensions on alternating cylinders in the firing order to locate different torque peaks for individual cylinders to broaden the torque range.

Most high-speed applications, such as drag racing or Bonneville, want to operate above the torque peak most of the time. So you have to adjust the peak to suit the application, particularly when horsepower is more of a factor in propelling the car and gear changes are calculated to fall no lower than the torque peak.

CHAPTER 4

INTAKE MANIFOLD

The type, configuration, and dimensions of the intake manifold greatly influence the production of torque and horsepower and their positioning within the engine's effective operating range. A poor intake manifold selection can make or break an engine's power curve, causing lost horsepower, misplaced torque, and poor throttle response. Selection criteria include determining the best type of intake manifold, how well it suits the particular dynamics of the application, and whether it can be suitably and legally modified to accomplish the designated task.

In today's racing environment, it has become critical to properly match the intake manifold to the application. That often means building a custom manifold rather than buying a commercially available version manufactured to suit a range of applications. Hence the proliferation of manifold specialty shops that modify existing manifolds to obtain more desirable entry angles, optimum plenum and runner shapes and sizes, and even port surface texturing for mixture enhancement.

As discussed in Chapter 3, you're concerned with recovering atmospheric pressure in the manifold plenum after you have accelerated it through the carburetor venturis. Each time you accelerate the air through a restricted opening it loses (static) pressure that must be recovered to maintain optimal supply pressure and, thus, cylinder filling efficiency.

Beneath the carburetor, you are concerned with the air's throttle-bore exit speed, the size and shape of the manifold plenum chamber, and certainly the discharge angle of air leaving the carburetor and expanding to fill the plenum area. The discharge angle from the carburetor(s) is critical to good pressure recovery.

Reher-Morrison developed unique carburetor spacers that provide a smooth transition for the air as it decelerates into the plenum.

Once enough airflow capacity is provided through the carburetors, the next element in the airflow equation is the intake manifold. A whole new world of airflow and pressure changes occurs beneath the Holley carburetors on this Chrysler cross ram intake.

INTAKE MANIFOLD

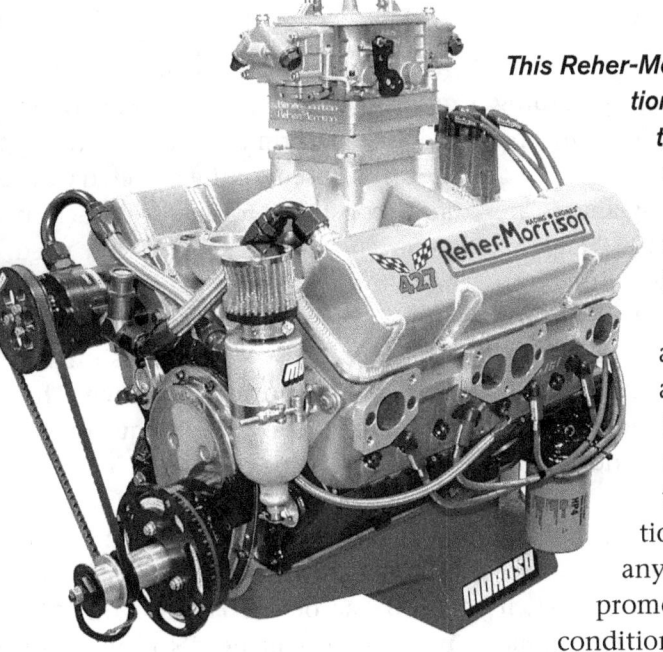

This Reher-Morrison big-cube small-block package demonstrates the application of a taller-runner 4-barrel intake with multiple stacked spacers to increase plenum volume and help the air make the turn into the runners. (Photo Courtesy Don Cooper)

Darin Morgan at Reher-Morrison says that the angle can be no more than 7 degrees for optimum performance. Although some small eddy currents appear at the upper end of the RPM range, 7 degrees provides the smoothest and most desirable discharge.

Without a tapered discharge, turbulence is severe, especially if the floor of the plenum is too close. Pressure recovery is diminished, and less natural air pressure is available to feed the cylinders. In other words, you might be running at sea level, but the pressure condition inside your plenum might be closer to, say, 3,000 feet of altitude. Hence, the artificial weather conditions inside the plenum are limiting performance.

As a rule, try to accomplish tuning on an individual cylinder basis if you have the necessary instrumentation. The configuration and dimensions of any intake manifold rarely promote perfectly equal conditions in each cylinder. So individual tuning consideration becomes necessary for the extraction of maximum performance from each cylinder. More often than not, it is highly beneficial.

Intake Manifold Types

Racing and high-performance applications typically have a choice of three manifold types: dual-plane, single-plane, and tunnel ram, which is effectively a taller single-plane intake capable of running either single or multiple carburetors or throttle bodies. Individual runner (IR) intakes are also employed in some applications, and they have their own unique characteristics and tuning requirements. Each of these manifold types has its strengths, weaknesses, and tuning characteristics that make it suitable for a particular high-performance or racing application.

Intake manifold type, dimensions, and characteristics exert tremendous influence on engine performance, helping to shape and position the power band within the operational RPM scale. The average performance application typically uses a commercially available intake designed for broad coverage. High-end applications trend toward custom-fabricated manifolds that are built with specific dimensions applicable to their exact competition environment.

Air movement through each type of manifold is influenced by the CFM demand created by the descending piston at the point of its highest velocity (approximately 76 degrees after TDC) on the intake stroke. It is further influenced by restrictions that include carburetor or throttle body size, manifold type, the dimensions and volumes of the plenum and separate distribution runners, valve event timing, wave tuning, and the overall operational RPM range of the engine.

Dual-Plane Intake Manifolds

Dual-plane intakes divide a V-8 engine into two independent 4-cylinder engines connected by a common crankshaft. Their design

The most common intake manifold in the performance world is the single 4-barrel dual-plane intake, which separates the intake into alternating flow requests based on the firing order. These intakes provide strong booster signals and deliver very strong low- and mid-range torque.

divides intake runners into two groups, so each is exposed to alternating induction pulses (airflow requests) submitted by opening intake valves and the accompanying pressure differential in a given cylinder. When a manifold is divided into separate cylinder groupings with alternating and evenly spaced pulses, it is said to have 2 degrees of freedom. This configuration produces stronger pressure waves, effectively emulating longer runners that tune to lower engine speeds.

Dual-plane intakes are highly effective as high-performance street manifolds because they promote strong torque at street engine speeds. Similarly, they are ideal for many Sportsman racing classes that depend on low- and mid-range torque for optimum performance, particularly with heavier cars in various circle-track applications.

Dual-planes submit stronger booster signals to the carburetor, which promotes crisper throttle response and increased runner energy for effective cylinder filling at lower engine speeds. In effect, each cylinder only sees half of the carburetor or, in a sense, a 2-barrel carburetor with a single primary bore and a single secondary bore, each requiring individual tuning according to plenum size, configuration, and engine speed.

Competition dual-planes are typically effective in the 2,500- to 6,500-rpm range. The runners in commercially available dual-plane intakes are dimensionally tuned to promote a torque peak between 4,000 and 5,500 rpm depending primarily on runner cross section and engine displacement.

Modifying Intake Runners and Primaries: When dual-plane intakes are specified for various racing series, it is necessary to consider their unique characteristics, and how they might best be manipulated to optimize power and performance in the most effective operating range. Some dual-plane intake runners, such as the Edelbrock Performer RPM Air Gap, have a fixed cross-sectional runner area that you can use to calculate the RPM where the torque peak occurs.

Once you identify the RPM where the intake builds maximum torque, you can manipulate supporting torque components to help boost torque above or below that point depending on how your car needs to perform.

In a typical application, you might, for example, add length to the header primary tubes, altering the arrival point of the reflected wave and boosting torque production below the torque peak. If you need more torque above the peak you can shorten the primaries or even change to a larger cross section to shift the peak higher in the RPM range. This broadens the overall torque curve and is the same procedure you can use to successfully pinpoint and position torque with single-plane and tunnel ram intakes.

To accomplish this on the intake side, you need to know the cross-sectional area of the individual intake runners because it is more difficult to alter their length. Race applications can, of course, do this to shift the torque bias above or below the peak by constructing an intake manifold with runner lengths appropriate to the desired effect based on wave tuning. That's why drag racing applications typically incorporate tunnel ram intakes with carefully calculated runner lengths to suit their high-RPM environment. They also

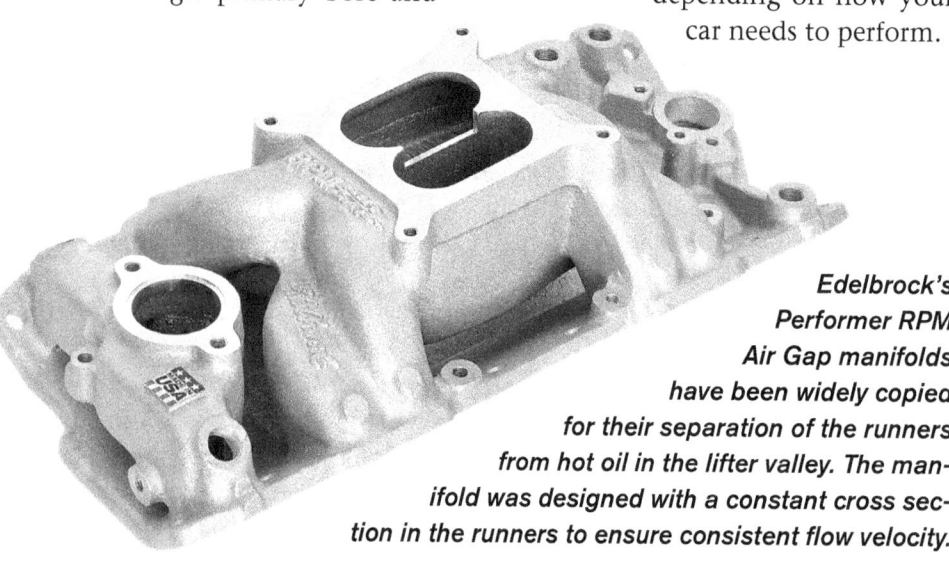

Edelbrock's Performer RPM Air Gap manifolds have been widely copied for their separation of the runners from hot oil in the lifter valley. The manifold was designed with a constant cross section in the runners to ensure consistent flow velocity.

Small ridges or other textured features are used inside the plenums of many dual-plane intakes to resist fuel separation and puddling when high-speed air exiting the carburetor slams into the plenum floor and loses control of the fuel droplets.

feature larger cross sections to move more air at higher engine speeds.

Other supporting torque components might include the camshaft; the designer may choose to close the intake valve sooner or later to strike the most favorable balance between cylinder filling and building cylinder pressure earlier in the cycle. In street, as well as many lower-class sportsman-racing applications, you are often stuck with fixed-dimension intake manifolds that are not easily modified to correct for more favorable torque positioning. Therefore, it is often easier and better to apply those changes from the exhaust side or alter the timing of events via the camshaft.

Finding Torque Peak: To calculate the cross section of a given commercial runner, measure the runner entry and the runner exit, and average the two dimensions. This yields the mean cross-sectional area of the runner, which can then be used to calculate the mathematically defined torque peak using the well-known formula developed by Jim McFarland:

Torque Peak = mean cross section x 88,200 ÷ volume of one cylinder

Where:
Mean cross section = (runner entry length + runner exit length) ÷ 2
88,200 = mathematical constant

Calculating the cross section by averaging runner entry and exit dimensions also incorporates any degree of taper that may exist in the runners. Runner taper provides additional flow volume while preserving increased port energy by encouraging a venturi effect with decreased runner cross section along the length of the flow path to help build velocity.

Depending on the engine, dual-plane intakes have unequal-length runners on the center cylinders compared to the end cylinders. The longer runners tend to boost torque below the torque peak; the shorter runners promote torque above the peak. The peak location on the RPM scale is governed by the mean runner cross section.

Runner cross section is the primary factor governing flow capacity. For any given cross section, flow efficiency peaks and then fades at a particular engine speed; it is lower for smaller cross sections and higher for larger cross sections. Peak torque or max efficiency occurs wherever the most efficient flow is established. So an intake with mismatched runners is creating dual peaks at slightly different engine speeds as the runners go in and out of phase. When the longer runners achieve maximum efficiency, the shorter runners have not yet reached their peak and vice versa.

Longer and shorter intake runners of the same cross section perform slightly differently. Two separate peaks are created and the overall, or average, torque peak lies between them. You can use exhaust dimensions to help crutch this problem by also adjusting primary tubing diameter and length.

You can strengthen this effect by providing complementary primary tube dimensions on the exhaust headers. Longer intake runners should be paired with longer primary tubes, and shorter runners should be matched with shorter primary tubes to broaden the overall torque curve.

High-performance small-blocks typically use 1¾-inch primaries; big-blocks use 2-inch primaries. But cross section relates specifically to engine size and speed. In a general sense a 302-ci small-block Ford typically uses 1½- to 1⅝-inch primaries unless it's a stroker and then it might accommodate 1¾-inch tubing. A 396-ci big-block performs better with a 1¾- to 1⅞-inch header, but a 454 typically wants a 2-inch header.

Think of these efforts as torque shifting if you want to bias torque one way or the other around the torque peak. You also have the option of employing larger or smaller primary tube cross sections on selected cylinders that are torque deficient due to a weak flow path, i.e., good port/bad port as found in big-block Chevys. This promotes a secondary torque peak that broadens the overall curve.

Modifying Hardware: When I speak of tuning efficiency peaks I'm talking about modifying hardware, not simply making an adjustment with a screwdriver. You move the torque peak up or down the RPM range by adjusting the cross-sectional area of the flow; it's not an easy thing to do from the intake side without a purpose-built intake manifold. People tend to expect dramatic movements, but it is generally a few hundred RPM at best. Because it is easiest to alter the exhaust, that's where most people do it.

A good example is a 427-ci big-block Chevy street engine with rectangular or square port heads. Factory versions of this engine made good power when revved to higher engine speeds, but they were a little doggy on the street with regular street gearing. The large ports do not provide adequate flow velocity for street-driven engine speeds. Smaller oval-port heads with less cross section often outperformed them because they maintained sufficient port velocity within the normal driving range.

Designers engineered the big port heads for high-RPM drag racing and they were inefficient on the street. The smaller cross section on the oval-port heads achieved maximum flow efficiency at street engine speeds. This shifted the torque to a more comfortable driving range and made the engines more accommodating for automatic transmissions.

In a race application, you might have a road race car that accelerates off the corners pretty hard but gets run down by faster cars at the end of the straightaway. So you want more power in the second half of the straight. You have to move the torque peak higher to make the power upstairs. Increasing the cross section by 10 percent or more helps you do this. If you can't get enough power with the intake manifold, you can add more by increasing the exhaust cross section. You can learn the exact numbers if you have a specific dyno sheet for your combination and good onboard data logging to tell you the engine speed at the troublesome straight.

Because manifold architecture is so tightly controlled by packaging, exhaust tuning is often the favored path. For example, if a 360-ci engine runs to 8,000 rpm with peak power around 7,800, peak torque likely occurs between 6,500 and 7,000 rpm. You might shift the torque upward a couple hundred RPM by switching the 1⅞-inch headers to 2-inch headers. And you might further support that change with slightly more aggressive second-, third-, and fourth-gear ratios in the transmission to make sure the transient torque through the gears remains high.

Each case is different and it is hardest to accommodate on the street because you mostly have to work with off-the-shelf parts that don't always offer the exact dimensions you are seeking. Again, that's why working with the exhaust is usually more effective.

Other supporting components that can help equalize power in each cylinder include Comp Cam's four-pattern cams, which feature more cam timing for the front and rear cylinders of domestic V-8s running single 4-barrel intakes with longer runners to the end cylinders. Although not specifically an airflow enhancement, it does address the flow path discrepancy between longer and shorter runner paths by giving the longer runners a bit of a head start. These cams get the air column moving a little earlier on the end cylinders to address the time and distance factors.

Using Carb Spacers: Recall that one of the primary goals in the manifold is to recover atmospheric pressure below the carburetor. This is typically easier with a dual-plane because of the smaller plenum volume, but still requires a throttle bore spacer with the desired 7-degree discharge angle to prevent excessive turbulence. From a strictly airflow perspective, velocity typically remains high, but the carburetor discharge varies because the tall plenum has more than double the volume of the short plenum.

Using Stagger Jetting: As previously noted, dual-planes generate stronger pressure pulses and carburetor signals due to the separation of the plenum area into two smaller volumes. In many cases, it can also be beneficial to investigate a different method of stagger jetting based on the high side versus the low side of the divided plenum. The high side generates a stronger booster signal than the low side does, so it tends to dominate jetting selection for the engine. It's entirely possible that the low (deep) side (generating a weaker signal because the booster is farther from the signal source and the plenum volume is greater) tends to deliver a leaner mixture because the weaker signal does not pull fuel through the jet as easily. Accordingly, it may be beneficial to run slightly more jet on the low side of the plenum.

The degree of side-to-side jet stagger varies with plenum depth and volume, runner cross section, and engine speed. Dyno testing can establish the ideal difference between driver- (low) and passenger- (high) side jetting based on power readings, exhaust gas temperature (EGT) levels, and oxygen-sensor readings if you have them. Once you establish the optimal spread, you can adjust accordingly at the track.

Automatically going richer on the low side may not always be the best choice because that side may already be rich, so it's best to take the jetting out of the high side until power falls off. Once you establish that point, you can tune the low side according to the best spread as indicated by the dyno or actual track performance. As a rule, the low side often requires at least one jet size larger once you have optimized the high side. This, of course, varies depending on the height and type of carb spacer and whether or not the spacer permits pressure pulse transfer between the divided plenums.

Depending on the type of spacer, you may compound the problem and require more jet stagger to equalize fuel delivery. Remember, the different-length runners resonate at different engine speeds, thus encouraging separate torque peaks and affecting the fueling requirement accordingly. A spacer's chief value is not necessarily in adding plenum volume per se, but rather in easing the ability of the high-speed air/fuel charge to negotiate the sharp turn into the runners without depositing most of the suspended fuel against the plenum floor.

With a dual-plane, there is no practical way to equalize the distance from the signal source to the boosters on all four barrels of the carburetor. Accordingly, fuel droplets may hit the plenum floor and fall out of suspension on the high side because there is less room to make the turn into the runner. Hence the low side of the manifold may generate better mixture quality than the high side. Juggling air bleeds might provide some relief, but they are usually too sensitive.

Stagger jetting is a more valid tuning strategy in the absence of a spacer design that is open on the high side while incorporating throttle bore extensions to enhance booster signal on the low side. Clearly, performance gains are available to those willing to investigate booster signal and jetting requirements on separate sides of dual-plane intakes.

Cutting Down the Center Divide: The most common modification to balance airflow on dual-plane intakes has always been to cut down the center divider so both sides can see the entire carburetor. Some manifolds are actually manufactured that way, but most are not. Cutting down the plenum divider offers more airflow, but produces only minimal gains.

For street muscle cars with very tall plenums you should not cut down the center divider, but rather rely on side-to-side jetting adjustments for optimal tuning. Very short dual-plane plenums are better off with an open spacer that exposes the entire carburetor to both sides.

Unless you have a very poor manifold design you're not going to get any significant airflow improvements, but you can gain performance by equalizing fuel distribution via jetting. You cannot significantly alter an existing dual-plane to shift torque position without major metal surgery that is costly and generally not worth the meager results.

Using Internal Porting: Some companies, such as Brzezinski Racing Products, offer internal porting of dual-plane intakes that are required for class racing with mixed results. As in the square-port/oval-port, big-block Chevy example, the chief value of a dual-plane intake manifold is high torque in the normal street driving range. Most popular engines have a choice between a low- and mid-range dual-plane and a high-performance dual-plane that already flows more air.

So the operative question is: Why bother? It's just not worth your time to mess with it. A stock factory dual-plane might be internally ported and textured to achieve minimal gains, but not really enough to contribute to the "sleeper mystique." Unless you're just hell-bent on grinding it, simply buy a good manifold and work with the exhaust to tune your combination.

Single-Plane Intakes

The open plenum on a single-plane intake manifold serves all eight cylinders at once and tends to promote more even mixture distribution of the fuel charge as engine speed increases. The physical details and dimensional specifics of various runner entries and runner lengths may also provide the opportunity for selected runners to dominate others via pressure wave exchange or "cross talk" within the plenum, particularly on adjacent runners according to each cylinder's position in the firing order.

A single-plane intake never quite achieves the full resonance found in dual-plane intakes. The lack of resonance limits low-speed torque, which can affect throttle response and drivability out of slow corners. It also impacts fuel economy in the sense that it requires more engine speed and more throttle opening to produce effective torque.

A large, undivided plenum exposes all eight cylinders to the carburetor collectively, reducing

A common plenum feeds all the intake runners on 4-barrel single-plane manifolds. They work best at high engine speeds; they sacrifice some torque production at low speeds due to insufficient and uneven signal strength to the carburetor boosters. This one is flanged to accept a Holley Dominator race carburetor.

CHAPTER 4

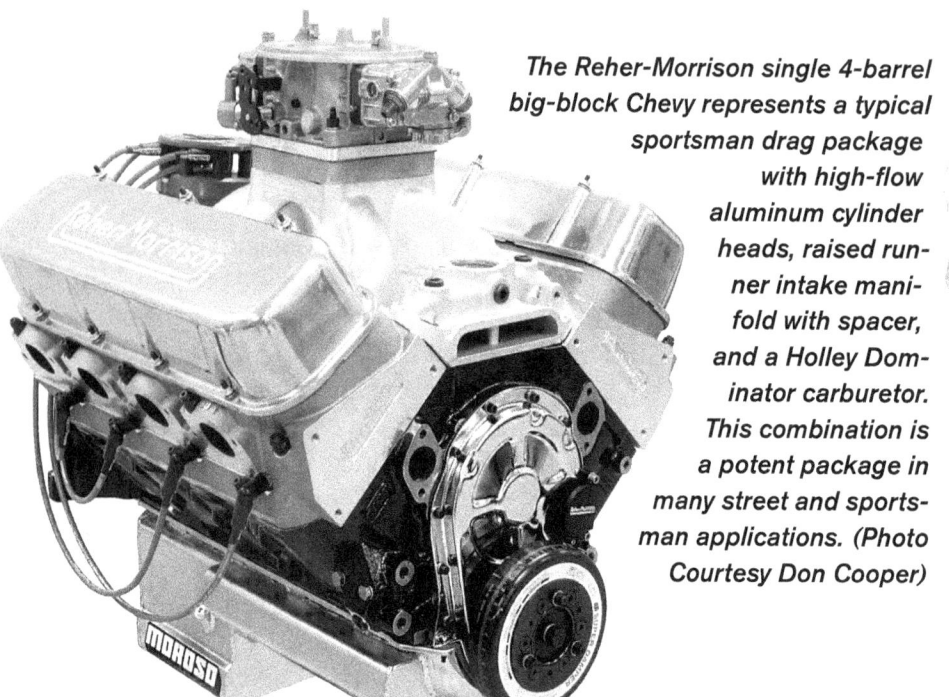

The Reher-Morrison single 4-barrel big-block Chevy represents a typical sportsman drag package with high-flow aluminum cylinder heads, raised runner intake manifold with spacer, and a Holley Dominator carburetor. This combination is a potent package in many street and sportsman applications. (Photo Courtesy Don Cooper)

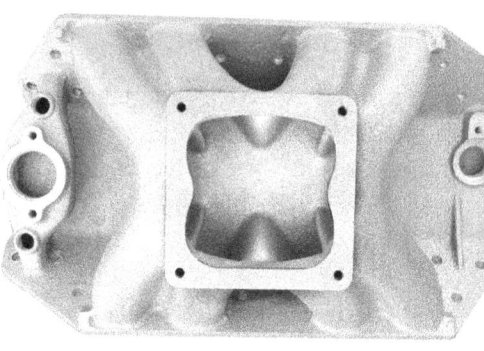

Here is a top view of a tall Edelbrock spread-port intake for Dart Big Chief and Brodix Big Duke cylinder heads. Runner length is very difficult to equalize with a centrally mounted carburetor, but this design comes close and the path to the ports is one of the best available.

booster signal and low-speed fuel metering consistency. Larger plenum volumes tend to dampen the effects of cylinder-to-cylinder pressure pulse influence, but open plenum manifolds in general sometimes experience fuel distribution issues caused by certain cam or cylinder head conflicts or in some cases the undue influence of poor exhaust tuning. Still, properly configured combinations typically provide more even fuel distribution than most dual-planes, particularly at elevated engine speeds.

The point is that you can't assume this. There is power to be gained by investigating fuel distribution and mixture-quality properties. This is usually done on the dyno with precision instrumentation. You can also gain some insight from plug readings, oxygen sensor readings from side to side if you have them on the car, EGT readings, and indications of reversion that may occur in individual intake runners or the plenum.

Despite potential problems, single-plane intakes offer superior high-speed power, and they come in different sizes and configurations to support higher airflow requirement as engine speed increases. They incorporate shorter runners that tune to higher engine speeds while promoting high-flow potential and greater charge density at high RPM. If you're willing to invest the effort, you can test the manifold's plenum and runner characteristics by using a

Holley 4500 Dominators provide high-flow capacity via their large throttle bodies. They also spread the bores farther apart to position them more favorably for the individual runners they serve. The raised-runner Team G intake helps ease the flow path to the intake port. (Photo Courtesy Holley)

INTAKE MANIFOLD

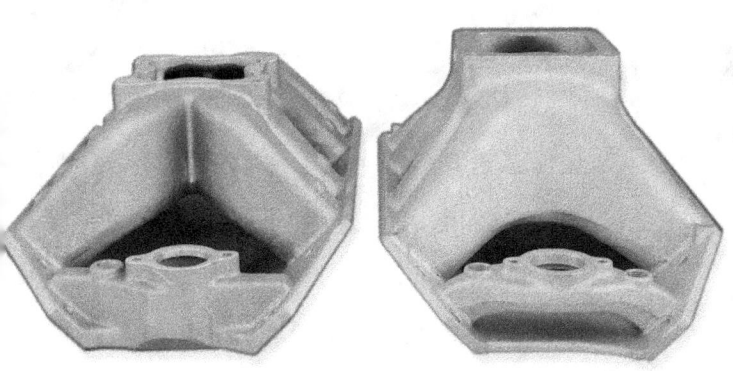

Here, a Dart Intake (left) is shown next to an Edelbrock big-block Chevy intake (right). The Edelbrock looks much taller, but only because of the raised carburetor flange. The runner height is about the same, but the Edelbrock runners take a straighter shot at the ports.

Two schools of thought exist regarding runner configuration and approach to the port. The Edelbrock approach is shown in the foreground while the Dart method is shown in the rear. Air exiting the carburetor at high speed has an easier turn into the runner on the Edelbrock manifold.

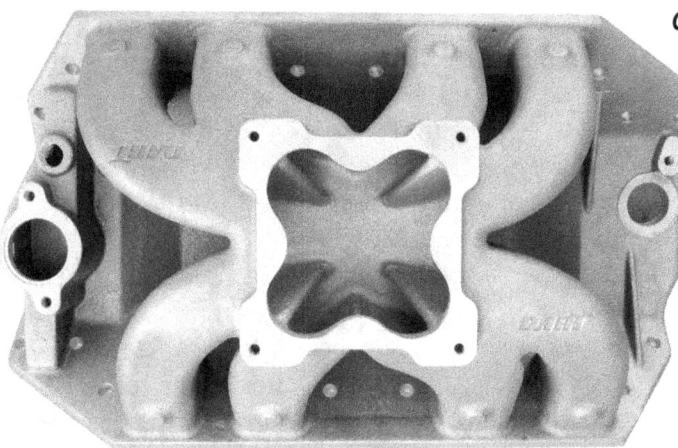

Compared to an Edelbrock, the flow path of this Dart intake has more directional changes. These differences are subtle, but can make a considerable difference depending on the application, RPM range, carb spacer, and carb size.

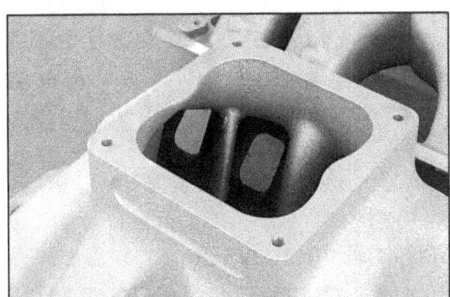

The Edelbrock manifold has a straight shot at the port so you can almost see the entirety of both ports. This design means that the carburetor has a relatively easy turn into the runners.

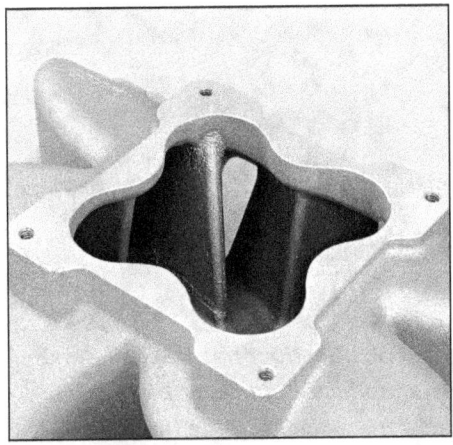

This earlier Dart version of the spread-port intake manifold has a more torturous path to the cylinder head and thus the valves.

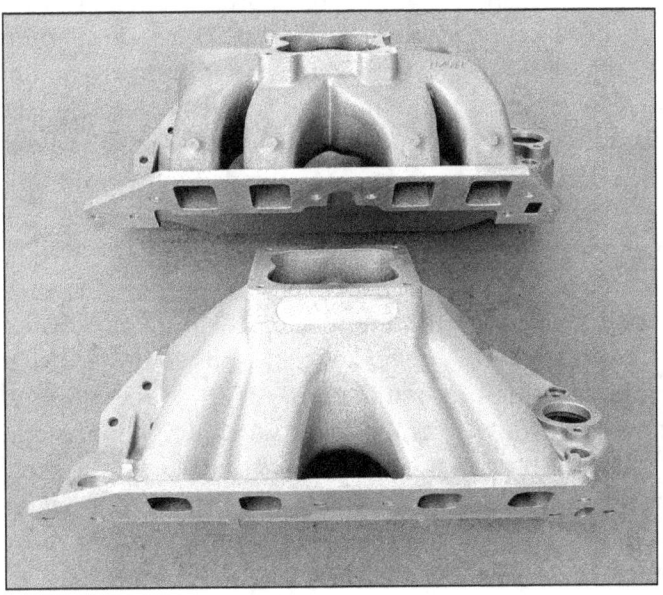

This comparison between the Dart (top) and the Edelbrock (bottom) clearly shows the advantage of taking a straighter shot at the intake ports.

PRACTICAL ENGINE AIRFLOW

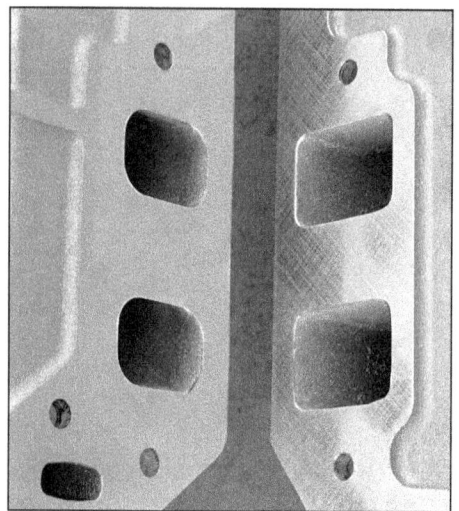

The Edelbrock (left) comes with smaller ports that can be adjusted for cross section and port matching without using epoxy. Nothing is really wrong with the Dart port (right); the Edelbrock simply requires significantly more preparation to match the head.

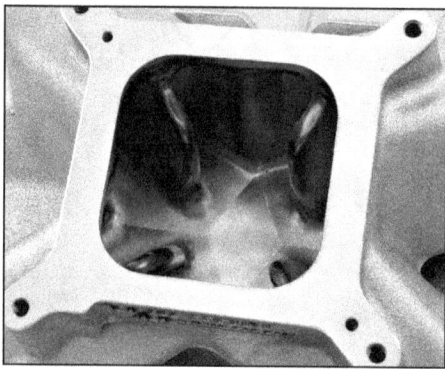

These runner walls are aero blended and extend into the plenum to gain runner length. For high engine speeds they perform better if they are laid back farther. Each runner shares a throttle bore above it, but flow and fuel distribution can be uneven depending on the angle of the throttle blade above the runners and the direction in which it opens. (Photo Courtesy Wilson Manifolds)

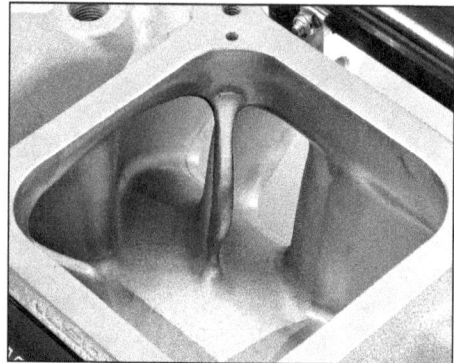

This setup has appropriate entry angles to the ports; the lower dividers are cut back to encourage flow and fuel motion after striking the plenum floor. (Photo Courtesy Wilson Manifolds)

pitot tube to check the runner entry velocity at various points, particularly the floor and the roof. The runner entries and shapes are pretty well tested and revised on most commercial manifolds, but you may identify a poor-performing runner that can be crutched by laying back the lower divider wall to match up flow.

Using Carb Spacers: Single-plane intakes can also be tuned with carburetor spacers. Open spacers are commonly used to increase plenum volume and aid pressure recovery, which softens the impact of cylinder-to-cylinder pressure influences that affect air/fuel ratio consistency. A 2-inch open spacer is almost always beneficial if hood clearance permits it. Open spacers add plenum volume and also ease the transition of the fuel charge from vertical when exiting the carburetor throttle bores to nearly horizontal in the runners.

In many cases, this is beneficial as long as it doesn't interfere with pressure recovery within the plenum. This is usually not a problem except on single-plane intakes running at very high speeds where the air demand is much greater. Four-hole spacers are the least desirable for most applications, but combination spacers are often useful in mid-range applications.

Combination spacers are usually open on the bottom, but have four holes on the top. They add plenum volume while attempting to maintain more effective booster signals. Many of them incorporate a tapered center core intended to help smooth and direct airflow coming out of the carburetor. They are not effective in every application, but they are worth trying in case their characteristics prove favorable on your particular combination. HVH Super Sucker combo spacers are quite popular and their exit characteristics most closely approximate the beneficial 7-degree exit angle previously described by Darin Morgan.

Flow velocities through the carburetor can exceed 600 feet per second, and at this speed, fuel droplets slam against the plenum floor as they attempt to change direction into the runner. Spacers can help alleviate this and for the most part they are not a hindrance to airflow or pressure recovery.

It has long been established that a mean flow velocity of 240 to 260 feet per second is desirable for best torque production. This, of course, depends on properly dimensioned

This plenum floor has been shaped with deflector angles to encourage flow from each throttle bore to its designated cylinders. It involves a lot of trial and error; flow-bench results don't always prove out on the track. (Photo Courtesy Wilson Manifolds)

INTAKE MANIFOLD

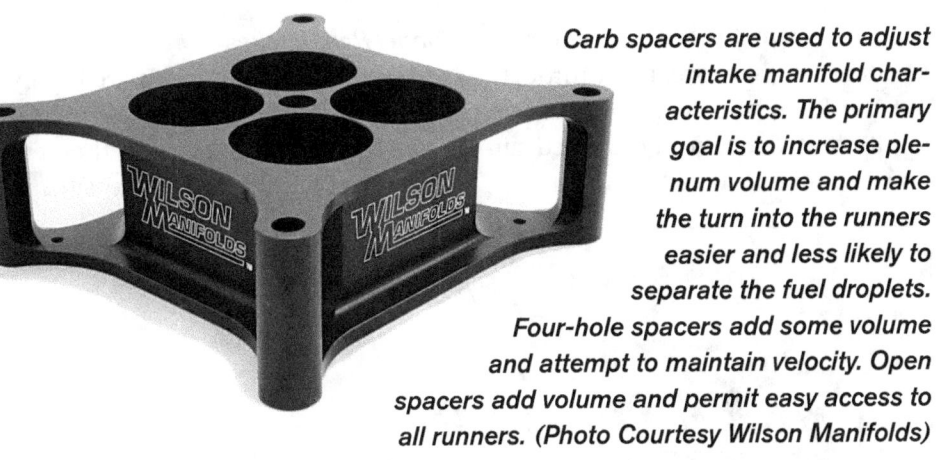

Carb spacers are used to adjust intake manifold characteristics. The primary goal is to increase plenum volume and make the turn into the runners easier and less likely to separate the fuel droplets. Four-hole spacers add some volume and attempt to maintain velocity. Open spacers add volume and permit easy access to all runners. (Photo Courtesy Wilson Manifolds)

Some carb spacers feature a tapered reverse cone to help direct airflow. It permits a greater degree of flow while still influencing flow direction for each bore as well as the neighboring bore. Results vary depending on the air speed and the depth of the plenum. (Photo Courtesy Wilson Manifolds)

ports and runners relative to engine displacement. And it depends on where you measure it along the flow path. An air/fuel mixture exiting the carburetor at 600 feet per second has to negotiate the relatively tight turn into the runners, and at that point the velocity slows to the mean rather quickly. Air (being compressible) tends to make the turn and decelerate more easily than the incompressible fuel droplets that fall out of suspension.

Fuel droplets fall out of suspension because of high-speed inertia in combination with rapid direction and volume changes. This becomes your first post carburetor opportunity to practice mixture conditioning. Highly atomized fuel produced by effective booster design changes direction more easily because smaller individual fuel droplets have less mass. Increased plenum depth and volume tend to support this cause. Although track testing provides the most accurate results, engine dyno testing can help pinpoint spacer configurations that improve single-plane performance by addressing mixture-quality issues. Although the problem only increases with engine speed and associated higher mixture demand, efforts to improve these conditions are often surprisingly worthwhile.

Four-hole spacers and various hybrid (combination) spacers are often used on single-plane intakes for similar reasons. In the long run, though, assisting mixture transition into the runner is usually more important than adding plenum volume to dampen plenum pressure excursions (you could also call them pressure changes or fluctuations). Another concern is pressure changes that tend to rob mixture from other runners under certain conditions. A spacer assists both of these concerns and, to a degree, they can also be crutched through other means, such as individual cylinder adjustments to valve and ignition timing.

Carburetor spacers typically accomplish two things: Increasing the plenum volume tends to soften inter-cylinder pressure disturbances, and greater volume also reduces inlet airspeed and encourages the smooth transition of air and fuel into the individual runners with less fuel separation and puddling. Open spacers that provide a significant increase in volume some-

Spread-port intakes for big-block Chevys added another dimension of performance as spread-port cylinder heads came online. The combination allowed for improved runner entry angles and taller raised runners for improved line-of-sight to the ports.

times allow a single-plane intake to modestly approach tunnel ram performance, depending on the application.

In some cases, a manifold sees more airflow near the lower end of its power band; a four-hole spacer improves booster signal and often sharpens low-speed throttle response. With fixed dimensions, all manifolds generate their own particular sweet spot (RPM) where they deliver maximum torque according to the displacement of the engine. Above and below this point, they tend to fall in and out of tune depending on dimensional influences on airflow and mixture quality that require evaluation and extensive tuning effort to optimize performance.

Adding Plenum Dividers: In the past, plenum dividers were often added to single-plane intakes to boost carburetor signal strength. This was only partially successful; the uneven firing pulses acting on each side of the divided plenum did not permit a second degree of freedom resonance. Instead, unpredictable resonant phases occurred throughout the RPM range with inconsistent results that dramatically affected airflow and mixture quality.

Tunnel Ram Intakes

Tunnel ram manifolds are highly desirable for all-out racing applications because they provide the very best configuration for equalizing

Here's a serious LS-based engine with twin Dominators on a sheet-metal tunnel ram. You can just make out the taper built into the intake runners. This much airflow capacity suggests a very high-RPM application. (Photo Courtesy Holley)

Sonny Leonard's injected Mountain Motor has twin 4-barrel throttle bodies, moderate plenum size, and tapered intake runners. The throttle bodies are positioned to provide the most direct path through the plenum to the runner to help maintain flow velocity. (Photo Courtesy Sonny Leonard Racing Engines)

Tunnel ram intakes have long been a staple of high-performance tuning. Earlier versions featured compromised runner lengths and cross sections to accommodate broader applications within similar engine families. Newer sheet-metal versions offer application-specific dimensions that generally perform better, but the older versions are still popular in nostalgia racing and for many street applications.

runner lengths and volumes. They provide the most direct and unrestricted flow path from the carburetor to the intake valve, and they offer the best possible design for optimizing flow velocity and mixture quality. They are particularly effective at engine speeds above 7,000 rpm.

Modifying Runners: If you set aside packaging issues, a long-runner tunnel ram can be an effective high-performance intake and a good choice for heavier drag cars needing a torque boost at lower engine speeds. Short-runner tunnel rams with appropriate plenum volume provide superior high-speed performance, which is why you see them almost exclusively on professional drag racing cars (Pro Stock) and their high-RPM Sportsman counterparts.

Tunnel rams present the best opportunity to optimize runner length, volume, and taper. You're less likely to see variations in runner dimensions in these applications because they operate in a very narrow power band that doesn't require the pursuit of multiple torque boosts via

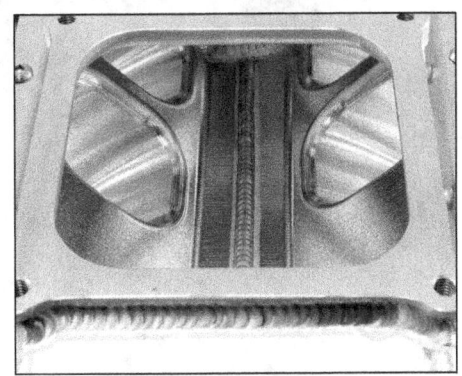

Internal texturing helps maintain fuel in suspension and the machined entries of the runners provide the smoothest possible entry into the runners. In this configuration, air must exit the carburetor, dodge toward the port with the greatest depression, and then make a relatively sharp turn into the runner without fuel dropout along the way. Minimizing turns and area changes is a vital part of successful intake science. (Photo Courtesy Wilson Manifolds)

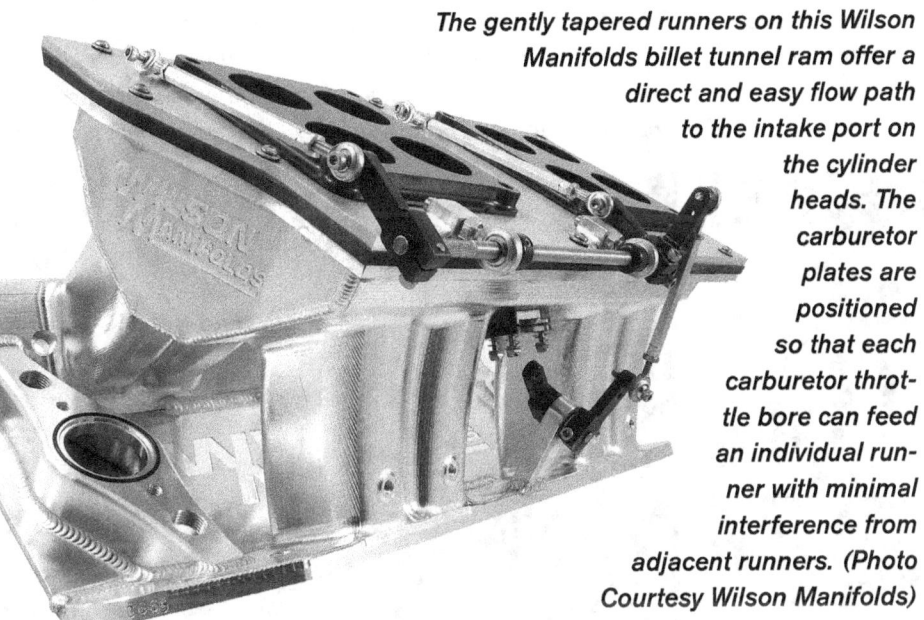

The gently tapered runners on this Wilson Manifolds billet tunnel ram offer a direct and easy flow path to the intake port on the cylinder heads. The carburetor plates are positioned so that each carburetor throttle bore can feed an individual runner with minimal interference from adjacent runners. (Photo Courtesy Wilson Manifolds)

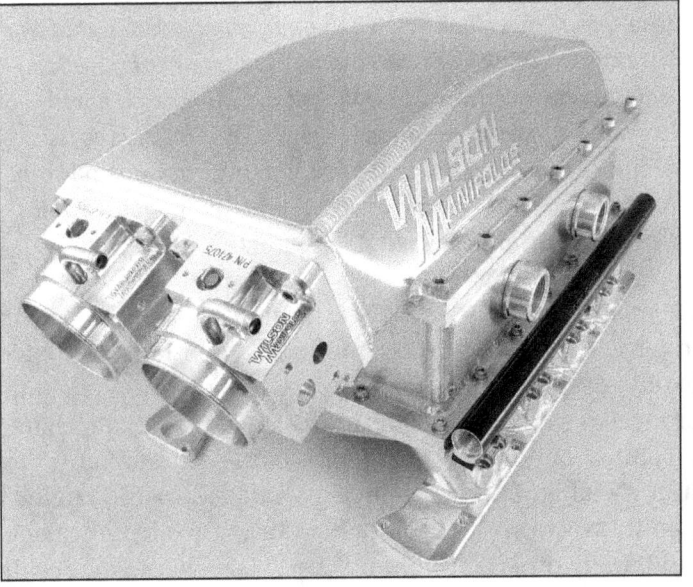

Manifold designs are many and varied according to the engine type. This Ford Modular engine intake for a boosted application has twin throttle bodies and a built-in intercooler. (Photo Courtesy Wilson Manifolds)

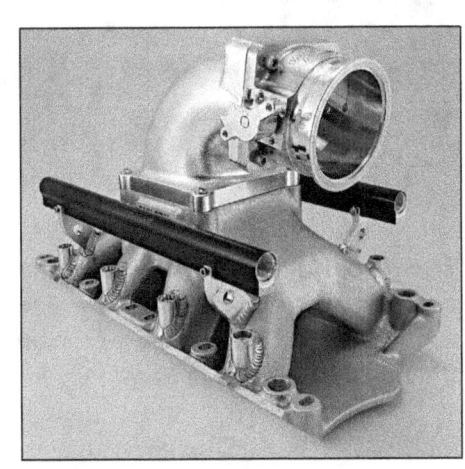

A large single-blade throttle body moves air efficiently in boosted applications. This configuration makes the most of boosted and intercooled air, but it does require some accommodation for hood clearance. (Photo Courtesy Wilson Manifolds)

CHAPTER 4

Here's a good example of runner length. Remember that runner length incorporates distance from the runner entry at the plenum all the way to the valve.

Once the plenum air box is set in place, individual radiused flow caps are bolted to the top of the runners. Plenum height can be further adjusted to suit the displacement and RPM range. (Photo Courtesy Mitech Racing Engines)

The front opening accepts a large throttle body. This application works best with boost. The back cylinders may be underserved without boost pressure to equalize them. (Photo Courtesy Mitech Racing Engines)

One thing you will notice when examining a fabricated tunnel ram is the plenum depth and top plate configuration. Builders have various thoughts about plenum size and pressure recovery within the plenum. You must recover atmospheric pressure in the plenum because it is all you have to work with on naturally aspirated engines. (Photo Courtesy Wilson Manifolds)

selective intake and exhaust dimensional matchmaking. Nonetheless, a heavier drag car might respond to manifold modifications to complement alternative exhaust dimensions to help broaden the torque curve, particularly if it operates over a greater RPM spread than a Pro Stock car.

Types of Tunnel Rams: The two basic types of tunnel ram intakes are "universal" fixed-dimension aluminum castings produced by most major intake manufacturers and custom handmade sheet-metal intakes made by Wilson Manifolds, Hogan's Racing Manifolds, and many others.

Custom intakes are built with very specific dimensions designed to closely match the engine's final application. Runner length, shape, taper, and cross-sectional area are specifically matched to the engine's requirements and the plenum shape. Volume and carburetor mounting

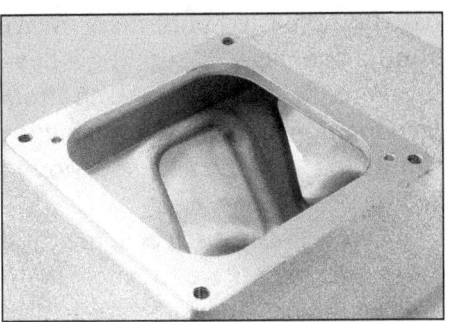

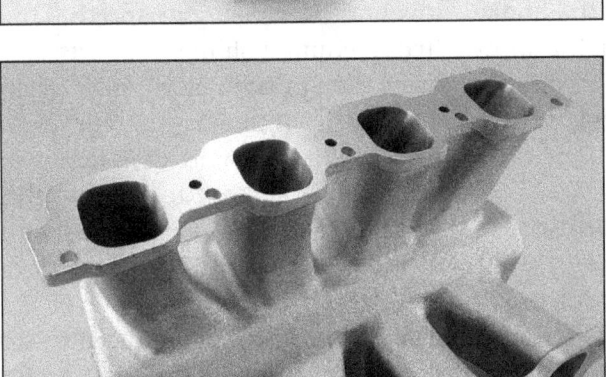

Wilson Manifolds' single 4-barrel small-block Ford intake features a tapered plenum roof to help pinch the air toward the end runners and equalize flow. Flow velocity into the plenum can be influenced by spacers to help the air make the turn and recover pressure quickly. (Photo Courtesy Wilson Manifolds)

This view into the tapered top of a Ford intake highlights the path of the runners. The taper helps build pressure toward the end runner to help overcome the more abrupt direction change compared to the nearer runner, which receives a pretty straight shot. (Photo Courtesy Wilson Manifolds)

This bottom view shows nearly equal-length runners and some curvature on the end runners to help the air into the runner. (Photo Courtesy Wilson Manifolds)

From the top of a Ford manifold, you can see that all cylinders have pretty good exposure to the carburetor baseplate and that the end cylinders benefit from the pitched roof pinching the air to recover pressure and build velocity into the runners. (Photo Courtesy Wilson Manifolds)

surface are sized to accommodate the exact requirements of the engine.

The handmade application permits the engine builder to pinpoint very specific intake characteristics depending on how the engine will be used. These intakes are very labor intensive to construct and are thus quite expensive. Used intakes are often available on eBay and other outlets, but the chances that one matches your exact requirements are pretty slim, and you could easily do more harm than good if you don't thoroughly investigate the manifold's exact dimensions prior to purchasing it.

Most tunnel ram applications operate at extremely high engine speeds; therefore, it is important to accurately match plenum volume to displacement and the actual air demand at the engine's most effective operating range. The established rule dictates that optimum performance is derived from the smallest possible dimensions that adequately support the engine's airflow requirement.

Optimizing Airflow: This is no more difficult than with any other manifold. It's primarily a matter of getting the shapes and sizes right for the application. These include runner cross section, runner length, runner taper, port entry angle, plenum volume, carburetor or throttle body offset, and top shape.

Runner cross section can position the torque peak relative to engine speed and vehicle requirements. Runner lengths returning multiple pulse reflections tune best to the second reflected pulse (wave) if the engine requires a peaky, narrow power band. Engines requiring a lower and slightly broader power band are better served by tuning runner length to the third or possibly even fourth pulse. To calculate the optimal runner length based on reflected pulses (see "Wave Tuning" on page 57), use the following formula, which is taken from Dynomation 5, the popular engine simulation program from Motion Software.

As previously discussed, the third and fourth pulses are the most desirable for performance use. To calculate the ideal length, divide the indicated constant by the RPM where you want the engine to perform best. Here's the formula:

Optimal Flow Path Length = pulse constant ÷ target operating RPM

Where:
2nd pulse constant = 108,000
3rd pulse constant = 97,000
4th pulse constant = 74,000
5th pulse constant = 54,000

If you have correctly identified a power band with the desired RPM spread between peak torque and peak power, you can use the McFarland cross-sectional area formula (page 53) to establish the optimal runner cross section for your chosen torque peak. Then you can use the reflected pulse formula to pinpoint the supporting runner length.

These efforts are more effective than you might suspect, particularly when combined with other known strategies to effect individual cylinder optimization. These include individual cylinder timing via specialty ignition boxes, such as those from MSD, within the software interface of most electronic fuel injection programs. A hot cylinder identified by higher exhaust temperatures may need more fuel or less timing depending on local conditions and the amount of data you have to identify the problem. In some cases racers make fine alterations by simply changing the heat range of the spark plug in certain cylinders.

For the most part these tricks provide minimal improvement, but are useful to crutch unforeseen circumstances or to prevent engine damage from detonation or over-lean conditions. When you tune each cylinder to its peak efficiency and take steps to boost torque across your required power band, it pays big dividends on the track. Accordingly, the intake manifold becomes one of the most influential components available for tuning and positioning torque effectively.

Plenum Characteristics

A cursory examination of manifold styles uncovers some differences in plenum shapes and volume. It also includes the possibility of adding volume to the plenum and specific airflow considerations.

Dual- versus Single-Plane Intakes

Dual-plane intakes typically have the smallest plenums because the manifold is divided into two separate manifolds functioning almost independently of each other. As previously noted, a major component of a dual-plane manifold is unequal plenum floor depth from one side to the other. This promotes uneven carburetor booster signals from side to side and leads to uneven fuel distribution if not compensated for by jetting adjustments.

The high-side plenum is more susceptible to high-speed fuel separation due to the minimal distance between the carburetor throttle bore exit and the plenum floor. The low-side plenum is more effective at directing the mixture into the runner with less fuel separation because of the reduced velocity and an easier path approaching the floor and the runner. The downside is reduced booster sensitivity on that side of the manifold and the potential for uneven fuel distribution.

That said, also note that both plenum volumes are still smaller than that found in a single-plane manifold and therefore tend to provide superior throttle response at low to moderate engine speeds. Limited plenum volume supports this even though both sides may generate slightly different fuel curves. A fixed volume occupies the plenum at all times so it's easy to see that this volume maintains a fixed amount of inertia (resistance to movement). One molecule has to get out of the way before the next molecule can replace it. This requires a certain amount of energy, which is easier to generate with reduced volume. Thus, the higher energy state of smaller plenums makes it easier to move the mixture and provides higher sensitivity (even if unequal) to the venturi boosters.

Another important component of dual-plane intake operation is carburetor size. For many years, builders sought to minimize carburetor size to maintain good flow velocity. But the newer generation of highly efficient dual-planes flies in the face of convention. Traditional thinking suggests that because each cylinder connected to a given plenum sees only half of the carburetor's total air capacity, the engine can effectively use a larger carburetor because the signal strength is greater. Although there is some truth to this, the greater benefit of using a larger carburetor is in more effective mixture conditioning.

INTAKE MANIFOLD

The larger carburetor reduces venturi airspeed, allowing the air/fuel mixture to make the turn into the runners more easily and with less fuel separation. The larger carburetor also allows more room around the fuel delivery cone for air to flow. Hence, like spacers, carburetor size can be an effective tuning aid for dual-plane applications when and if carburetor size is not restricted. Single-plane intakes are a different story. They may present more evenly matched signal requests to the carburetor boosters, but they are dampened because of increased plenum volume. This often requires more jet to compensate for weaker signal strength. When a spacer is added, volume increases, signal strength degrades further, and jetting must be readjusted to service fuel demand and establish adequate flow sensitivity at the jet.

Volume Increase

Spacers are a means of adding plenum volume to both single- and dual-plane intake manifolds. Their primary purpose is to encourage mixture quality by easing the turn into the runners without detrimental fuel separation. There is a fine line between adjusting plenum volume for the promotion of mixture quality and the invisible dynamics of airflow inertia. Larger plenums, as found in tunnel rams, tend to soften inter-cylinder pressure excursions.

Some engine builders feel that added volume is also necessary to ensure adequate mixture quantity at elevated engine speeds. In reality, every combination has a select "sweet spot" that strikes an ideal balance among mixture quality, pulse tuning, and airflow inertia management within the plenum. Although it is sometimes difficult to pinpoint exactly, calculations to identify torque peak RPM and pulse-tuned runner lengths can put you not just in the ballpark, but well on the way to home plate.

Airflow Assessment

The best combination is not easy to determine, particularly on engines with a broad power band. Still, it is possible to increase your accuracy by conducting an airflow assessment of the manifold you intend to use; assuming, of course, that you are using a commercially available intake of fixed dimensions. Builders with flow-bench access can flow test the manifold and cylinder head together, and it's a good idea to include the carburetor with the throttle plates locked open. This often requires some jury-rigged props and adjustments to set up on the flow bench, but it's worth the effort.

The preferred procedure is to flow each runner and port combination separately with the other runners sealed off. This constitutes a basic airflow study that does not specifically address wet-flow conditions or potential pressure influences from adjacent runners. Nevertheless, it does establish a basic airflow map of the manifold and what each runner is capable of, independent of outside interference. It does not evaluate compensation for runner-to-runner pressure influence or the unsteady flow of dynamic valve operation, but it can illuminate airflow weaknesses and inequalities that should be corrected or compensated for if possible.

With the carburetor in place, flow testing also considers plenum volume; at least to the extent that it affects total airflow and the identification of problematic flow paths. For most race applications, the valve opening action occurs so quickly that it isn't necessary to evaluate low-lift flow, except perhaps in the case of lower-performance circle-track applications. It's also not necessary to flow at all valve opening increments, but you'll want to evalu-

This Ford V-8 application has Weber carbs and tuned stacks. Carb size limits airflow at high speeds, but delivers sharp response and good torque in its intended environment.

PRACTICAL ENGINE AIRFLOW

CHAPTER 4

These individual runners have a direct shot at the valve on every cylinder. This is very effective depending on the configuration of the plenum above the runners. (Photo Courtesy Mitech Racing Engines)

ate intake flow at about 65 percent of net anticipated valve lift.

If the manifold/port combination supports the calculated volume requirements and runner performance is relatively equal at this point, you'll probably find it sufficient at peak lift as well. Recall that the valve is only at peak lift for a fraction of a second, but it typically resides at or above the stated percentages for most of the valve event. These percentages represent known values relative to piston position and port flow demand for optimal VE and efficient exhaust blowdown.

You'll likely discover that cylinder-to-cylinder flow variations are greatest with a dual-plane and least with a tunnel ram. Careful flow mapping of the manifold in this manner helps identify runners that may need individual tuning assistance. This most often takes the form of rocker ratio adjustments, individual cylinder cam lobe profiles, header dimension compensation, and even timing and jetting adjustments based on runners that exhibit weaker or uneven flow characteristics relative to the others.

Once you have created this flow map, you'll be surprised at the follow-on thought process it provokes, all based on a keener awareness of your equipment's characteristics and recognized methods of compensation to increase and equalize torque.

Mixture Conditioning

Fuel atomization is central to the practice of mixture conditioning. This is particularly true for carbureted applications, which are limited to wet-flow fuel delivery methods. First and foremost, you want the finest, or smallest, possible fuel droplets in the airflow mixture. You also want the highest degree of homogeneity (consistent size) among the smallest fuel droplets. For a given fuel volume, a higher percentage of smaller and evenly sized droplets presents more combustible surface area, which burns faster and more evenly.

Droplets that vary in size slow the rate of combustion relative to exclusively smaller droplets because the larger ones are more difficult to burn. They also degrade mixture quality by falling out of suspension more easily whenever they encounter abrupt changes in direction, cross-sectional area, runner volume, or mixture velocity.

Mixture quality is particularly sensitive to booster design, plenum volume, runner configuration, surface texture, and flow path velocity. Any issue of mixture quality can lead to fuel separation and localized wetting

Here's a proven application. This Duttweiler-spec'd Hogan-built intake is the fastest intake manifold in the world. It came from the 2,700-hp twin-turbocharged 388-ci first-generation small-block Chevy in George Poteet's Speed Demon streamliner that owns the 439-mph piston-powered record at Bonneville.

The Speed Demon manifold has a unique fueling arrangement using a mechanical injector. With turbos, it is easy to supply massive airflow, but getting enough fuel is difficult.

Dual 225-pound injectors are not enough so Duttweiler supplements them with a computer-controlled mechanical injector that turns on as boost increases.

This is the mechanical injector centered between the openings for the twin electronic injectors. Boost pressure negates the restriction offered by the mechanical injector, so airflow is not compromised.

of plenum and runner walls and floors. In severe cases, fuel may puddle on the plenum floor, particularly on the upper plane of a dual-plane intake. This makes degraded mixture quality partially responsible for the diminishing efficiency of these manifolds at elevated engine speeds.

Successful mixture conditioning maintains the finest homogenous mixture while reducing dynamic influences that cause fuel separation. These include fuel contact with runner walls, valves, cylinder walls, piston tops, and the various surface textures they present. Excessive velocity can separate fuel transitioning in the bowl area below the valve. It can also fling fuel against the opposing side of the combustion chamber causing fuel wash that is compounded by rapidly increasing piston motion and a potentially inhospitable piston dome configuration.

Be sure to consider every portion of the flow path from carburetor to combustion chamber. This includes carburetors, plenums, runners and runner entries, port shapes, valvestems, valveseats, combustion chambers, cylinder walls, and piston top configuration. All of them are potential sources of mixture degradation.

Smooth or polished surfaces are particularly troublesome and should be eliminated from the flow path

A compact late-model Hemi intake emulates factory curved-runner design with shorter, straighter runners and more plenum volume. (Photo Courtesy Wilson Manifolds)

The Mopar Hemi intake has tall, long runners for strong low- and mid-range performance.

An LT5-5 C7R Corvette race engine incorporates combination carbon-fiber and aluminum cross ram intake with each air box feeding the opposite side of the engine. Note the radiused runner entries and opposite-side runners passing between them.

If you trace the flow path from opposite sides, you note relatively long curved runners angling for a straight shot at the valves. The long runners promote mid-range torque to support the requirements of road racing Corvettes.

Similar to Corvette race intakes, MSD Air Force intakes for LS-based performance engines also have tuned-length runners feeding opposites sides of the engine from separate plenums. Radiused entries are used on the runner inlets inside the individual plenums.

wherever possible. Dimpling, port surface striations perpendicular to the flow path, or simply a rough surface texture tend to support good mixture quality by reducing fuel separation. These depressions activate the boundary layer near plenum and runner floors by providing a tumbling effect that tends to maintain flow velocity while keeping fuel droplets in suspension.

In-cylinder mixture motion (in the form of swirl and tumble as the mixture enters the cylinder) promotes mixture quality and cylinder filling. In practice, most high-speed competition engines favor some degree of swirl to help direct the burn toward the exhaust valve, but tumble has been found to have little effect at very high engine speeds. Successful efforts to encourage quench and active mixture motion typically permit a reduction in spark timing, which lessens negative work against the piston as it approaches TDC. Accordingly, equalization of EGTs, lower BSFC numbers, and an increase in torque typically accompany successful mixture conditioning.

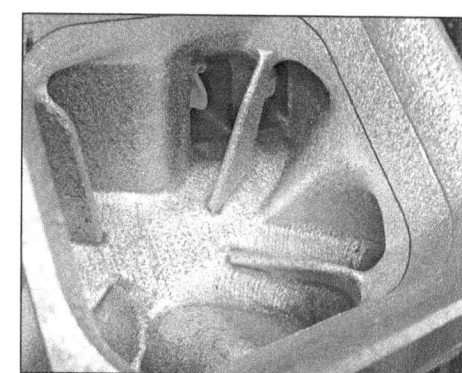

Meaux Racing Heads applies this rough-texture porting treatment to intake manifolds, cylinder head ports, and combustion chambers to enhance mixture atomization and prevent fuel separation. (Photo Courtesy Meaux Racing Heads)

Surface Texturing

Surface texturing is useful anywhere in the flow path, particularly in areas that are prone to fuel separation because of changes in direction or charge velocity due to area variations. Manifold runners should never be polished, and any place in the plenum that has been ground to match a spacer or modify a runner entry should be retextured. (This primarily applies to carbureted wet-flow applications.) Fuel droplets tend to stick to smooth surfaces so avoid them wherever possible.

Depending on accessibility, plenum and runner floors can be dimpled with an appropriately blunt tool (1/8-inch rounded top) to promote rolling vortices, or eddies, that tend to return fuel into suspension and prevent further dropout. Dimpling is commonly used on piston tops and in combustion chambers that are easy to reach. However, without prior engine operation, there is no burn pattern to guide you relative to areas of fuel wash and incomplete combustion. You may want to reserve this tactic for use after the engine has been run.

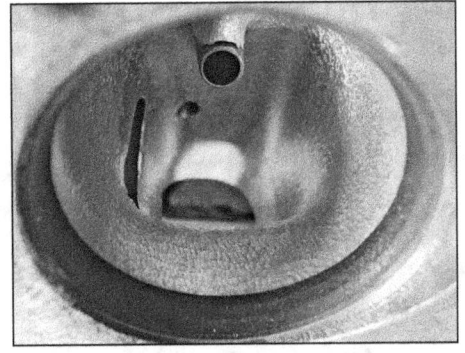

Meaux Racing Heads uses this texture-porting technique on most carbureted applications to minimize fuel separation and enhance mixture quality. It has regularly proved to be worth significant power. (Photo Courtesy Meaux Racing Heads)

An interesting example of dimpling is found in the Tork-Link manifold offered by Hi-Tech Engine Components; the tall dual-plane intake is specifically designed for some circle-track applications. Hi-Tech also offers the Swirl-Quench piston design that incorporates dimples and a tapered ramp on the piston top to optimize homogeneity and direct mixture motion and, thus, the burn toward the exhaust valve. Other applications attempt to do the same thing by reading combustion patterns on previously run pistons and dimpling clean areas that exhibit little or no combustion residue.

Some builders don't believe using dimples and a tapered ramp are effective. Instead, they prefer to glass bead piston tops, apply piston top coatings, and texture manifold passages. Some racers also extrude-hone manifolds to increase runner volume, but this may be a bad idea for carbureted intakes because it tends to polish the runners, and there is no inexpensive way to retexture them. Extrude honing is reserved for dry-flow manifolds on EFI systems where fuel separation is not an issue. At the very least, texturing manifold runners by glass beading or sanding with 80-grit or coarser sand paper at 90 degrees to the direction of airflow may help improve mixture quality in manifolds with very smooth runners.

Reversion

Reversion is present in all engines to some degree. It varies with engine speed and the particular combination of parts and timing events that encourage it. Reversion occurs at IVO when cylinder pressure is still greater than manifold pressure, causing remaining combustion residue to migrate into the intake manifold. This continues briefly until manifold pressure, cylinder pressure, and exhaust pressure equalize and a pressure drop is initiated in the cylinder.

The incoming fuel charge then enters the cylinder contaminated with residual exhaust particles that

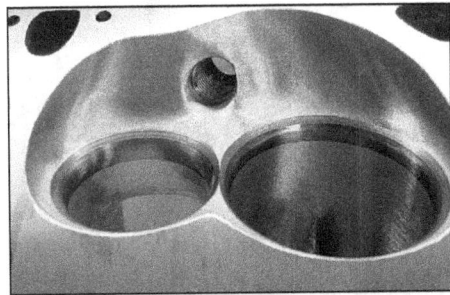

This well-shaped and de-shrouded chamber predates the current move toward rougher surface textures. This is what a lot of head shoppers are looking for; in most cases, it performs well. However, textured surfaces as espoused by Larry Meaux are rapidly becoming a favorite.

The extended runner walls will likely benefit from being cut back more to provide a freer path to the runner entries. This photo is somewhat misleading because it doesn't show the exact view of the plenum that each throttle bore sees. Recalling the goal of pressure recovery below the carburetor, many things are obstructing flow, particularly when you consider the way the throttle plates are opening.

previously entered the manifold. Charge contamination reduces power by replacing usable fuel mixture with unburnable combustion residue, which is a version of EGR that works to limit power production in all competition engines. This typically forces the need to crutch the system with more timing and more jet to get enough fuel into the engine and burn it as well as possible. More timing increases pre-TDC work against the piston (negative torque), and excessive fuel compounds the mixture quality issues. As a result, these issues reduce power and increase fuel usage unnecessarily. Crutching a poor configuration is always less desirable than resolving it.

Various manifolds are resistant to reversion depending on the application. Dual-plane intakes with smaller plenums and high-energy runners tend to dampen the effects of reversion. Single-plane intakes with large plenums and larger runners are more sensitive to reversion pressure. They frequently permit a greater level of charge contamination depending on the IVC point and exhaust back pressure during the camshaft overlap period.

Efforts to reduce reversion include later-closing intake valve timing to allow more time for cylinder pressure to fall. Also, a properly timed EVO helps evacuate the cylinder and draw in the next fuel charge without the pressure difference that encourages reversion. Carburetor

This FE Ford engine from Mitech Racing Engines is primed for serious performance in a Ford Cobra application. This unique EFI application has pretty short stacks, but the cross section is sized to optimize performance in the desired RPM range. The rounded entry radius on the stack smooths air entry. (Photo Courtesy Mitech Racing Engines)

The intake flow path length on carburetors with direct individual runners can be adjusted for best performance by altering the stack length: taller for more low-end response and shorter for optimal high-speed power. (Photo Courtesy Wilson Manifolds)

Individual runner applications are traditionally more difficult to tune, except with EFI, but they have been favored in many track cars because of their good throttle response. And they look awesome on street rods.

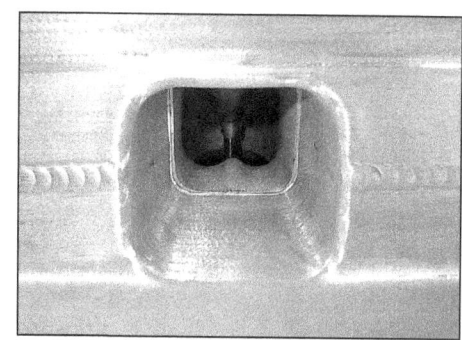

This is a good example of how you taper a runner to the intake port to build pressure for the intake ramming cycle. It's what keeps filling the cylinder after BDC when the piston starts to rise and the intake valve is still open. (Photo Courtesy Mitech Racing Engines)

INTAKE MANIFOLD

Multiple Weber carbs provide smooth street operation, but limit airflow at elevated engine speeds because of an insufficient flow-path cross section.

This imposing big-block Chevy, with mechanically injected individual runner setup, is a hard-core engine for the street. Throttle plates are located high on the runners and just above the injector entry. Long runners promote superior torque and stacks can be resized to help shift torque higher or lower in the RPM band.

spacers tend to encourage reversion by weakening manifold pressure. This can usually be corrected with properly matched cam timing.

Consult your cam supplier with the specifics of your package. They can determine cam specs that resist the effects of reversion, particularly in the usable power band of your engine.

Additional Intake Considerations

A universal caveat of intake manifold application reminds us to be sure that the runners in the manifold never flow less than the intake port they support. You will never see the cylinder head's full potential if a poor-flowing intake manifold pinches off airflow. You must check and verify this for every cylinder.

Although specific runner and plenum dimensions, as well as the shape and style of manifold, hold the most potential for power production and power band positioning, additional factors must be considered depending on your exact requirements. Recall that there are very few, if any, universal racing engines that deliver top performance outside their intended environment. So once you have established the ideal manifold configuration and dimensions for your application you may wish to apply additional techniques to help the manifold do its job at peak efficiency.

Insulation

Modifications include heat management in the form of thermal coatings or types of insulation to isolate the plenum and runners from radiant engine heat. These coatings may be applied to the entire manifold or specific areas such as the bottom, which is exposed to splash oiling from the lifter gallery.

Various companies, including Dart Machinery, offer specialized

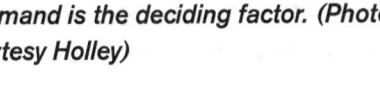

Many EFI applications use larger single-blade throttle bodies, such as this 95-mm Holley unit. They work because they don't rely on velocity to facilitate fuel movement. With EFI, you have a choice between this and a four-hole throttle body version. Available capacity to serve engine demand is the deciding factor. (Photo Courtesy Holley)

anti-corrosive coatings and marine jacket coatings for marine applications. These coatings prevent saltwater corrosion in the water jackets of cylinder heads and intake manifolds and act as a shielding treatment that resists galvanic corrosion in blocks and cylinder heads.

You may also wish to incorporate modifications for "four-corner" or "center" cooling fittings to optimize coolant flow through the cylinder heads. Some manifold manufacturers specifically accommodate these needs. Others do not, so you have to choose from commercially available intakes or specify your exact requirements for a custom manifold.

Injectors

Even if you are running carburetors, it may be prudent to select or build a custom manifold that already incorporates bosses for nitrous-oxide injectors or bungs for fuel injectors. This saves you time and expense later if you decide to switch to port fuel injection or nitrous-oxide injection. Most good racing manifolds now incorporate dual-distributor hold-down clamp bosses so you can choose the most convenient location for locking down the distributor. Many also incorporate threaded openings at the front and rear water jacket openings where you can install bleeders to eliminate all air from the cooling system. You'll probably want these so make sure you get them.

Spacers, Adapters and Shear Plates

Although you may incorporate some form of carburetor spacer, depending on your final application, you should never choose to incorporate a carburetor adapter if you are seeking top performance. Most manufacturers offer adapters for 2-barrel carbs or to adapt 4150-style intakes to 4500 carbs and vice versa. Although these components offer tremendous convenience and utility, they almost never complement the ideal flow path and volumetric requirements that promote optimum power and, more important, power band positioning. If you are a top-level engine builder, you already know to avoid them.

Many people don't recognize that Chevrolet's fuel-injection systems of the late 1950s and early 1960s were essentially side-inlet tunnel rams with properly sized plenums. Their performance was derived largely from the airflow configuration and not the fuel injection. Runner lengths and cross sections for the 283- and 327-ci V-8s were optimized for the engine's specified power range.

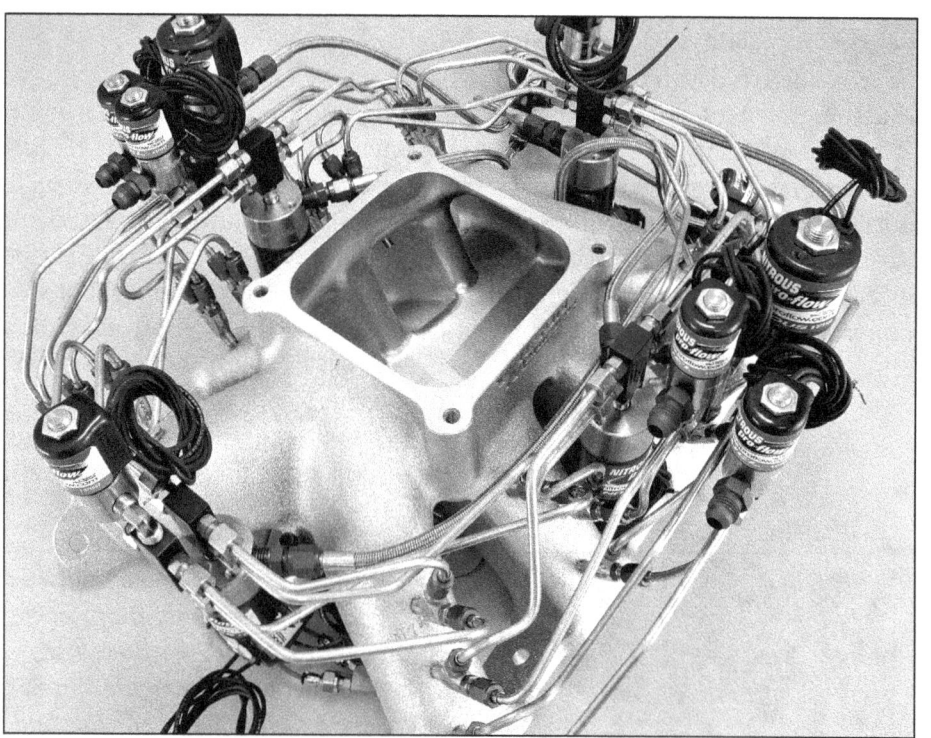

A Holley Dominator flanged on a single-plane intake has a very good shot at all the ports. This system requires a lot of RPM to retain high flow velocity without being affected by the intense fog of triple nitrous oxide injectors. (Photo Courtesy Wilson Manifolds)

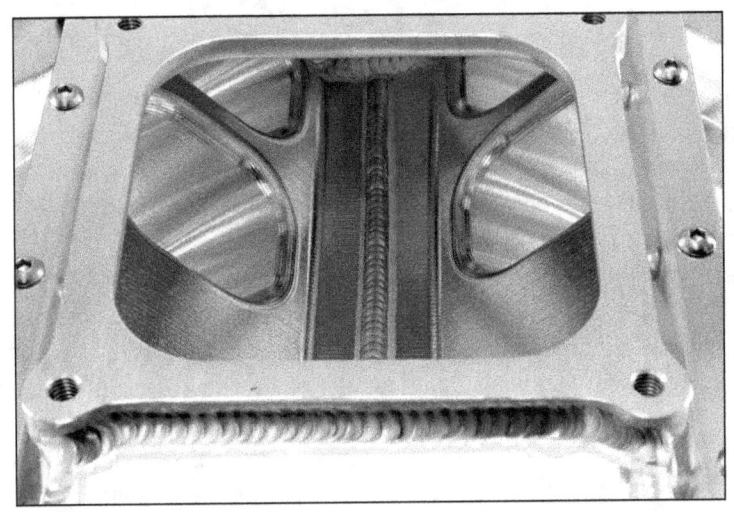

One controversial aspect of some sheet-metal intakes is the configuration of the central valley. Many experts feel that this area should be fabricated or otherwise filled flush with the lower edge of the runner entry to avoid a flow interruption entering the runner. (Photo Courtesy Wilson Manifolds)

Shear plates, such as those offered by Wilson Manifolds, are an exception. They are not adapters but rather airflow enhancement plates specifically designed for tunnel ram intake manifolds. They integrate 1/2-inch-thick carburetor plates with 5-degree tapered-throttle bore extensions with anti-reversion grooves that may be beneficial if you have missed the call on camshaft selection. If you need them, however, you have probably missed your best cam selection. Their primary benefit comes from the throttle bore extensions that help maintain velocity and mixture quality via fuel shearing at the lower openings.

Some builders swear by them. You can decide for yourself by observing what other winning combinations are running. Make sure your cam designer or supplier agrees with the use of shear plates, and you absolutely must do the math to see how they affect plenum volume and flow velocity.

Manifold Material

If light weight and top performance are your goals, a sheet-metal manifold is your best choice. If you're popping for a max-effort custom-built intake, make sure it incorporates all of the above considerations and any others that may be necessary.

Extrude Honing

Extrude honing became a popular porting process in the 1990s when it was used primarily to improve flow characteristics of dry-flow EFI-based intake manifolds. Many of these manifolds incorporated abrupt turns and reversals with rough edges and casting anomalies. It became hugely popular as a modification on 5.0L Ford engines.

The extrude hone process forces an abrasive sludge-like medium (generally an abrasive-laden polymer) through the internal passages under pressure to smooth, blend, and in some cases enlarge the internal air passages. It is often referred to as abrasive flow machining or abrasive flow deburring.

Polishing is necessary depending on the abrasive quality of the medium and the time and flow rate as it moves through the passages. Although it doesn't directly offer the capacity to dramatically enlarge passages, it is generally seen as overall beneficial to the flow path surface.

The greatest amount of material removal occurs at points where the flow of material is restricted because the flow velocity tends to increase and gain pressure. It tends to round off the radius of turns, remove or diminish obstructions, and polish the flow surface. It is still widely popular with the import crowd despite the fact that their manifolds only flow air and hence it is quite unnecessary.

Extrude honing is a process adapted from industrial applications that require flow improvements for liquids moving through pipes and the internal passages of machinery. In that regard it offers benefits, but in my opinion it has very limited performance value in terms of airflow. If performance gains are realized, they are generally slight and mostly the result of enlarging the passage and raising the torque peak RPM, which I have witnessed on a dyno.

Extrude honed heads and manifolds have little or no performance value on carbureted engines. The fuel dropout that occurs is highly detrimental. My advice? If you're looking for maximum performance spend your money on CNC-prepared heads and forget you ever heard of extrude honing.

Flow Testing Intake Manifolds

Flow testing your intake manifold with the carburetor(s) and cylinder heads you intend to use can be very instructive even if not always scientifically precise. Most commercially available intake manifolds incorporate necessary compromises to accommodate manufacturing and

CHAPTER 4

CNC Porting and Texturing

CNC stands for computer numerical control, an automated machining process used in the manufacturing sector to control machine tools that make or modify parts. CNC can be used to control lathes, mills, grinders, and a variety of multi-function automated machining centers. In the automotive performance aftermarket, CNC systems are used to precision machine cylinder blocks, heads, manifolds, carb spacers, and other components that are made more affordable by the automated machining process. CNC cylinder head porting is by far the most common use we are concerned with in this book.

CNC allows cylinder head manufacturers to automate most, if not all, of the manufacturing process so that high-quality parts with repeatable performance characteristics can be manufactured quickly and affordably. The process is referred to more correctly as CAD/CAM or Computer Aided Design/Computer Aided Machining. Originally derived from the aerospace industry, it is now the machining standard for nearly all manufacturing of machined parts.

In addition to traditional manufacturers of cylinder heads, countless small shops and companies have acquired CNC machining centers to make their own parts and/or modify existing parts. It has become common practice for many small shops to digitize known good designs so they can reproduce them in-house. Port piracy is common and you would be amazed at how much easier it is to cast your own aluminum parts today than it was a few decades ago. With a little study and advice, a small shop can accomplish the necessary tooling and molds and have molten alloy castings relatively quickly. Suddenly, everyone is either making parts or copying parts.

Full-service machining centers are offered by numerous manufacturers. Among them, Rottler Manufacturing has emerged as a recognized leader in specialized automotive machining equipment. Rottler offers a wide variety of machine tool equipment for cylinder head shops including automated, CNC and manual surfaces, seat and guide tools, and valve refacers. They also provide fully automated machining centers that digitize and reproduce a cylinder head (intake port, exhaust port, and combustion chambers) or an intake manifold with remarkable speed and accuracy. Rottler's P55 and P69 cylinder head machining centers are fully automated five-axis machines incorporating automatic digitizing, CNC porting, head resurfacing, and port texturing. They incorporate an automatic tool changer and provide walk-away performance for cylinder head machining operations. They can process any digital design file to make identical parts all day long.

Existing digital files are easily modified in the computer to alter shapes, bends, turns, cross sections, and port locations. Designers and engineers work with these files constantly to refine design elements or make modifications that have been

Blueprinting plenum chambers and runner entries ensures the smoothest transition from the carburetor to the intake runners. The objective is to blend the plenum opening from the carburetor and eliminate abrupt turns, sharp edges, and any other obstructions that might interfere with the smooth flow of air. (Photo Courtesy Wilson Manifolds)

Modifying port entry angles via specific port matching produces power. The match between the runner exit and the intake port entry should be almost seamless with no sharp edges or area change. Epoxy filling is sometimes required to accomplish the smooth finish. (Photo Courtesy Wilson Manifolds)

found to improve performance. Rottler uses Windows OS with touch-screen technology so nearly anyone can learn to use it quickly. The full software package allows operators to design tool-accurate tool-path programming to precisely cut ports and combustion chambers. It also allows ports to be designed and refined on stand-alone computers that may also incorporate CFD (computational fluid dynamics) analysis for initial evaluation.

CFD is a computational method of numerical analysis and algorithms. It is used to predict and evaluate flow path characteristics based on simulating the interaction of liquids and gases across surfaces defined by boundary layers. Final files can then be imported to the machine for turn-key production. The best head porters around the country can do a great job, but more and more of them are using hand porting for R&D and CNC for reproduction just like the manufacturers.

Rottler's progressive approach also incorporates a texturing technique some porters have considered a closely guarded secret for many years. It's well known that roughening the port surface or port texturing offers power gains by improving flow and, in the case of carbureted applications, maintaining good fuel atomization. Rottler has refined these methods by incorporating a texturing procedure based on the aerodynamic properties of a golf ball. Small vortices created by the dimples in a golf ball help it fly farther by smoothing the airflow across its surface. And the reduced surface area reduces drag. The same thing occurs in the port.

Rottler's tooling and software are such that they make nearly perfect surface dimples of uniform size and depth without altering the basic port shape and cross section. Cylinder head people we spoke with generally confirm that they do see power gains and the Rottler process is a refinement of something they have been fiddling with for years. Rottler says that their customers report a 1½– to 2-percent power gain on average.

A few years ago, cylinder head expert Larry Meaux offered the following comments in an interview conducted by Hot Rod Engine Tech:

"This was one of my speed secrets, but I've had to include and account for its effects in the new PipeMax version 4.0 to make it correlate with my new dyno and dragstrip data. In 2010 I talked my best engine building customers into letting me try something I've wanted to test for the past 30 years or so. I took one of my old chipped and slightly bent Alumina Burrs and rough ground just the entire intake ports on a big-block Chevy Dart head all the way to the bottom valve job angle cut. Back on the dyno the engine gained almost 15 hp on a 950-hp engine. You could theorize that the intake ports are now slightly larger and it should have made more horsepower.

"We kept testing this on the next five or six various types and engine sizes, grinding over the previous 60-grit finish with the rougher alumina burr finish and gaining anywhere from 10 to 15

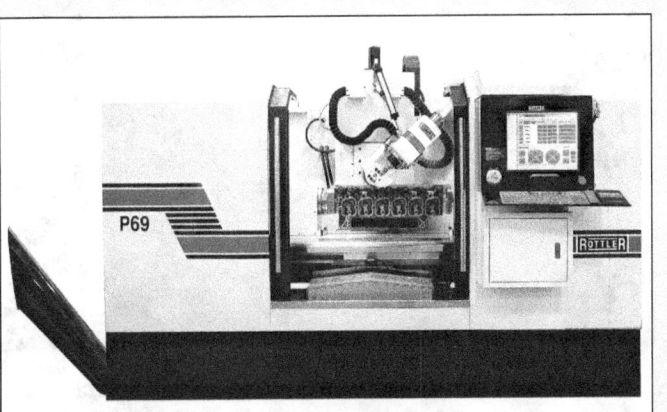

Rottler's P69 digitizing and porting machine provides fully automated porting capability with remarkable speed. It can also digitize existing ports so files can be modified to suit different requirements. (The same port can be applied to a replacement head.) It can digitize a port in about 30 minutes. And it can apply Rottler's exclusive port dimpling technique as required.

CNC porting makes it possible to mass produce highly developed high-performance and racing cylinder heads. Precise numerical control of the cutting heads allows extraordinary reproduction of flow paths and combustions chambers for each cylinder.

CNC Porting and Texturing CONTINUED

hp and lower BSFCs and sometimes shifting Peak HP 100 or 200 rpm higher.

"Again, I removed the heads and went back to 60-grit finish everywhere. Back on the chassis dyno it lost the 17 hp and was basically back to where the engine was originally. That was the only A-B-A tests I've done so far. I wish those tests would have been on my engine dyno instead.

"We kept going with the rough carbide finish everywhere in the intake, exhaust ports, chambers, and intake manifold from that point on. So far every engine has responded with 15- to 25-hp increases (or more), a wider power curve, sometimes 100-to-300-higher RPM point of peak horsepower, less fuel consumed on the Dyno (lower BSFCs), and dryer exhaust ports.

"On the flow bench, there were basically no flow gains from roughing up the entire heads/manifold surfaces. On the dyno and down the dragstrip, we consistently see more HP and quicker ET/MPH times. In 2010 Jeff Colletta won the NMCA NPS Championship with the rough carbide finish everywhere in the intake and exhaust ports, chambers, and intake manifold.

"My dyno tests so far show around a maximum gain of .018 percent times peak HP as the typical HP gain from a rough carbide finish everywhere including the intake manifold. The majority of the tests were with VP's Q-16 race gas; the rest of the tests were with VP C23, C25, C16, and Exxon 93 premium. I agree with Jim McFarland about the reasoning; it appears to be trapping a greater amount of higher quality mixture by IVC point and also burning it more efficiently during combustion."

Although the value of CNC machining lies in the speed and accuracy of reproduction, it's also clear that refined surface preparation plays a significant role in modern cylinder head technology. The ability to measure, store, and accurately reproduce top-performing flow-path profiles has revolutionized cylinder head technology and made it available to more people than ever before. ■

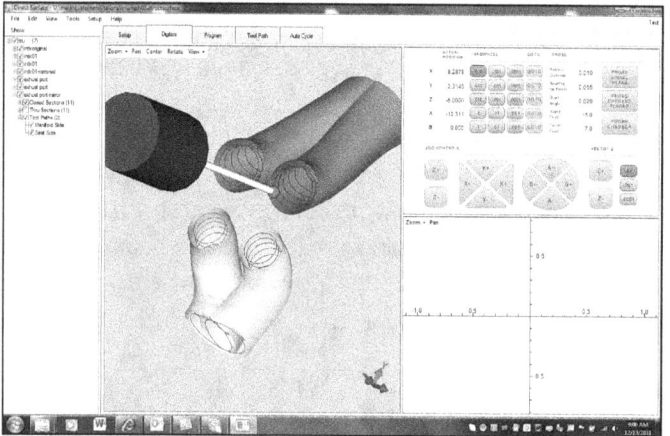

This is the machine's main digitizing screen that allows the operator to record very precise measurements. The advanced software permits direct manipulation of the port design. The operator can use positioning data to "tweak" the design right on the screen.

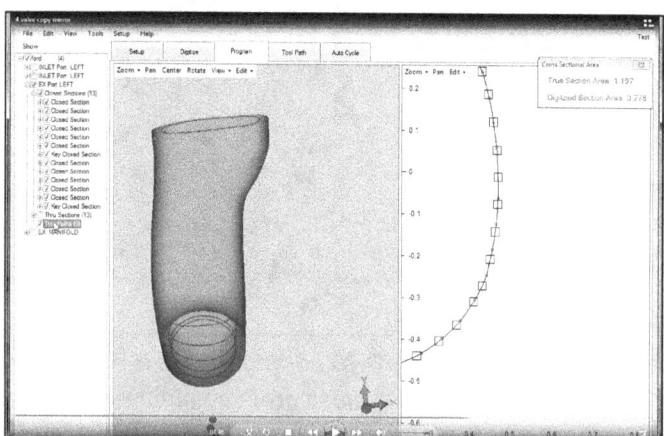

The program function allows the entire process to be performed on the machine. Unique software lets the operator import and export to and from common CAD/CAM design files such as those produced by Master Cam or Surf Cam software programs.

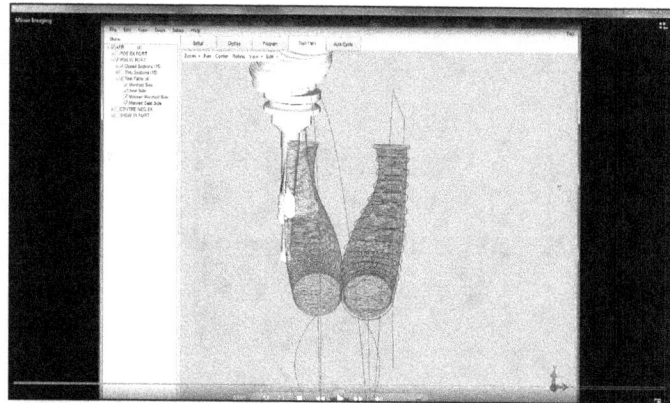

The tool path function allows the operator to check and adjust the path of the cutting tool to ensure smooth transitions and minimize stepping of the port area where different tool paths meet.

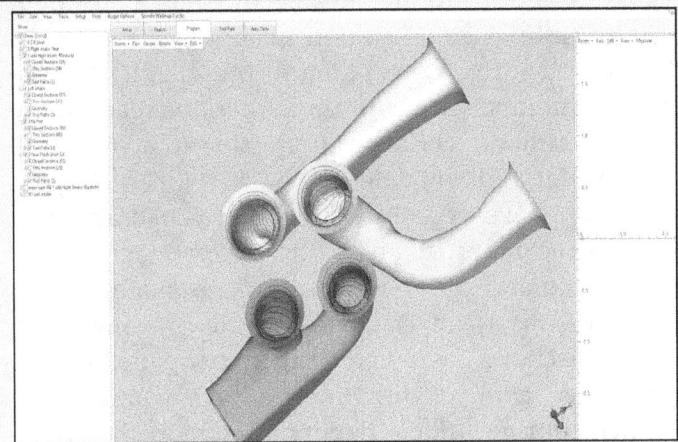

The wire-frame model helps the operator visualize the ports being created so the machine can execute multiple repetitive machining tasks without error. The system uses a Windows-based operating system that incorporates touch-screen management and facilitates factory support via Skype and other direct-interface options.

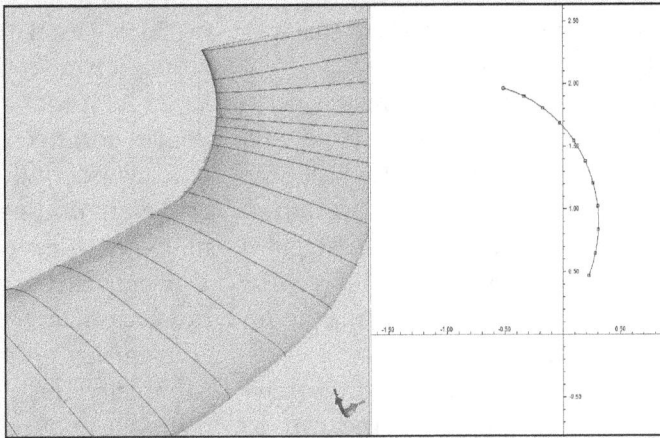

This screen shows a detailed picture of a port wall with a small radius. The operator can refine the design and tool path to accommodate various requirements. Once a design is finalized, a typical V-8 cylinder head with all ports and combustion chambers can be fully machined in about an hour.

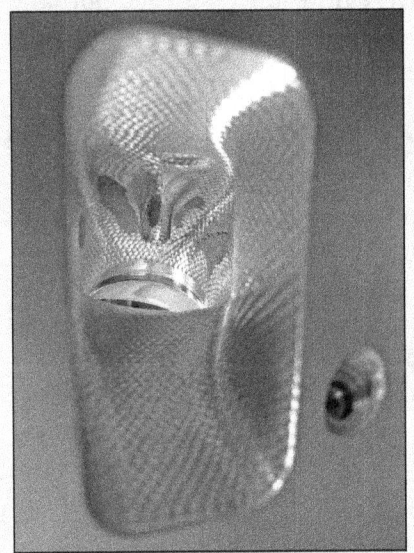
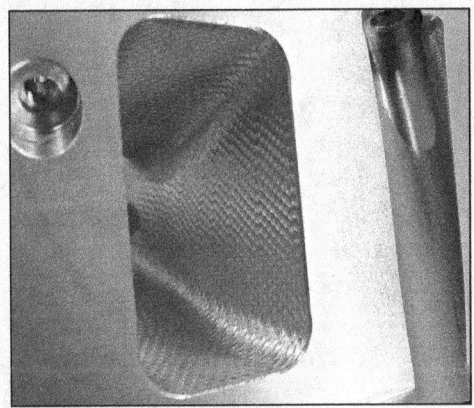
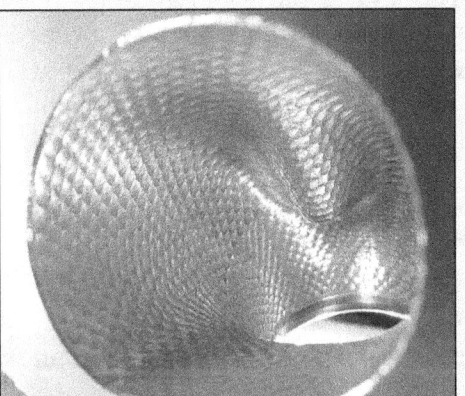

These photos show the dimpling technique applied to two different port shapes. They illustrate the uniformity of the process as it applies to shape and area changes and obstacles such as valveguide bosses.

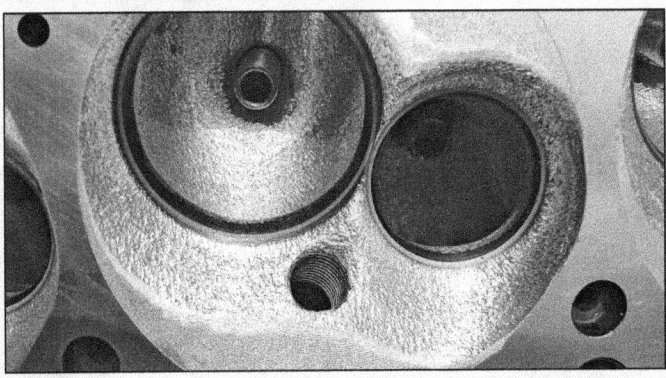

This Meaux Racing Heads' rougher, but equally effective, hand-textured combustion chamber was accomplished with a modified, rough carbide bit and lots of patience.

CHAPTER 4

production necessities and often to meet broad marketing demands that require a more universal approach to application and fit.

These compromises include packaging restraints (manifold shape, size, and height) necessary to keep the fueling components underneath a stock hoodline. That often requires port and runner shapes and lengths that are not ideal for maximum performance, but necessary to production line assembly and fit requirements or the need for the part to fit a broad range of engines such as a small-block Chevy in a dozen different displacement configurations. In such cases, the manifold is likely very good for one displacement and increasingly less effective as displacement moves further away from the sweet spot. It's the same reason that we have different carburetor sizes and a compelling reason for flowing components together to get an overall picture of total flow efficiency.

Custom sheet-metal intakes are a different story, but it is still a beneficial exercise to flow the manifold and companion components together to investigate potential anomalies and gather an overall snapshot of the airflow characteristics of the entire intake flow path. Although this approach lacks the essential dynamics of a running engine it identifies the overall capability of the components and exposes any major flow deficiencies that may exist in one or more inlet paths.

Most intake manifold castings reduce cylinder head airflow by 10 to 15 percent, which may prompt you to rethink your overall airflow and cylinder head requirement for achieving optimal VE. Proper intake manifold selection does not include choosing the best-flowing head and then handicapping it with the most convenient manifold selection. Complementary components and using the applicable mathematics are essential for top performance.

You may find it worthwhile to return a poor-performing manifold for a refund if it doesn't pass the flow test with your high-dollar heads and carburetor(s). In many cases, flow problems can be corrected with various modifications, but this may not be cost effective. A different manifold may indeed provide a better solution.

To perform these tests successfully, you have to isolate and flow each runner in an identical manner to determine the available airflow potential without any outside influences. These may affect individual runners via dynamic pressure wave influences in the actual environment of engine operation. Recognize from the outset that this is an imperfect evaluation designed to help determine which way is up. Still, you can learn from it if you consider the data thoughtfully.

When mounting the manifold to the head, pay the same attention to port matching that you did when building the engine. Do the same for the carburetor(s) and make certain you are able to achieve full throttle and lock it open. If your application is other than drag racing (e.g., oval track or road racing), you may wish to also evaluate flow at several part-throttle openings such as 50 to 75 percent. Note that all of this almost always requires some fancy rigging to support the whole mess while it is attached to the flow bench.

Tape off every port that is not being flowed. You're not going to see any outside pressure influences from other cylinders, but you can observe how much air each port and flow path is capable of flowing independently. And you can identify any paths that are much better or much worse and decide how they might be modified. It is tedious work, and some builders are tempted just to spot-check a few ports, but remember that it's a racing engine. You *must* check everything twice, three times, four, or more; as many times as it takes to make it perfect.

In the end, the port you pass over may turn out to be flow deficient. The engine will be down on power in that one hole, and you may never figure out why because everything else seems correct.

INTAKE MANIFOLD

CHAPTER 5

CYLINDER HEADS

Selecting cylinder heads is a crucial decision; they make up a substantial portion of your racing engine budget. Properly suited heads help ensure that you build an efficient, high-horsepower, competitive engine. The airflow enhancements discussed thus far combine to influence the performance of the ports, valves, and combustion chamber in your cylinder heads.

If you've done a good job so far you have maximized inlet airflow through the carburetor or throttle body and optimized the recovery of atmospheric pressure in the manifold plenum. You've calculated the best runner cross section and length for the application and applied the desired amount of taper to help accelerate the air toward the intake port.

All of that is fundamental to good performance, but critical details within the cylinder head itself also need to be addressed. Always keep in mind that a big flow number rarely tells you much about how well a given cylinder head performs. If you're seeking answers about a particular head you're better off learning what the airspeed is in the port, the RPM range it is expected to serve, where the valves are relative to the cylinder wall, and how the port is set up to feed the combustion chamber. Most engine power comes from the cylinder heads and their ability to fill the cylinders and evacuate them efficiently. The differences among short-blocks assembled by a broad range of competent engine builders are relatively minor, but builders who follow up with superior well-matched cylinder heads usually excel. Many commercially available high-performance and racing cylinder heads are designed to meet the specific requirements of their application. They are almost always a compromise of sorts because they don't directly accommodate specific engine sizes or operational parameters. Many of them are very good when applied within their intended range of performance, but you can often do even better.

The overriding idea is that this is a team effort, and the goal is not always maximum flow numbers. The

Cylinder heads are the most influential component of an internal combustion engine. They are the gatekeeper that regulates the amount and quality of the air/fuel mixture entering the engine.

CHAPTER 5

flow number is simply a benchmark. You can pit two similar heads against each other and the one with the lower flow numbers often performs better on the track even though it appeared to be inferior on the flow bench. You want good flow, but you also want it to be smooth, non-turbulent flow that holds onto the fuel and helps distribute it evenly around the valve and into the cylinder with the best pressure recovery possible.

Component Compatibility

The shape and specific dimensions of individual ports and combustion chambers exert enormous influence on the shape and positioning of the torque curve and the overall power band of the engine. If maximum power spread across an application-specific power band is the primary goal of competition engine building, cylinder heads have the greatest influence on the volumetric efficiency and cylinder filling ability that make this possible. Although the camshaft commands the precise timing of flow path events, the cylinder head flow passages (ports and valves) manage the rate and volume of flow into the engine based on engine speed and piston position (CFM demand) as dictated by stroke length and rod length.

All of these components work in close concert and must be appropriately matched to ensure compatibility, optimal cylinder filling, and combustion efficiency. Incompatible components anywhere in the system not only fail to deliver the anticipated level of performance, they also restrict the optimum performance of other components operating within the flow path environment.

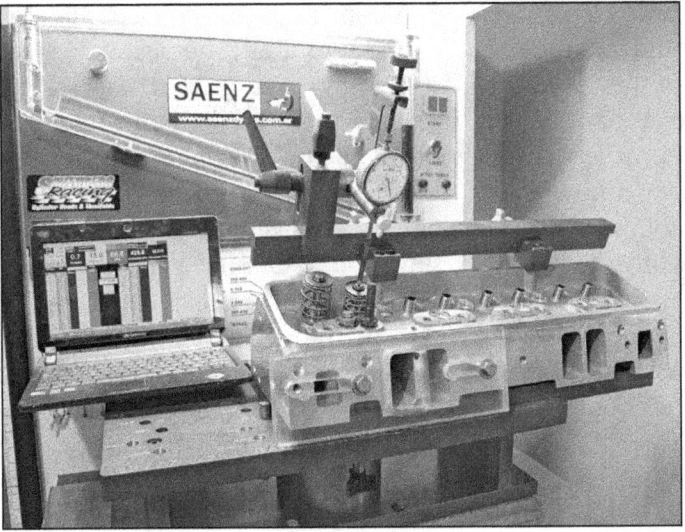

Naturally aspirated applications typically require much more flow-bench work to extract maximum performance for each application. Experience pays off, but it still may require long hours of trial and error. (Photo Courtesy Smithberg Racing)

Airflow Control Point

The most critical point in the head is the valveseat and the valve throat area. This is where savvy head porters begin their investigation because it is the choke point that controls airflow into the engine. At lower valve lifts, the valve curtain area is the primary restriction, but once the valve opens far enough so that the curtain area equals the throat area, the valve lift becomes irrelevant and the throat area dictates flow. This is primarily true, although Stock and Super Stock

Port Taper

Port taper generally ranges from 2 to 4 degrees with the port becoming smaller as it approaches the valve. Some builders refer to it as a percentage based on the port exit area divided by the port entry area. Taper is incorporated to encourage greater intake ramming by accelerating the air mass toward the valve throat. Taper is typically only accommodated on racing and high-performance intakes. Most cylinder head ports incorporate some taper, but manifolds don't always support it.

An Edelbrock dual-plane, such as the Performer RPM Air Gap, is known to maintain a constant cross section all the way to the runner exit at the manifold flange. So it isn't as effective at supporting a cylinder head with a lot of taper (say 3 degrees) because the runner exit is smaller than the average port entrance.

A tall single-plane intake with taller, larger runner entries tapers to the runner exit with a much closer match to the port entry on the cylinder head, thus accommodating the desired taper over the full length of the runner/port flow path. This makes the taper more effective and promotes ever better intake ramming.

Taper works best on tunnel ram intakes and you can easily see it on sheet-metal manifolds. The port entrances at the plenum are always larger and taper toward the port entry on the head. ∎

racers long ago realized that even higher valve lifts could still promote performance because they tended to add duration or the amount of time the valve is open with the full flow area available. Many other factors enter into the equation, such as valve size and location relative to the cylinder bore.

The ratio of intake valve size to bore diameter works best within a fairly narrow range of about 50 to 52 percent. The port size and taper exert enormous influence over the filling and intake ramming process, as does the shape, height, and efficiency of the short-side radius.

Street versus Race Heads

There's a tremendous difference between a high-performance head and a race head. On a street or high-performance head, low-lift flow is frequently considered an important quality. On a race head, it is virtually irrelevant. When you're lifting the valve nearly an inch very quickly, you blow right by the low-lift flow opportunity in milliseconds.

From the point of valve opening to about mid-lift, the piston is either still rising as it approaches TDC, or its velocity is virtually nothing as it traverses the TDC region. The piston's initial departure from TDC on the intake stroke is relatively slow and it doesn't achieve enough velocity to generate a good depression in the cylinder until the valve passes mid-lift, at which point it generates a strong flow demand. So, high-speed engines, such as for drag racing applications, really need very efficient high-lift flow, particularly because the duration of each flow event becomes shorter with increasing engine speed.

It's also common to see race cylinder heads with beautifully polished ports and chambers and/or high-tech-looking CNC porting patterns, but that is no guarantee of superior performance. In most cases, even a CNC'd port may be

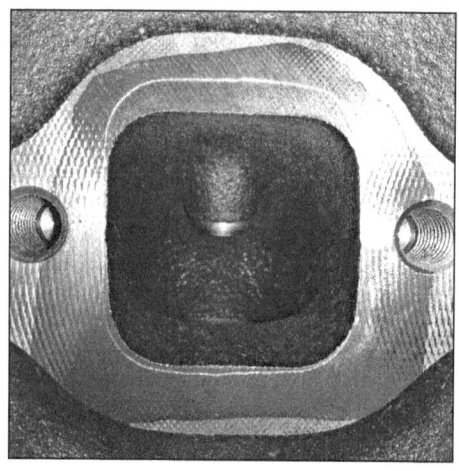

As cast, exhaust ports look pretty restrictive. This one is being prepped to raise the roof to provide a less restrictive exit angle. (Photo Courtesy Smithberg Racing)

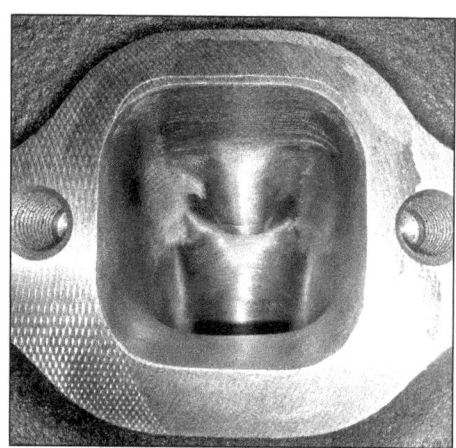

This finished iron exhaust port shows the raised roof and blended exhaust valveguide. It offers a freer-flowing exhaust path. (Photo Courtesy Smithberg Racing)

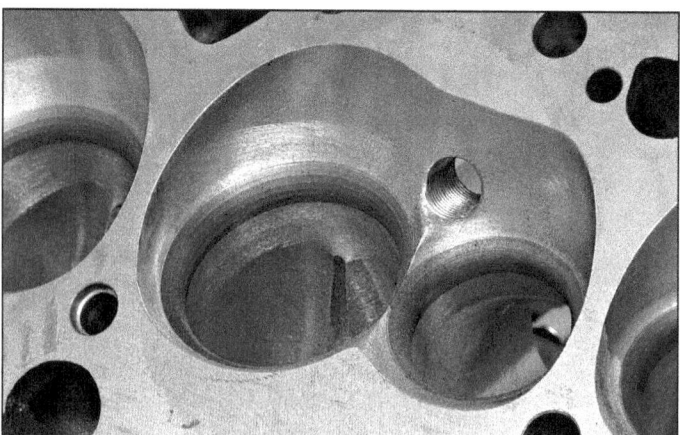

The diameter of the throat area immediately ahead of the intake valve is the most critical part of the head. It is the choke point that limits maximum flow and usually represents the minimum cross section of the intake port.

A similar choke point exists on the exhaust side. It also represents the minimum cross section and typically has a larger radius to encourage smooth exhaust flow, which exits under high pressure.

CHAPTER 5

Here you can see the basic valveguide blending to reduce flow obstruction. (Photo Courtesy Smithberg Racing)

Chamber prep seeks to equalize chamber volume and optimize airflow entering the chamber. Note the scribed lines indicating the location of the cylinder bore relative to the chamber. (Photo Courtesy Smithberg Racing)

An old-school deep chamber resists efforts to unshroud the valves. The modern trend is toward shallower chambers with decreased valve angles to have a straighter shot at the valve. This is a good effort to save a chamber that is deeply shrouded. (Photo Courtesy Smithberg Racing)

This intake port has a pushrod pinch area with the port smoothly arcing around it. (Photo Courtesy Smithberg Racing)

This is the throat area where you want the throat diameter to be between 91 and 92 percent of the valve diameter. (Photo Courtesy Smithberg Racing)

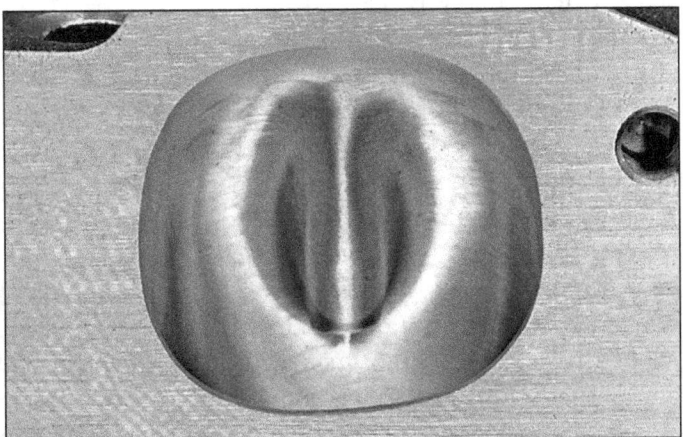

Here's the proper way to shape and blend an exhaust valveguide.

compromised because it is essentially a copy of a port design developed to yield good performance across a range of engine applications. In a general sense, it often performs well, but it is unlikely that it is optimized for your specific application, nor does it provide the final bit of performance gain required to make you a consistent winner.

In a similar sense, highly polished ports attract attention and are often viewed with envious eyes. The port design may be good, but the shiny surface is generally not. Most head porters now concede that a rough surface typically provides better performance, particularly in a well-shaped port. Many heads come with polished ports as a sales incentive because customers believe that racing heads should be ported and polished. Old habits die hard.

Where the Power Comes From

The intake and exhaust ports lead to and from the combustion chamber where air and fuel are processed into power. The cylinder head is the core of the power process. It provides the all-important combustion space where energy is released from the burning of the air/fuel mixture, and it provides the valves and flow paths that escort the air/fuel mixture into the combustion chamber and usher it out via the exhaust system. But there's really no magic involved other than a thorough understanding of airflow behavior and how it moves efficiently through the engine. How all of this is coordinated, managed, and properly tuned for maximum VE is largely a matter of sizing the ports and valves and managing the transitions to suit the application.

Chamber Function

To fully appreciate the dynamics of gas exchange in a competition engine, it is logical to start by examining the combustion space for the critical keys to its function. For the purpose of this discussion, you can view the combustion space as having a roof (chamber with valves), a floor (piston top), and walls (chamber and cylinder).

Within this captive environment, the roof and floor approach and depart from each other rapidly many times per second. This motion exerts a profound influence on the fuel mixture as it enters the combustion space, combusts and expands, and exits at a very high rate. Although the spark ignition is initiated at a specified distance before TDC, the piston (floor) is still approaching the roof with rising pressure creating negative work.

Turbulence driven by increasing piston motion and the quench effect against the roof drives the denser fuel charge toward the spark plug where it ignites. In the best cases the flame expands smoothly depending

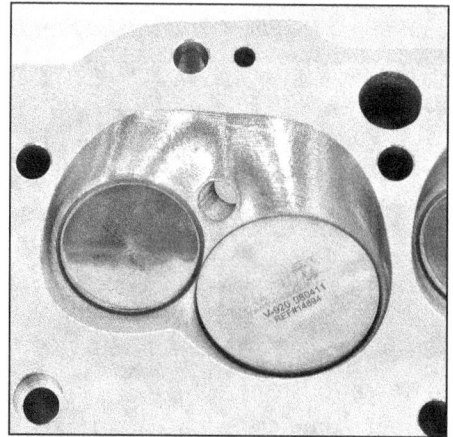

The combustion chamber shape and the valves play a major role in determining how air enters and exits the cylinder. Large valves typically support high airflow and increased power levels.

on mixture homogeneity, piston area, and the effects of any obstructions, such as compression domes. The higher the mixture quality, the better the burn; a smooth combustion event occurs.

Most combustion chambers are designed to drive the advancing flame front toward the exhaust valve, hastening the burn and improving the exhaust cycle, which often increases power.

Power Improvements

In recent years, combustion chambers have become smaller, and some specific shapes have been refined to encourage swirl and tumble within the fuel mixture as it enters the cylinder through the intake valve. Swirl is a rotational motion of the incoming fuel mixture that tends to assume a circular path defined by the cylinder walls. Tumble is a similar but vertical motion where the mixture enters the cylinder with a waterfall effect.

The mixture-enhancing qualities of swirl and tumble are known to encourage power improvements even though they tend to restrict net airflow to some degree. At the higher engine speeds associated with racing applications, swirl is commonly accepted while tumble is generally thought to be ineffective due to insufficient time for effective charge motion to occur.

With advances in port design, spark plug placement, valve design and placement, and CNC-machining processes, we have reached a point where few builders undertake major cylinder head mods. Choosing the ideal cylinder head for a particular engine package is a dilemma, even with the vast selection offered by specialized cylinder head manufacturers.

CHAPTER 5

Best Racing Combo

As previously discussed, the wide array of cylinder head offerings still leaves something on the table, and hardcore builders are determined to find it. Smaller, high-efficiency chambers have proven their value via lower BSFC numbers, better burn characteristics, and (obviously) more power. The chamber's combustion efficiency can't really be quantified on a flow bench, but you can observe its improved filling characteristics via reduced turbulence and increased flow due to efficient pressure recovery in the cylinder.

With application specifics in mind, builders tend to evaluate cylinder heads (when not specified or restricted by rules) based on mid-range and high-flow numbers; port turbulence; chamber shape and efficiency; valve size and angle; spark plug placement; port shape, size, and position; and other critical attributes that affect power production.

Nearly all modern race heads now incorporate more optimized valve placement, thicker deck surfaces, optimized cooling jackets, and

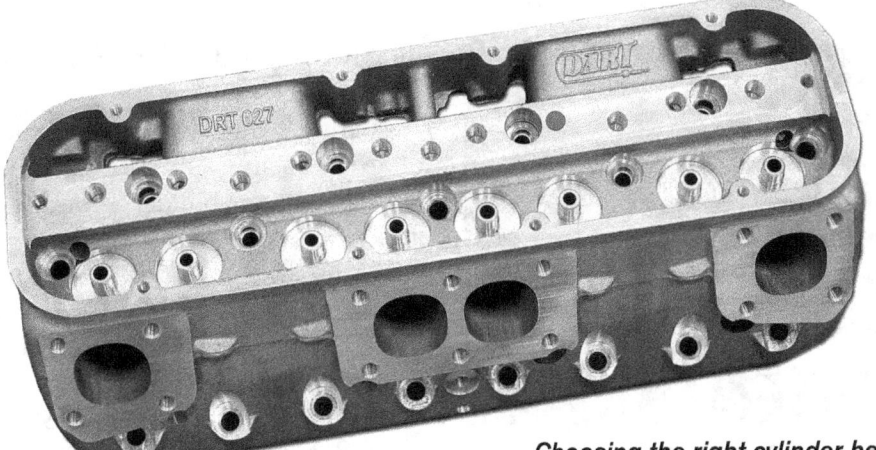

Choosing the right cylinder head for the application can make or break any high-performance or racing application. Primary considerations include port shape and dimensions, valve angle, valve size, intake valve throat diameter, and available valve gear. (Photo Courtesy Dart Machinery)

The Dart 11-degree Little Chief aluminum cylinder head from the 462-mph Speed Demon LSR car does not sport massive exhaust ports despite running more than 40 pounds of boost to produce close to 2,700 hp on a 388-ci Duttweiler-built small-block Chevy.

The Speed Demon intake ports are geometrically symmetrical with a tall, short-side radius to increase flow efficiency. These heads flow about 420 cfm as delivered. That's massive flow for a small-block. Then add boost and stand back.

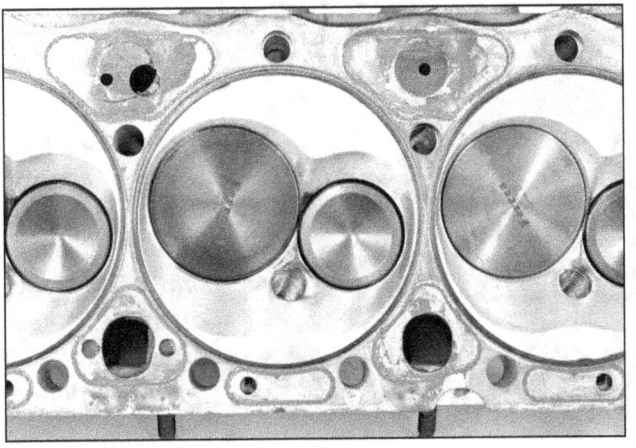

Chambers on the Speed Demon Dart heads are very shallow to accommodate the steep valve angles. This view shows the coated valves and shallow chamber after more than 70 runs on the dyno at max boost.

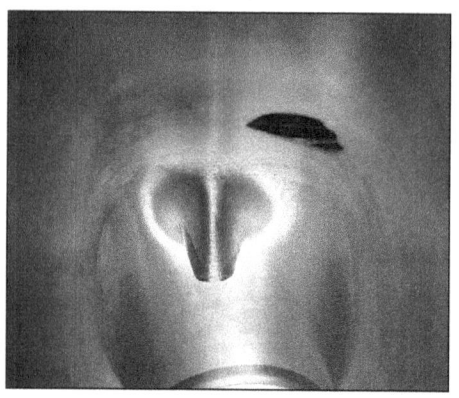

The shape of the airflow around the valveguide is a matter of personal preference. Some head porters prefer a bulbous leading edge facing the flow and tapering with the flow. Others prefer a sharper and thinner edge against the flow. Many believe that the shape shown here is best for splitting the air around the valve. (Photo Courtesy Meaux Racing Heads)

better oil control. Some recommend using the smallest ports and valves that support the target power level. Smaller ports with high-flow velocities offer better flow and cylinder filling qualities accompanied by more desirable mixture qualities that promote power. These qualities encourage strong low- and mid-range power even as they encounter a sort of power ceiling based on the head's flow capacity. Larger ports and valves are superior at high RPM, and when suitably cammed they create big power at high revs.

A critical balance must be struck for every racing application. Experienced engine builders routinely probe the limits while trying not to harm the desirable flow velocities generated by smaller ports and/or the enhanced mixture qualities that promote good power.

With the exception of Stock Eliminator drag racing and various lower-level circle-track applications, most racing engines now use aluminum heads. Some applications are restricted to the stock-type iron heads and valve sizes with no porting allowed, but most applications allow aluminum heads with a variety of valve sizes and porting configurations. When selecting a cylinder head for a particular application it is important to closely match the desired RPM range based on port dimensions that include port length, cross section, and mid- and high-range flow rates.

Flow Factors

The primary factors affecting cylinder head flow rate include valve size, port shape and dimensions, short-side bend radius before the valve, and surface texture of the port surfaces. This is particularly true of the port floor and the port roof to prevent fuel separation. Inertia tends to push the bulk of the fuel mixture above the port centerline toward the roof where the runner makes the turn to the valve. The short-side radius influences flow rates considerably, and is one reason for the evolution of high-port heads with shallower valve angles.

Most manufacturers publish valve sizes and flow figures for their cylinder heads, and some provide port volumes. The best ones also provide port dimensions including height, width, cross-sectional area, and port location. Port length along the centerline of the port is also useful, but few provide it. The more of this information you have, the easier it is to pinpoint the ideal head for your combination.

Flow figures help you determine the head's ability to fill and evacuate the cylinders efficiently according to the engine's displacement. Port dimensions help you calculate the torque peak and the spread of the power band. This information is particularly useful if you are performing some initial brainstorming on one of the many engine simulation programs available for your PC.

Valves and Valve Sizes

Valves are a necessary evil in any IC racing engine. They represent a variable-flow restriction that must be dealt with to effectively feed the engine. Bigger valves are generally better for obvious reasons, but valve size is always limited by bore size. Under naturally aspirated conditions intake mixtures must find their own way into the cylinders at relatively low pressure; hence bigger valves are

Pro Stock–style semi-oval–shaped intake ports are pretty much the norm today. Many porters favor them and most high-end heads incorporate this shape.

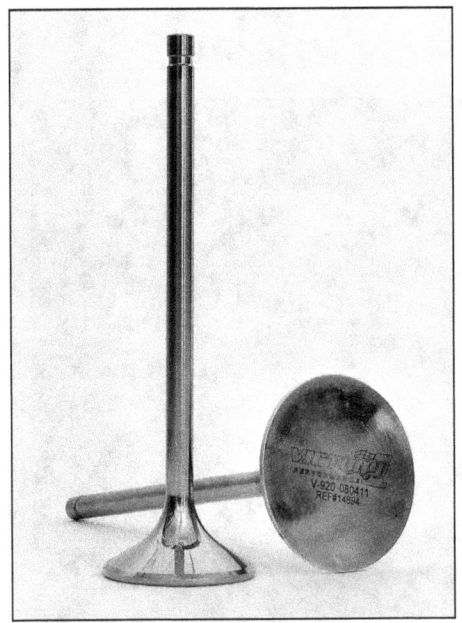

Valve size, shape, and seat angle are critical to flow. This titanium racing valve incorporates standard 45-degree valveseat faces, but many racing valves now use 55-degree seats that flow more air at the expense of shorter valveseat life.

In addition to the reduced stem diameter, this polished intake valve also incorporates a thinner, straighter margin around the circumference. It also features minimal curvature on the bottom to encourage the fuel mixture to shear away from the valve when it passes over it.

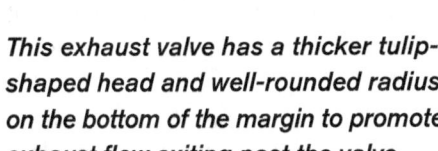

This exhaust valve has a thicker tulip-shaped head and well-rounded radius on the bottom of the margin to promote exhaust flow exiting past the valve.

required on the intake side. Exhaust gases are discharged under higher pressures, which means that smaller valves can be used.

In most racing circles, the intake valve is typically about 50 to 52 percent of the applicable bore size (31 to 33 percent on four-valve heads). Exhaust valves are generally about 72 to 76 percent of the intake valve diameter. These sizes are not set in stone, but they have been found to yield an effective combination in most high-speed racing applications.

Part of the complication with valves is shrouding, caused by proximity to cylinder walls and some deeper combustion chambers. Shrouding presents a barrier that closes off part of the valve curtain, or flow window. It reduces net flow, redirects the optimal flow path, and often influences the combustion process with negative results. This is the main reason that many successful racing heads used canted or splayed valves that move away from the cylinder walls as they open. Typically, the largest valve that follows the 51-percent rule works best, but in the case of severe shrouding, smaller valves may flow better because they are farther from the cylinder wall and present less restriction.

Valves are somewhat delicate compared to most other components. It is very easy to burn or damage a valve to the point where the head breaks off and you lose an engine. Thus it becomes necessary to show them plenty of respect in order to avoid serious consequences.

Valveseats must be perfectly concentric to seal properly and the valvetrain must be configured to minimize the severity with which it opens and closes the valves, avoiding valve float at all cost.

Valve angles are critical to maximizing performance. Many race heads use a radiused seat or up to five different angles on each seat. Although 45-degree seats are still the norm,

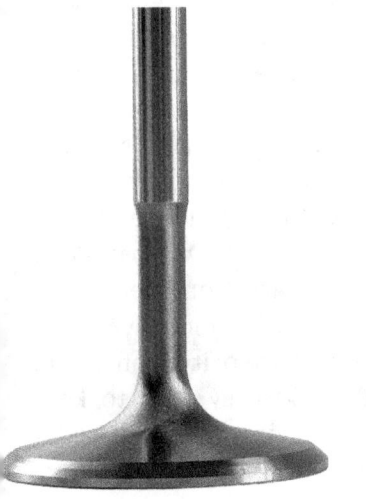

A comparison between typical intake and exhaust valves reveals common differences. The intake valve on the left features reduced stem diameter in the throat area to present less flow restriction from the exposed stem. The exhaust valve on the right features more robust construction to withstand extreme heat.

The Bowl Area

The expanded bulb-like portion just ahead of the valve is the bowl area. When you hear porters speak of a modification in the area just below the valve, the head is upside down on the bench. What they really mean is upstream of the valve. When installed on the engine, below the valve actually means anywhere in the cylinder or combustion chamber.

The bowl area, valveguide, short-side radius, and port all reside above the valve when the head is on the engine. Head porters often speak of performing work below the valve because that's how they see it when they're working on it.

The short-side radius is part of the bowl area where the vertically shaped intake port converts to a round port as it approaches the valve.

The throat area is the round area just before the valveseat. It is generally the point of maximum restriction (cross-sectional area) and controls the choke effect, which ultimately limits its airflow. ■

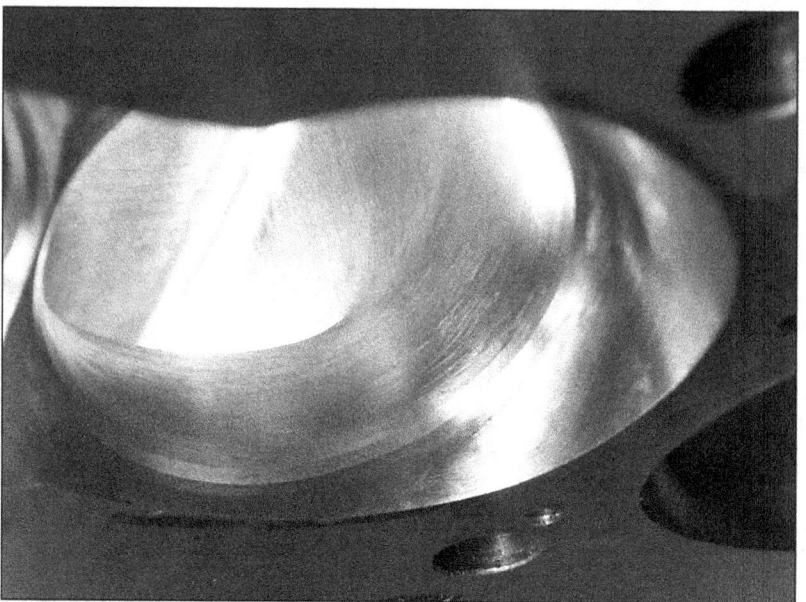

The short-side radius is a critical area of the intake port. The turn into the valve must be minimal and gentle to ensure that air laden with fuel droplets can negotiate the turn without having the fuel drop out of suspension. It is also important in equalizing flow around the valve, so that the flow doesn't overrun the valve and stack up against the opposite side of the chamber. (Photo Courtesy Smithberg Racing)

Pro Stock applications use 50- to 55-degree seat angles to take advantage of their superior airflow characteristics at higher engine speeds.

Valve weight is another important factor in high-RPM engines. RPM potential and overall valvetrain dynamics are largely influenced by the mass of the valve and what it takes to open and close it with a perfect seal at very high engine speeds. Lightweight titanium valves are standard equipment in all serious racing engines, except those applications where they are not permitted.

Cylinder heads are all about using ports, valves, and combustion chambers to manage and optimize airflow through the engine. To achieve the highest degree of success the cylinder heads must be carefully matched to the specific requirements of the desired power band and its associated racing application. Getting close to the desired result is not difficult with the broad range of available racing cylinder heads, but it is expensive. As a rule, top-performing cylinder heads are almost always the most expensive component of any racing engine. Even then, there are still modifications and tweaks to be made if the head is to deliver to its full potential.

Evaluating Cylinder Head Potential

Two primary restrictions dictate airflow through an engine; one is variable and one is fixed. The carburetor or throttle body is a variable restriction necessary to provide engine throttling. The fixed restriction is the valve throat diameter approximately 0.25 to 0.30 inch above the valveseat. It is the single most important factor in determining a cylinder head's ability to move air and make power.

In some cases, there is also a pushrod pinch area where the port is required to dodge around the pushrod. Depending on the cylinder head design this can present a substantial restriction, but in many cases it can be used to help accelerate the air toward the valve. One particular caveat that comes from head guru Darin Morgan is that most oval ports have a smoother velocity profile than square ports. So they tend to keep the fuel mixture in suspension better than square port heads.

CHAPTER 5

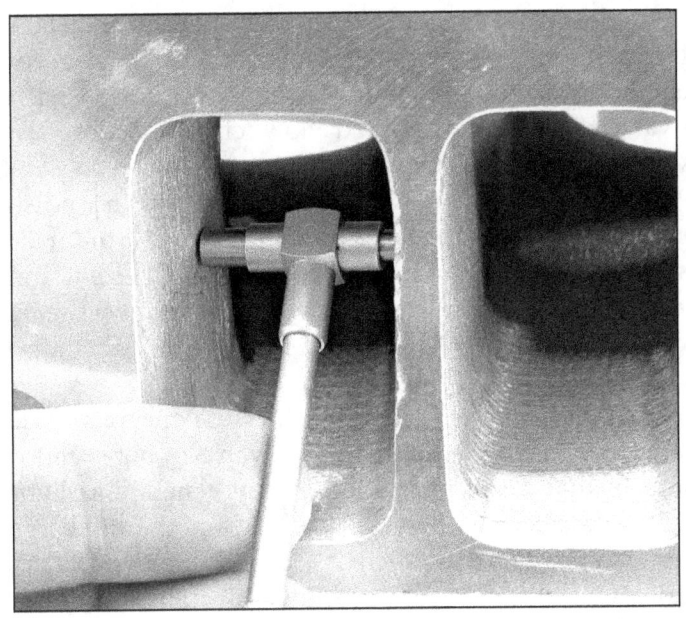

In some cases, a smaller cross section exists ahead of the throat area. It is usually located at the pinch area adjacent to the pushrod. The port is forced to contract here to provide pushrod clearance. This pinch accelerates the air, but then velocity slows as the port widens and transitions to the valve throat.

Do the Math

At Reher-Morrison, Darin Morgan checks the intake valve throat diameter before anything else on the head. If the throat opening is larger than 92 percent of the valve diameter he discards the head as unworkable.

To determine the maximum critical ratio (MCR) on your engine, use this formula:

MCR = throat diameter ÷ valve diameter

For example, if the throat diameter measures 2.196 inches and the valve diameter is 2.4, the max critical ratio is 91.5 percent (2.196 ÷ 2.4 = 0.915), which is workable for a high-powered engine.

You can adjust the formula to find the throat diameter when you know the desired ratio and the valve diameter:

Throat Diameter = valve diameter x maximum critical ratio

For example, if the desired percentage is 91.7 on a 2.4-inch-diameter intake valve on a big-block, the throat diameter is 2.2008 inches (2.4 x .917). This means that the throat diameter can be no larger than 2.2008 or the air does not move efficiently past the valve.

As one of the top cylinder head guys in the performance industry, Darin Morgan is vocal but confident about what makes a cylinder head perform. Airflow is the last item on his list. Although you might imagine that he spends his days chasing airflow flow numbers, the opposite is true. According to Darin the average airspeed is the most important factor affecting induction system performance. He ranks the relevant factors in the following order:

- Average velocity
- Instantaneous velocities
- Shape and design
- Rate of velocity change
- Airflow

In his view induction system performance is all about velocity, shape, and airflow. Airspeed rather than airflow is king. Darin reminds us that a bad port can flow as much air or more than a really good port, and the last thing you should be concerned about is the age-old question, "How much does it flow?" Achieving the ideal velocity profile for the intended application is far more important and it is one of the primary reasons that cylinder head specialists exist and prosper. Darin says he can teach anyone how to make an intake port flow in a relatively short time. It's not difficult, but getting a port to flow a lot of air smoothly and with the appropriate air velocities for a given engine combination is a lot more work and quite likely not something you can do at home in your garage. So don't try it at home, but do be aware of what's involved so you can talk intelligently with your head porter. And try not to ask what it flows.

There's an old saying about welders that can be applied to porting your own heads and manifolds. Unless you have a lot of experience and a way to evaluate what you do, it only makes you a grinder, not a head porter. Any improvement you might achieve is usually minimal and the chances that you will ruin the head are a lot greater. Blueprinting your own heads is the stuff of legend and magazine lore. It's not worth it unless you are pursuing a career as a porter.

A number of books and articles have been written on exactly how to port your cylinder heads, shape your combustion chambers, or prep your intake manifold, but they are very basic and thus not the best way to ensure maximum performance. Morgan conducts regular classes on cylinder head selection and preparation and you won't find a better instructor. He notes that cylinder heads are largely promoted based on port volume and advertised flow numbers. They are usually exactly what they say they are, but that's not the whole story when it comes to cylinder head selection.

It's very difficult for people to accept that port size must complement velocity to achieve optimum performance. The average velocity profile must accommodate the engine size and the desired power band. Everyone understands that you don't put the biggest square-port heads on a street-driven 396-ci big-block Chevy. The result is very poor velocity and thus performance. To cite the obvious you also don't build a high-RPM large-displacement big-block with oval-shaped peanut-port heads. That results in a ton of velocity at one low engine speed and then a complete choke off.

The same logic applies for port volumes. Smaller port volumes apply to small displacements and low RPM power bands; larger volumes equal larger displacements and higher power bands. Darin cautions that you can only compare "like" cylinder heads (port volumes) with similar-length ports.

Port Flow Efficiency

Most all-out engines perform best when the throat diameter is about 91.7 percent of the valve diameter. Drag racing engines typically shoot for 91.5 percent to maintain good signal strength at the carburetor with optimized power. It's very much tied to the engine's application.

For example, engines such as the Chevrolet LS3-LS7 typically incorporate an 89-percent ratio to help maintain air speed at part-throttle operation. In that case they're pinching the air a bit more to gain velocity over the valve. If your cylinder head falls within that 91- to 92-percent range it is probably workable for maximum power production. If the throat diameter exceeds 92 percent of the valve diameter many builders are tempted to simply install a larger valve. This rarely works because it upsets the bore-to-valve ratio, which is critical within 1 to 1.5 percent.

On a typical wedge engine (chamber type) the intake valve can be no more than 52 to 52.5 percent of the cylinder bore diameter. Canted-valve engines, such as the Mopar Pro Stock Hemi and other true hemis, can accept up to 53- to 53.5-percent bore-to-valve ratio because of their improved flow characteristics past the valve.

According to Morgan, it's possible to decrease the exhaust-to-intake ratio to about 70 to 71 percent and then increase the intake valve size by 0.5 to 1 percent. Exceeding that ratio loses power.

You can increase the valve size so that the valve-to-bore ratios noted above may generate a slight increase in CFM, but the discharge coefficient (see sidebar "The Mach Index" below) all but disappears and you lose power. Morgan also emphasizes that highly shrouded valves contribute considerably to a reduction in discharge coefficient and an increase in reversion on both sides of the intake-tuned power band. This reduces peak power and decreases overall power across the power band.

In Chapter 3, I described the vena contracta and how it functions to move air efficiently through an orifice (see the sidebar "The Vena Contracta" on page 50). In a

The Mach Index

Another measure of port-flow efficiency is the mathematical description of the intake charge velocity in relation to the speed of sound (known as the Mach Index). This is the ramming effect described in Hale's horsepower chain.

In the case of intake ports, it has been shown that Mach 0.6 (with 1.0 being the speed of sound) is about the maximum velocity you want to see in your intake ports at peak engine speed. The higher the Mach value (up to 0.6), the later you can close the intake valve to achieve more filling (VE), up to the point where inlet pressure and cylinder pressure equalize. Port cross section and shape are critical to achieving a high Mach value with smooth flow. The camshaft must appropriately time the intake closing event to take advantage of the intake velocity and accompanying pressure wave.

On the exhaust side the Mach Index is much different because the speed of sound is temperature dependent, and the temperature and pressure are much higher. That's why the exhaust valve is always smaller than the intake valve. Residual cylinder pressure is the primary contributor to efficient exhaust flow. For most applications, the exhaust flow capacity falls within the range of 65 to 80 percent of the intake capacity as seen in flow-bench numbers tested at the same delta P pressure with a stub pipe. Anything greater decreases the pressure ratio and diminishes the efficiency of cylinder evacuation. ∎

cylinder head the vena contracta exerts its influence approximately 1 inch on either side of the valveseat. The area leading into and out of the seat area controls approximately 45 percent of total airflow under dynamic conditions. This critical section helps support Patrick Hale's intake (inertia) ramming cycle and builds pressure for the wave.

The air must be set up for the turn into the valve. The bowl area is larger than the valve so you can help the air make the turn. Remember, the air does what it wants, but you can influence its choice by offering it the most desirable shape leading into the valve. If the turn is too abrupt the air can't make the turn and it slams into the far side of the bowl, creating turbulence and spoiling flow efficiency.

All of your efforts are centered on providing the smoothest flow path with minimal turbulence. The more you can do to smooth the flow, the better the results, but it's a tall order because the valve keeps slamming the door, up to 80 times per second or more depending on the maximum engine speed.

You are seeking high velocity (low pressure) to fill the cylinder quickly, but once the air enters the cylinder it must recover as much atmospheric pressure as possible. The pressure recovery dynamic within the cylinder depends a great deal on the valveseat and the divergent region of the vena contracta, which determines how the air expands after exiting the valve. A proper valveseat feels more like a radius and the layback of the chamber around the valve is critical. You're basically creating a variable venturi that must work efficiently at all given valve lift values.

Piston CFM Demand

For any given combination of bore, stroke, rod length, and RPM, maximum piston flow demand is at maximum piston velocity. In any racing engine application you're seeking to meet the flow demand (CFM) created by the piston at peak velocity where it creates the highest depression.

As the piston descends, it exposes more and more cylinder volume and gains speed until it reaches its peak velocity at about 76 degrees after TDC. Here the rod is perpendicular to the crankpin, and at this point, it is asking for a certain amount of flow, say, 480 cfm on a particular engine or perhaps 475 cfm with the manifold attached. Formulas are available to calculate this, or it is calculated for you in simulation programs, such as Engine Pro and PipeMax. The following formula was written by Larry Meaux, creator of PipeMax:

Piston Airflow Demand = (displacement x RPM x 0.0009785) ÷ number of cylinders

$(28/105)^{.5}$ x CFM = corrected CFM
105 inches WC = about 678.5 fps
678.5 fps ÷ speed of sound = 0.6078 Mach

Where:
.0009785 = mathematical constant
WC = water column depression (inches of water)
fps = feet per second

This equation calculates an instantaneous value that does not specifically accommodate any minor effects of rod ratio, but many years of testing and evaluation have proven it to be accurate and reliable. Meaux's extensive research indicated that 105 inches of water depression created enough energy to support intake mixture ramming

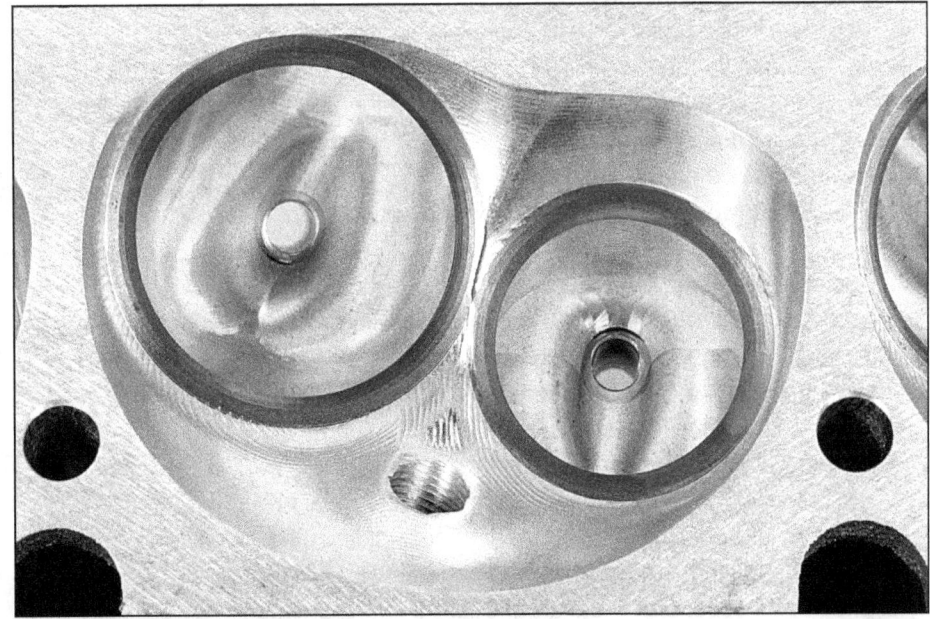

A primary objective of porting is to improve and prepare the flow path so that the air flows smoothly in the transition from the intake plenum all the way to the valve. Blending and minimizing obstacles is an important step. Surface preparation is another requirement to help keep fuel droplets in suspension as they negotiate the path to the valve.

Discharge Coefficient

In relation to engine airflow the discharge coefficient is based on the standard definition of fluid discharge through a specified constriction, or nozzle. Simply put, it is the ratio of the actual discharge value to the theoretical optimum, or best attainable discharge value. The key is that you are constricting flow through a nozzle (port and valve curtain area) in order to transfer conditions (air volume and pressure in the plenum) from one side to the other. It is done with minimal loss and the same exit pressure you began with, i.e., atmospheric pressure or as close as conditions permit depending on the degree of pressure recovery in the plenum and inlet path ahead of the valve.

A number of factors act on the fluid (air) transfer action including friction, pressure before the constriction, shape and size of the constriction, and divergent characteristics exiting the constriction, which include the volume and pressure delta within the discharge area or cylinder. Other influential factors include the density and viscosity of the flow medium (air laden with fuel droplets of varying size), influence of flow path obstructions, area changes, and certain directional changes. All of this, of course, takes place in a highly dynamic and relatively harsh and violent environment.

Also recognize that a static discharge coefficient models somewhat differently because it is generally a fixed opening or restriction with no moving parts and relatively steady-state flow. The jokers in the dynamic airflow deck are the rapidly opening and closing valve, the quick-moving piston and the instantaneous flow hiccups that occur (pulsating flow), the pressure changes due to engine speed variations, and the influence of powerful finite amplitude waves within the airflow path.

So, the discharge coefficient is the ratio of how much air you're actually flowing versus the theoretical maximum. Many years ago SuperFlow Corporation conducted extensive analysis and testing, which determined that the maximum achievable flow value for a single port is 146 cfm per square inch of flow area at 28 inches of water.

In practice, it is quite difficult to achieve more than 133 cfm/in^2 due largely to the action of the previously stated influences. Experienced head porters who achieve 137 cfm/in^2 for two-valve heads, or more than 140 for four-valve heads (but never more than 146 at 28 inches of water), rejoice at their good fortune.

It's a delicate balance, and it applies similarly to a Pro Stock engine with massive valves and to a motorcycle engine with relatively small valves. The percentages and ratios remain the same. The head porter's job is to chase that discharge coefficient as hard as possible without upsetting it.

The term *discharge coefficient* is somewhat loosely applied because by definition it actually applies to flow between two stagnant sources or reservoirs via a frictionless nozzle. More correctly it refers to a flow-loss coefficient that engineers apply to either steady (flow bench) or pulsating flow through a cylinder head as found in an actual running engine. Discharge coefficient conveys a descriptive mental picture because it implies the positive rather than a loss. Hence it has become the default term in discussions of engine airflow.

All of this applies for the duration of valve opening at a point somewhere before TDC to the full length of the intake stroke, plus that portion of the compression stroke where the intake valve is still open. From the point of IVO to BDC on the intake stroke you are "intake pumping" at whatever rate the discharge coefficient provides. After BDC you are "intake ramming" based on the efficiency of the discharge coefficient and the charge ramming effect contributed by favorable flow path dimensions, pressure wave activity, and, you hope, the stability of the renewable resource, or air pressure, in the plenum. ■

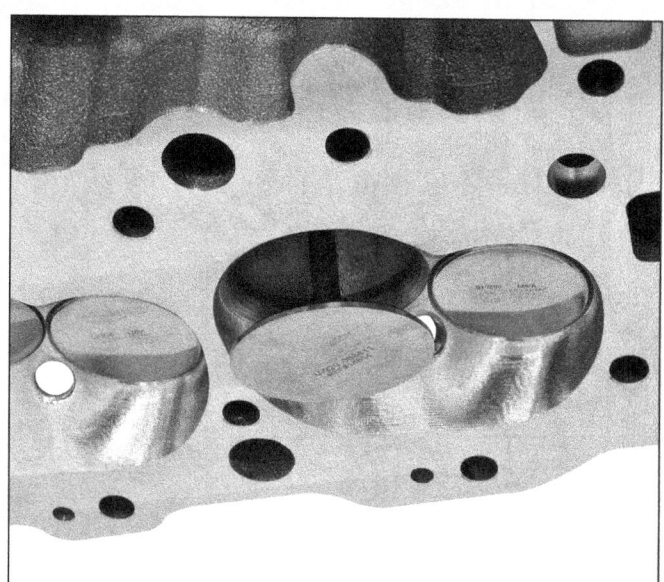

An open valve provides a variable-flow window into or out of the cylinder depending on the cycle. The rate and amount of valve opening are the primary factors for controlling airflow through the engine.

velocity plus wave tuning to create the potential for 125.8 VE. Accordingly he set up his PipeMax program so that 105 inches of water equals 126.5 VE. Above 105, column depression pumping losses begin to overcome efficiency. Using the standard flow-bench test pressure of 28 inches you can calculate the desired piston airflow demand.

Meaux also determined that 132.4-percent VE is the theoretical maximum because trapped VE percent on earth is 14.696-psi atmospheric pressure. This occurs before pumping losses to create the energy to overcome any gains from increased VE. Note that this is a close approximation because the speed of sound is dependent on local temperature.

Critical Valve Transitions

With the intake valve size properly matched to the valve throat diameter (91.5 to 92 percent) and the cylinder bore diameter (51 percent in most cases) you have nearly optimal conditions for moving air past the valve. This depends, of course, on the available air supply as dictated by atmospheric pressure; carburetor or throttle body configuration; pressure recovery in the plenum, runner length, and cross section; runner taper; port shape, dimensions, and texture; and seat configuration.

You must also consider restriction presented by the valvestem and valveguide. You can't do much about the valvestem except run a smaller diameter, which is common on many racing cylinder heads. Standard prep for valveguides depends on the application, the length of the valveguide, and the amount of stability it imparts to the valve. Although valve stability is critical to proper sealing it is also important to prevent excessive valve rocking in the guide.

On some heads, builders cut off the guide at the roof of the port so that only the stem is exposed to airflow. Most applications, however, taper and streamline the guide on both sides of the stem so air is directed smoothly around it. This also presents an opportunity to help direct airflow if you need to change it.

Bore Size

Bigger is almost always better when it comes to bore size. When the bore size and the stroke length are the same an engine is said to be "square." If the bore is smaller than the stroke the engine is "undersquare." The opposite, "oversquare," is true when the bore is larger than the stroke. Large bores almost always hold an advantage over smaller bores.

The larger bore/stroke ratio of an oversquare engine supports superior breathing characteristics and generates higher specific outputs in most cases. Bigger bores favor airflow in a big way. They unshroud the valves by moving the cylinder wall farther away from the valve curtain. Even if cubic inches are limited, builders tend to choose the largest bore and reduce the stroke to ensure good breathing. This generally results in an increase in engine speed, but the improved breathing easily keeps up.

Larger bores can also provide increased displacement (where permitted), which is generally advantageous depending on the application. The friction increase of a larger bore is far less than that generated by sweeping the entire ring pack an extra 1/2 inch (or whatever increase you might derive in a stroker application). So, increasing the bore without increasing the stroke generally amounts to a bit of free lunch as long

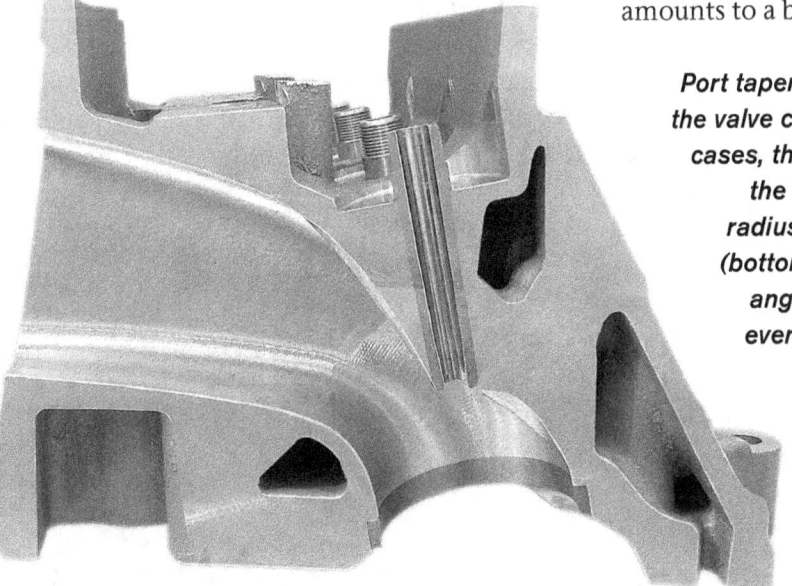

Port taper and the entry angle to the valve control the flow. In most cases, the higher the port entry, the better. This softens the radius on the short-side turn (bottom), improving the entry angle and promoting more even flow around the valve. Taper, or the gradual decrease in area, imparts velocity to the charge to optimize the intake ramming effect.

as cylinder wall thickness is not compromised to the point that flexing affects ring seal.

Port Taper

Most intake ports incorporate some amount of taper even if you can't easily see it. By taper I mean that the intake port narrows to a smaller size as it approaches the valve. In the case of a manifold it looks like a tunnel ram as it approaches the port entrance on the cylinder head, which is commonly matched to continue the taper into the port.

Port taper seeks to accelerate the flow column as does a venturi. The constriction (vena contracta effect) forces the air to accelerate as it approaches the valve. The increasing air velocity specifically supports the intake (inertia) ramming effect. It provides a considerable increase in flow energy and volume at low- to mid-valve lifts to the convergence point where the flow curtain area equals the maximum port restriction (area) at the throat. The inertia effect continues ramming beyond the convergence point, applying maximum flow energy to the restriction at the valve throat. From here overall port volume and flow efficiency determine the maximum flow available, assuming that the carburetor, plenum, and manifold runners are sized to support the flow demand.

A typical port tapers about 2 to 4 degrees from the intake flange to the valve area. Depending on the cylinder head configuration and port layout, taper can range from less than 2 degrees to as much as 7 degrees. Taper generally ends at the bowl area where the air travels through the short-side radius (floor) and throat opening, and transitions to the valve.

When port cross-sectional area increases, the charge decelerates and gains pressure. When the port constricts, the charge gains velocity and loses pressure. Losing velocity decreases port energy and inertia, subsequent filling ability, and volumetric efficiency. Increasing velocity raises port energy and reduces static pressure.

Raised intake ports generally support superior mixture quality because the accelerated air does not encounter abrupt direction changes as typically found in a stock- or low-port head. Hence fuel droplets tend to remain in suspension.

Turns must maintain a gentle bend on the short-side radius and port roof so the air follows without losing hold of the fuel. Higher ports typically reduce the port-length difference between the floor and the roof, balancing the frictional characteristics and further supporting efforts to distribute the flow equally throughout the valve curtain area.

Porters typically avoid lowering the port floor, which causes the short-turn radius to turn more abruptly into the valve and encourages fuel separation. They also try to maintain consistent taper all the way to the bowl area to ensure maximum effect from the ramming process.

Porting Pointers

As you may have guessed by now most of the performance in a cylinder head comes from the intake port. Although the exhaust is still important, it maintains the luxury of pressurized blowdown to do most of its work. The intake port is where the magic happens, but only if you have done a good job of improving flow and mixture quality at the same time.

An overriding prerequisite of flow arriving at the intake valveseat should be that the flow velocity at any RPM maintains good fuel atomization so the fuel remains suspended as a fine mist in the airstream and does not "rain out" in big droplets onto the cylinder wall. The flow in the intake port should not separate and form vortexes before it turns into the combustion chamber.

If you can meet all of these requirements, the conditions are set for sufficiently ram filling the cylinder to create a powerful expansion event in the combustion chamber.

CHAPTER 5

PRACTICAL ENGINE AIRFLOW

CHAPTER 6

COMBUSTION CHAMBERS

Efforts to improve airflow into the engine should result in good cylinder filling and high VE because you have taken the correct steps to optimize airflow through the induction path and have created the ideal conditions for maximum intake ramming. But the journey is far from over.

The combustion chamber in the cylinder head exerts enormous influence on the whole process. Once the air/fuel mixture departs the valveseat and enters the combustion chamber a whole new set of conditions apply. The way the air moves past the seat and expands into the cylinder has a great deal to do with cylinder filling and the pressure recovery process necessary to accomplish maximum VE. If you have done your homework correctly you will achieve high-velocity air with minimal turbulence through the port and the valve curtain window.

Cylinder Filling and Pressure Recovery

The most critical point is the throat area and what the air does immediately after exiting the valveseat. Upon leaving the valveseat, high-speed air wants to fill the larger space in the cylinder. Airspeed drops off and cylinder pressure increases slowly at first because it has to fill the cylinder first. This is the filling and pressure recovery process.

Researchers have opened a whole new window on engine performance with their ongoing study of wet flow. It helps them visualize how the air/fuel mixture enters the cylinder so they can characterize its behavior more accurately. Whether the air tumbles or swirls depends a good bit on engine speed and port entry angle.

The intake entry on most two-valve engines often involves an entry angle that tends to swirl the inlet mixture into the cylinder, particularly as airspeed increases. Slow-speed engines with reduced port velocity are more prone to tumble the air, causing the air to cascade over itself as it falls, rather than swirls, into the cylinder. Swirl

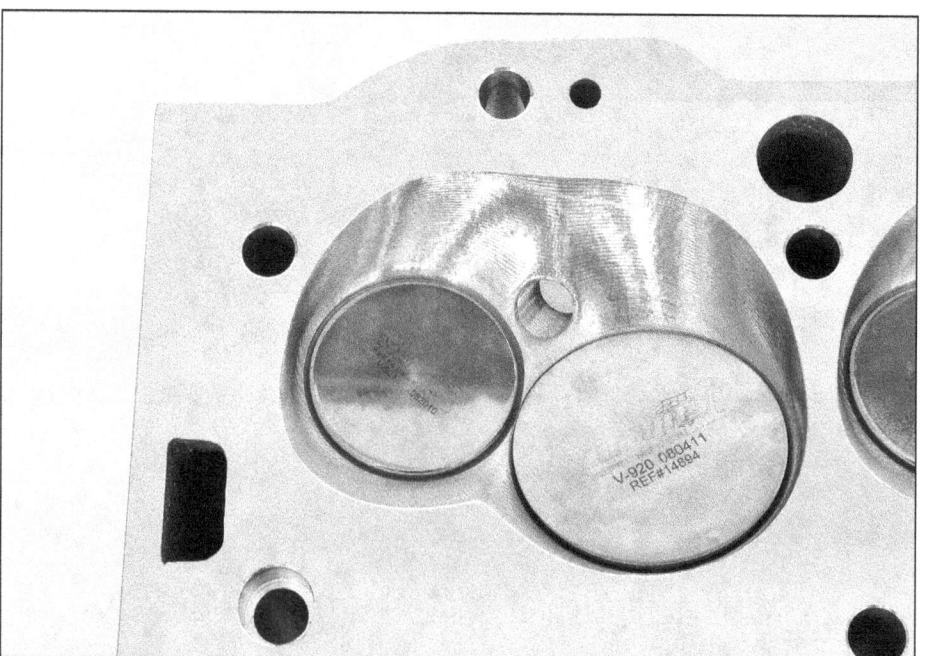
Combustion chamber shape, volume, valve size, and orientation influence airflow and the ability to fill the cylinder as much as any other component in the system.

COMBUSTION CHAMBERS

The descending piston creates the void that the atmosphere attempts to fill. Within this space, the most critical function is to recover full atmospheric pressure in addition to increased air mass via intake ramming before compressing the mixture.

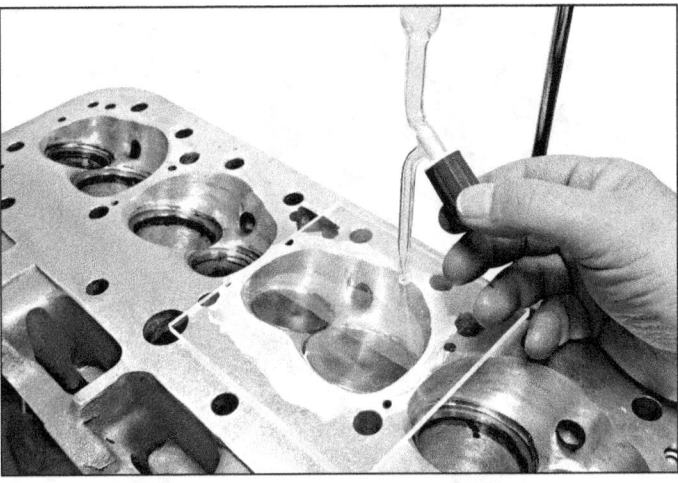

Equalizing chamber volumes helps maintain cylinder-to-cylinder consistency. Depending on the application, a grossly unequal chamber size may contribute to a lazy port with less efficient filling.

and tumble are surprisingly complex phenomena and their dynamics are not yet fully understood.

When contemplating the movement of the air/fuel mixture past the valveseat and into the actual combustion chamber it is important to recall the concept of the vena contracta as it relates to airflow. The minimum cross-sectional area (CSA) should be at the throat area adjacent to the valveseat. If the minimum CSA is located farther up the port, it interferes with effective pressure wave tuning. Pulses moving away from and toward the back of the valve are disrupted by the area change. This triggers velocity and pressure changes and leads to fuel dropout and the subsequent loss of power.

Some engines are affected more than others. Good examples include Chevy and Pontiac V-8s, which suffer from pushrod interference near the port entrance. The port may flow well on the flow bench, but its

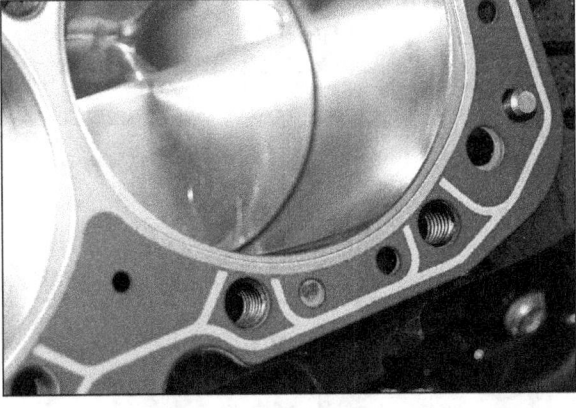

The head gasket doesn't influence flow per se, but you must take care to ensure the correct gasket shape and fit to the bore with no overhanging edges that might upset the flow stream.

Piston-top shape affects mixture motion as the piston approaches the chamber. Although not a direct influence on intake flow capacity, it contributes to combustion efficiency by helping to preserve the mixture quality you have strived to maintain at the carburetor exit.

Primary Factors of Cylinder Filling and Pressure Recovery

- Engine speed
- Intake air velocity and ramming pressure
- Valve size and throat area
- Valve curtain area and flow efficiency
- Combustion chamber shape and efficiency
- Valve shrouding
- Temperature and air density
- Camshaft timing

CHAPTER 6

Old-school pistons with large domes to achieve compression are flow resistant because, by necessity, they are teamed with deep chambers that shroud the valves and require considerably more lift before they overcome the shrouding restriction.

operational dynamics invite other problems in that area as the flow is pinched, gains velocity, and then loses it with the area increase after the pushrod bulge. Fuel dropout often occurs at this point. So you may see good flow numbers but inefficient transfer of the fuel mixture to the seat area where it is distributed to the cylinder. When these problems are fixed, power increases.

Careful grinding and port wall thickness measurements are often employed to minimize the pushrod bump. In some cases epoxy is applied after the bump to help smooth the flow and make the transition back to a larger area less abrupt. Head porters confirm that controlling and maintaining consistent velocity through the port and across the valveseat into the combustion chamber is critical to the way the mixture acts as it enters the chamber. The importance of the port-to-chamber transition cannot be understated.

Because of the physical structure of the port, airflow around the circumference of the valve and seat is rarely even. The ideal flow dynamic takes maximum advantage of the available flow window by moving air consistently around the valve. However, airflow quantity and velocity often differ at points around the circumference of the valve due to interference by the valveguide boss, valvestem, shape of the bowl area, chamber shape, and expansion characteristics of the flow mixture exiting the seat into the chamber. The transition must be smooth and non-turbulent to ensure optimal pressure recovery and efficient filling. Mixture quality should not be compromised by efforts to speed up pressure recovery.

Combustion Power and Efficiency

Most of the factors of combustion power and efficiency depend on engine airflow for maximum power and efficiency. High power output requires a chamber with good anti-detonation qualities so that higher compression ratios can be used. Detonation resistance derives from chamber characteristics that provide good squish (quench) and turbulence to drive the charge toward the spark. It also requires optimal mixture quality to ensure the best possible burn.

This piston top is from the Speed Demon engine. For each combustion event, the airflow column completely halts and restarts when the exhaust cycle begins. The clean portion under the exhaust valve indicates complete combustion. The darker sooty area actually results from residual unburned fuel because the engine has to be run quite rich to avoid detonation.

Requirements of a High-Performance Combustion Chamber

- High specific power output
- Good pressure recovery
- High combustion efficiency
- High thermal efficiency
- Low BSFC

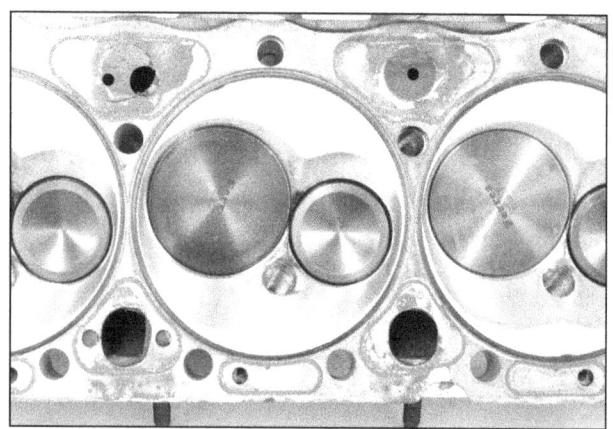

Shallow chambers on this turbocharged Dart head exhibit little distress after 400-mph runs on the Speed Demon land speed–record car. The exhaust valve has minimal shrouding to handle the large volume of exhaust generated by the 2,700-hp engine at 40 pounds of boost.

COMBUSTION CHAMBERS

High output also requires good pressure recovery to ensure maximum filling and volumetric efficiency. Pressure recovery depends on incoming charge velocity and airflow characteristics exiting the intake valve. Charge motion within the chamber can improve power by minimizing resistance to follow-on flow via swirl and the direction of vortices that form around the valves. The rising piston completes the chamber at the top of the stroke and plays an important role by providing the squish effect and compressing the mixture. Optimizing intake ramming via effective port shape and sizing is also required to increase VE beyond 100 percent, thus achieving a natural supercharging effect.

Combustion efficiency is a result of the burn characteristics of a particular chamber design. With proper squish and good mixture quality a chamber can deliver high efficiency. As noted, the piston deck serves as the floor of the combustion chamber and its shape can dramatically influence flame propagation. Increasingly the trend is toward shallower fast-burn chambers and pistons with little or no compression dome. Spark plug placement in the combustion chamber is also a prime consideration as manufacturers try to improve the burn and eliminate dead areas of incomplete combustion.

High thermal efficiency is necessary to reduce heat loss during the combustion period. A fast-burn event takes advantage of minimal heat loss and greater pressure. Again the trend to smaller combustion chambers offers reduced surface-to-volume ratios and reduced flame travel so the combustion event occurs rapidly. Once the all-important expansion has taken place, the cooling system will take care of residual heat over a longer period for effective cooling.

Lower BSFC stems from combustion efficiency and getting the most work possible from the fuel. It is often cited as a key component of efficiency-based competitions where a car can run longer between

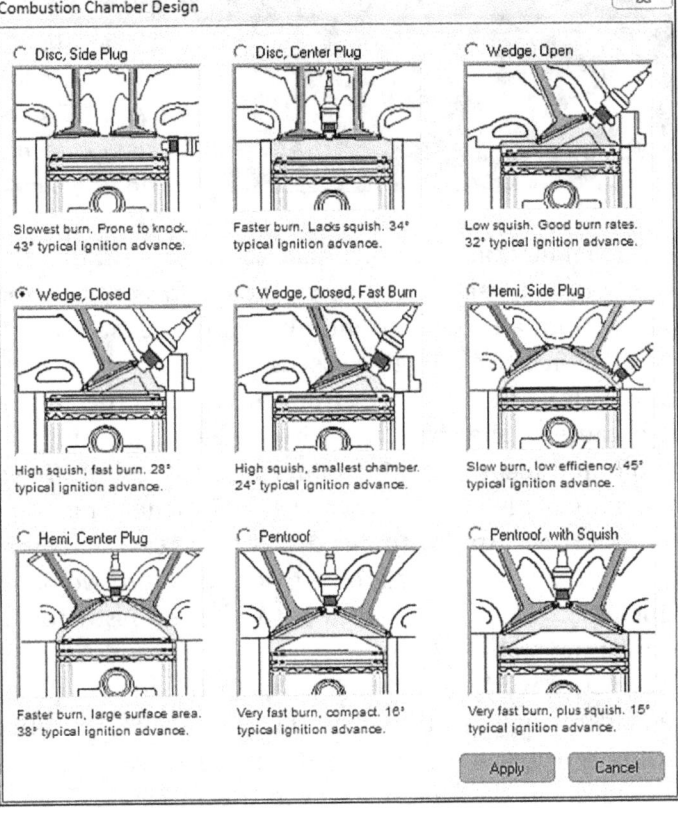

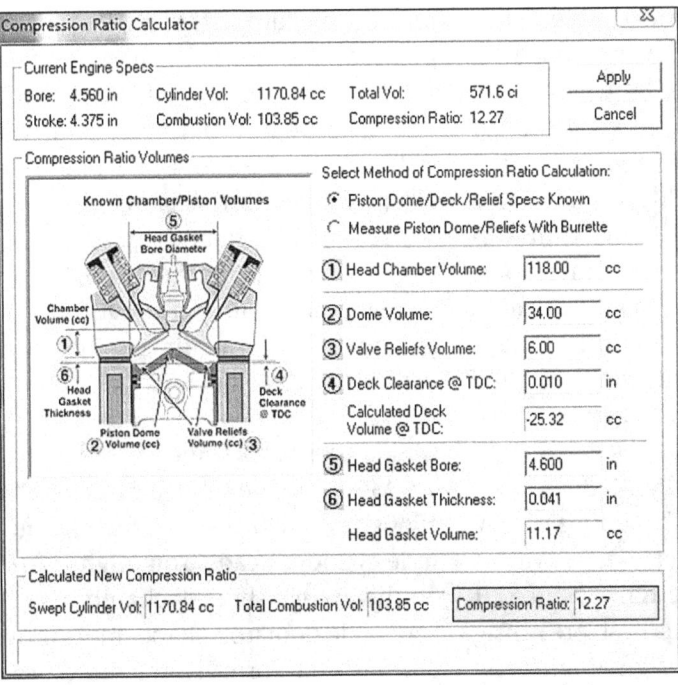

Engine simulation programs, such as Motion Software's Dynomation and Desktop Dyno, recognize the importance of combustion chamber configuration and provide for chamber selection input to perform their calculations related to mass airflow.

Motion Software incorporates a compression ratio calculator that allows you to input the appropriate specs and dimensions to automatically calculate the compression ratio. This still requires you to take very precise measurements of chamber volume, dome volume, valve reliefs, and other parameters to ensure accuracy.

fuel stops. But it relates more specifically to the ability of the chamber and its combustion characteristics to extract every last bit of power from the fuel. A faster burning chamber can, up to a point, effectively burn a somewhat leaner mixture. As long as it avoids the threshold of lean misfire it often provides fewer cyclic power variations compared to slower burning chambers attempting to fire poor-quality mixtures.

Chamber Types

Because combustion chamber shape, size, and layout exert enormous influence on cylinder filling and combustion efficiency, a variety of chamber types have been designed to meet various needs. In the real world of performance you mostly work with the following types of chambers: hemi center plug, wedge closed chamber, wedge open chamber, wedge closed, fast burn, pentroof, pentroof with quench, and flathead.

Each of these chambers has different airflow and combustion qualities. The hemi and pentroof versions are geometrically similar and generally have better line-of-sight port entry angles relative to the centerline of the cylinder. Wedge-type chambers are often favored because they package easier and make engines externally smaller. As the three distinct types of wedge chambers have evolved power has improved accordingly. I throw in the flathead because it is a traditional hot rod engine still much in favor with performance enthusiasts.

Hemi Center Plug

The hemi chamber has long been lauded as a great design, but in reality it is not as good as once

A traditional hemi chamber complements airflow because the valves are not shrouded. (Photo Courtesy Mitech Racing Engines)

thought. It gained its reputation because it allowed the use of larger unshrouded valves and performance was improved. It is still difficult to achieve a lot of compression with a hemi chamber. Also, because of the matching chamber and dome shape, the surface-to-volume ratio is high, making it difficult to hold heat in the chamber long enough to achieve a good pressure increase. Hemi chambers also have an unfavorable exhaust port for performance work; a fault that was tolerated for many years until Dart Machinery stepped up and fixed it for fuel racers in the early 1980s.

Despite the undesirable port, they tend to over-scavenge on overlap. Without careful cam selection, much of what you gain with a larger intake valve rushes right out the exhaust. Hemi builders know this and compensate for it with cam timing and proper header dimensions. Another problem is that the valves move toward each other on overlaps causing you to limit camshaft lift/duration. It also limits further valve size increases.

To be fair, the hemi does present the least valve shrouding of any design and can accept larger valves than most other designs. Hence, it offers potentially the best breathing per valve of any design if properly cammed and configured. Still, the entire hemi valvetrain is robust and quite heavy, which resists higher engine speeds.

Over-porting is often the biggest mistake with these heads and that tends to minimize any gains offered by larger valves. Hemi chambers with maximized valve size require offset plug placement and two plugs per cylinder to ensure a fast enough burn time.

Minimal quench and turbulence also affect mixture quality to reduce combustion efficiency. Without sufficient quench the mixture motion is less active and there is a greater chance for large fuel droplets to fall out of suspension. Because of their shape and volume, most hemi chambers provide a moderate-speed burn rate and typically required 36 to 40 degrees total timing for best performance.

The hemi's reputation was built largely on success in fuel and alcohol racing because it was tough, and it could move a lot of air and fuel, particularly with a supercharger.

Wedge Closed Chamber

Most muscle car engines of the 1960s had closed-chamber wedge-style cylinder heads. You might think of the wedge-shaped chamber as a very wide doorstop shape. In its most pronounced form it resembles the

COMBUSTION CHAMBERS

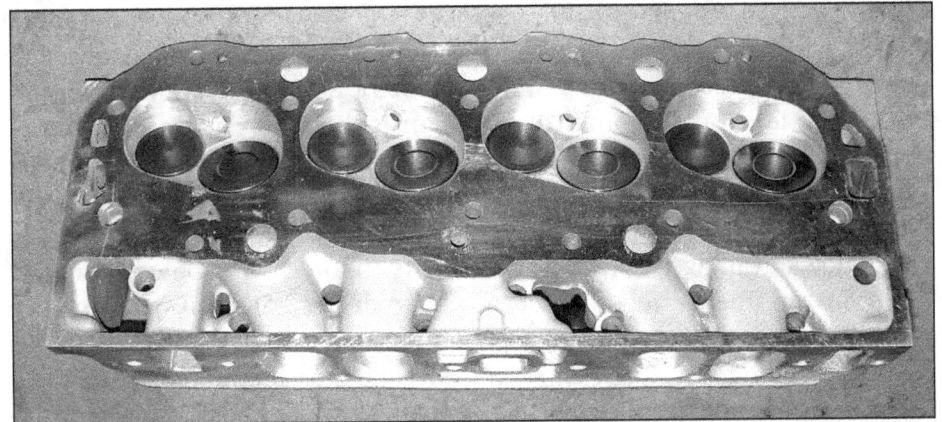

The early Chevy aluminum head with "bathtub" closed chambers had good quench but suffered from severe shrouding, which limited flow at high engine speeds.

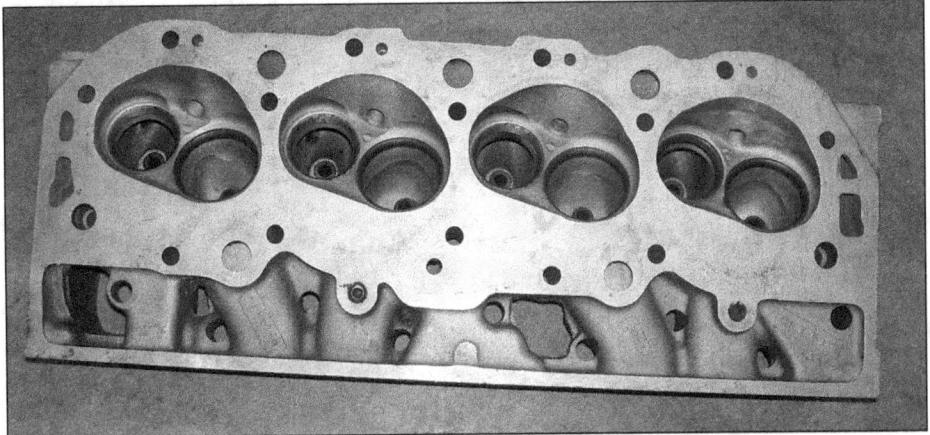

Open-chamber big-block heads attempted to unshroud the valves and succeeded to a degree, but it became more difficult to achieve a good compression ratio.

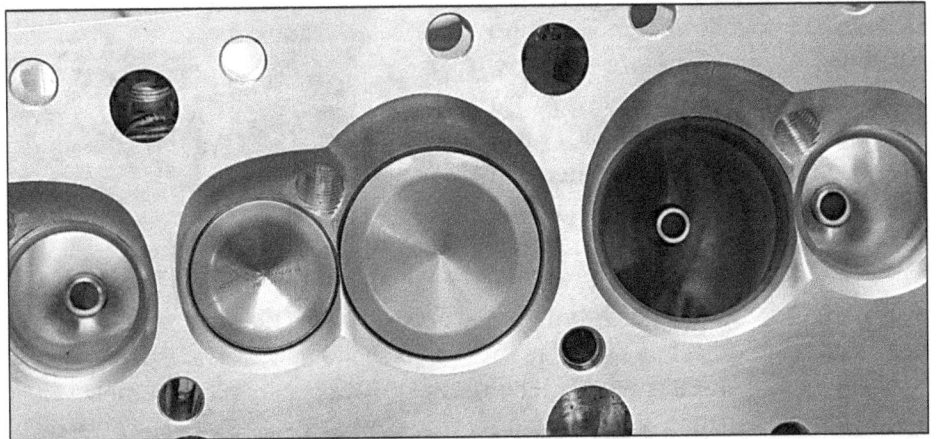

This Dart 9-degree small-block Chevy head has unshrouded valves resulting from the shallow valve angle and advanced chamber shaping. The valve angle and intake port positioning achieve maximum potential air/fuel flow around the circumference of the valves. The mirrored valve configuration used with inline valves permits a more compact intake manifold with even distribution between the runners.

deep, closed bathtub-style chambers of early Chevy big-blocks.

Wedges incorporate a relatively deep chamber offset by a large quench area or flat surface on one side. Valve size is limited and the sunken chamber shape, which effectively shrouds 30 to 45 percent of the intake valve curtain area, restricts airflow.

Earlier chambers have low squish and typically require 34 to 38 degrees of timing. Deep chambers also require substantial piston dome shapes to realize good compression. Closed-chamber heads can still make reasonable power, but you really have to give the spark a head start to get it.

Wedge Open Chamber

Open-chamber wedges, such as the later Chevrolet big-block heads, are an attempt to gain flow efficiency at the expense of reduced quench. Shrouding is also reduced, but builders still find it difficult to build compression without significant dome height, which often compromises spark efficiency and smooth flame propagation. The larger volume and surface area tend to cool the burn to the point at which sometimes it simply extinguishes without making any power.

Open chambers are generally more efficient when used with matching piston domes. They can often reduce the total to 30 to 34 degrees depending on the bore size. In large-bore applications, such as a 454, the greater flame travel distance may still require as much timing as a closed-chamber head.

Wedge Closed, Fast Burn

Fast-burn combustion chambers are smaller and the squish-to-bore ratio is maximized to improve turbulence and mixture quality. The intent is to speed up combustion and build cylinder pressure more quickly while also resisting detonation. This permits higher compression ratios for greater efficiency and reduced ignition timing, which reduces negative force against the rising piston before TDC.

Fast-burn chambers are typically smaller and shallower and are often accompanied by reduced valve-to-head angles for better line-of-sight airflow. They often accommodate an ignition advance of around 24 degrees and in some cases as little as 18 degrees, which really reduces negative force between the spark point and TDC. Most modern two-valve engines now incorporate fast-burn technology.

Pentroof

Pentroof chambers are commonly employed on newer four-valve-per-cylinder engines where two intake valves and two exhaust valves are mounted opposite each other with a centrally located spark plug.

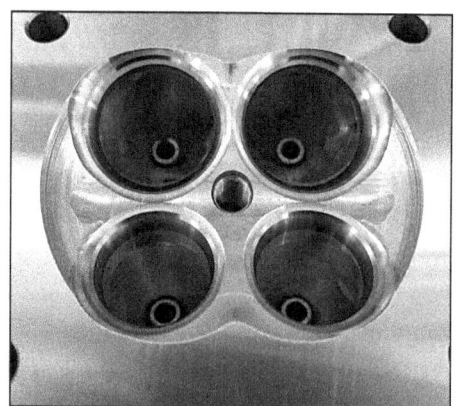

Like a hemi, four-valve ports often have a straighter approach to the valve. This means that the flow tends to exhibit more tumble motion as opposed to the swirl motion imparted by the tangential port approach on conventional two-valve heads.

These fast-burn chambers minimize flame travel requirements relative to bore diameter thus requiring minimal spark lead on the order of 16 to 18 degrees. They are effective on smaller-bore engines, such as the Ford Modular engine. In addition to the airflow advantages of four valves per cylinder, they offer a reduced surface-to-volume ratio for good heat retention and improved power.

Pentroof with Squish

A pentroof chamber with added squish pads is one of the most efficient modern chambers. With the addition of squish to provide improved turbulence and mixture conditioning, the chambers offer high efficiency, good power potential, and effective emission control. The burn takes place so quickly that they can often accommodate initial spark timing in the 12- to 15-degree range, which boosts power and reduces negative force accordingly.

Flathead

The Ford flathead is undesirable from a performance standpoint despite having dominated the hot rodding industry for better than two decades during its heyday. It was all they had until overhead valves debuted. The 1939 and later flatheads are favored, as are the later cylinder blocks manufactured in France. Performance aluminum heads are still made for the flathead, but they are primarily a nostalgia replacement for current hot rodders who still run flatheads. Other than a little blending and, in some cases, larger valves, there is little that can be done to wring performance out of a flathead cylinder head.

The head itself is little more than the roof of the combustion chamber; the valves and valvetrain are in the cylinder block. The chamber has a lot of surface area and compression is limited by valve lift because the valves open directly toward the chamber roof. You can boost performance a little by cleaning up the ports in the block, but not to any great degree. Modern performance efforts often route the exhaust out through the valley and more extreme versions reverse the flow by using the exhaust port as the intake and vice versa.

With all due respect for tradition, this was an appliance cylinder head that provided suitable packaging and efficiency for its day. Hot rodders modified and worked on it because it was all they had.

Chamber Flow Concerns

When critical mass flow is the greatest possible for existing upstream conditions and the mean

This simplified view of a valve curtain area shows flow around the intake valve. Although it is considerably more complicated than shown here, the colored portion illustrates the variable-flow window. Having a high valve lift and long duration is beneficial to most performance applications. High valve lift tends to negate valve shrouding at some point in the lift curve.

COMBUSTION CHAMBERS

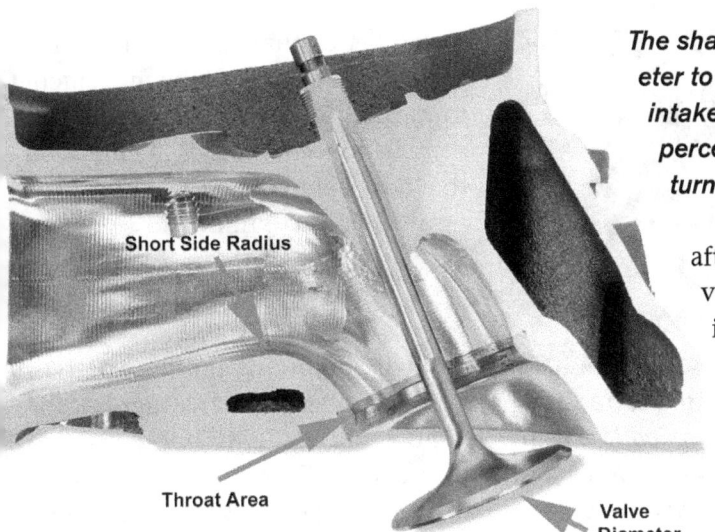

The shape of the short-side radius and the ratio of the valve diameter to the throat diameter are the most critical components of intake flow. For most applications, the ratio must be close to 91.5 percent and the short-side radius cannot be too abrupt on the turn into the combustion chamber.

velocity approaches local sonic velocity (speed of sound in air), the port achieves a high mach number and provides the greatest possible mass flow and port energy with minimal draw (pressure differential) from the cylinder. The pressure difference between atmospheric pressure and the pressure in the cylinder should be minimal, which indicates high flow and fast pressure recovery from the initial pressure drop.

Intake ramming notwithstanding, pressure recovery is largely affected by the air's behavior just after it exits the valveseat and expands into the cylinder. The area and volume increase initiates a rapid velocity reduction as the flow begins to fill the cylinder. Flow resistance remains relatively low until equilibrium is achieved (atmospheric pressure) and intake ramming is called upon to force more air into the cylinder to increase density.

If you can pack additional air into the cylinder, you have effectively supercharged it via natural means.

Studies have shown that air exiting the valve behaves differently depending on velocity, throat diameter angle of attack, valve opening and shape, seat angle, and localized shrouding by chamber walls and/or cylinder walls around some fixed portion of a valve's perimeter. Although it is said that air does not like to change direction, it does tend to follow the roof of the chamber as it exits if velocity is not sufficient.

Top cylinder head specialists, including Darin Morgan at Reher-Morrison, have made entire careers out of investigating the behavior of air entering a combustion chamber. They have determined the best exit angles (see Chapter 5).

This Arias hemi head for the big-block Chevy incorporates pistons with nearly flat tops to achieve the desired compression ratio for supercharging. Because of the natural high-flow capacity of the hemi chamber, this arrangement results in a very high flowing combination.

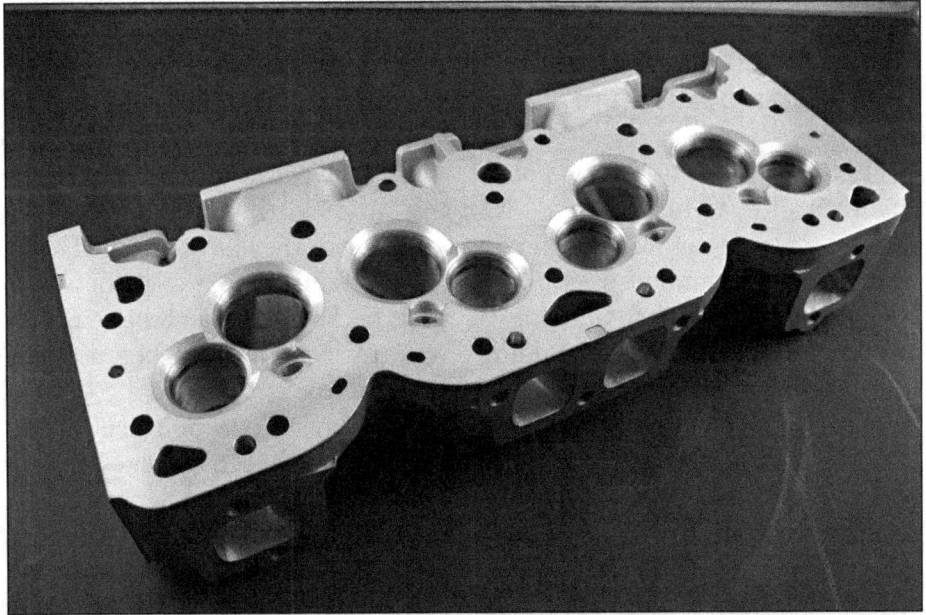

When is a combustion chamber not a combustion chamber? When the head is nearly flat with only a shallow chamber on a Chevy 409 and the rest of the chamber is actually in the cylinder due to a 16-degree block angle. Smithberg Racing prepped this head with the laid-back discharge area around the valves to encourage smoother flow.

PRACTICAL ENGINE AIRFLOW

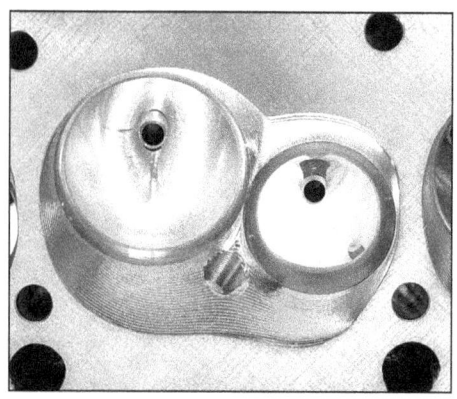

Modern chambers are shaped to help direct flow for efficient filling and to help achieve the desired compression ratio. The CNC tooling helps maintain fuel droplet suspension as high-velocity air exits the valve, loses velocity, and attempts to recover pressure without deteriorating mixture quality.

This is an example of the surfacing-texturing treatment applied to a combustion chamber by Meaux Racing Heads. It promotes better mixture quality in the chamber. (Photo Courtesy Meaux Racing Heads)

And they have used wet-flow studies and computational fluid dynamics (CFD) analysis to pinpoint the conduct of air flowing around valves, across valveseats, and across combustion chambers.

Chamber Texture

Head porters used to polish chambers to a high-gloss finish because it was thought to help retain heat in the chamber during the combustion event. That thinking is changing now that others, including Larry Meaux at Meaux Racing Heads, have been rough texturing chambers in the same manner as the ports to pick up power. The practice remains controversial, but Meaux and others have gained faith in it.

Meaux has conducted extensive testing with textured ports and chambers and has achieved good results. Rottler's P69 CNC machining center not only ports heads, but includes a dimpling program that machines golf ball–like dimples into the ports and chambers.

Ken Sperling at Airflow Research and Jim McFarland identified dimples in earlier efforts and have pointed out their benefits many times. Originally cited to help crutch problem areas in the ports and chambers, dimpling and texturing processes have matured with further research. Some porters feel that you almost can't make the surface rough enough. Others avoid it like the plague because it is easier to sell the bling. When customers look at a set of heads they have just paid a fortune for and it looks as if they have been hacked up by an amateur, they want their money back because they want "shiny."

Proponents of polished chambers cite the reflective value of holding heat and the tendency to not permit a carbon buildup. They further contend that heavy texturing leaves sharp edges that can cause pre-ignition. Perhaps, but the benefits of improved mixture conditioning likely outweigh all of this.

You can also still apply reflective coatings to a textured surface, which works better than polishing. Nonetheless, there is a growing movement toward rougher finishes and the combustion chamber is included in that movement depending on who is furnishing the opinion.

Valve Shrouding

It is important for the combustion chamber to fully support the airflow process and not present a restriction. This primarily refers to size, shape, and valve positioning. Minimal shrouding around the intake valve is a major consideration. Shrouding occurs wherever the chamber wall and, in some cases, the cylinder wall are in close proximity to the valve. Airflow through the curtain area is limited because the chamber wall is blocking the way. Not only are you losing a substantial portion of the airflow path, but you can also encounter turbulence as the air stacks up and tries to find another direction into the cylinder,

The valve throat area controls flow volume and efficiency. The chamber walls typically shroud the air entering the chamber, and the shrouding obstructs as much as half of the valve diameter. Chamber work to unshroud the valves is delicate. This chamber wall has been laid back in an attempt to encourage more even flow around the valve.

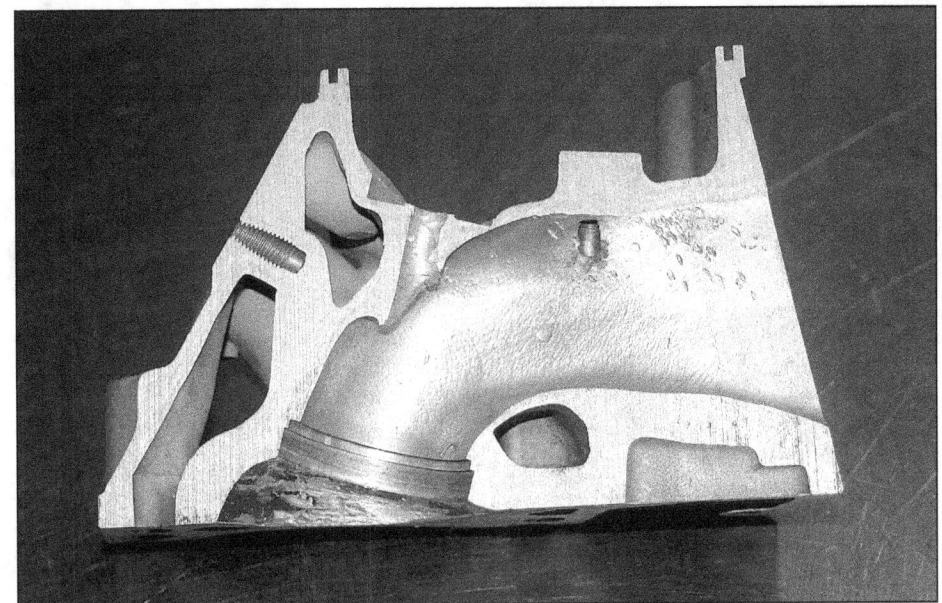

This cutaway view of a head shows a typical wedge-shaped chamber. The short-side radius of the port (bottom) is critical because it discharges to the unshrouded area of the chamber that promotes efficient flow. The wall side of the port discharges to a shrouded area that must achieve a reasonable amount of valve lift before shrouding diminishes.

thus affecting the smooth flow of air past the rest of the valve.

A valve is considered unshrouded if the clearance from the valve head to the chamber wall is 0.20D at 0.25D-inch valve lift (D representing valve diameter). For a 2.02-inch intake valve, it means that the valve can be no closer to the wall than 0.404 inch (2.02 x 0.20) at a lift value of 0.505 inch (2.02 x 0.25).

This indicates an angle of 36 degrees to the valvestem. From the valveseat to the actual area around the valve, it is the same as the geometrically calculated valve curtain area. If you can achieve this angle without opening the chamber so much that it negatively impacts compression ratio and incoming swirl characteristics you have a good chance of creating a high-flowing unshrouded chamber.

But your work is not finished. Depending on the shape of the short-side radius, air reacts differently at the higher velocities (same as test pressure) found in a running engine. As velocity increases, it wants to overrun the valve to the long (far) side. Geometrically unshrouding the valve is usually a great start, but there is no point in fixing it if the air is never going to go there anyway. This is where chamber shape and directional aids can help control it.

In most cases only a small portion of the short-side radius is affected by shrouding and it's not as big a deal at low lift and slower engine speeds. But you should probably pay attention to it on a high-speed engine. That's not to say it is a problem in every case, but air rarely enters evenly all around the valve. You need to carefully identify its characteristics at the highest test pressure possible to fully understand its preferences and determine how to work with them. Among these considerations you must also endeavor not to affect the squish characteristics of the chamber when the piston is at TDC.

Hemi combustion chambers are the most efficient from a shrouding standpoint. The valves move away from everything as they open so flow area is always increasing. And the chamber geometry is such that there are no adjacent chamber walls to resist flow. So hemi valves enjoy the full benefit of curtain area from right off the seat to full valve lift. Four-valve-per-cylinder heads also experience valve shrouding particularly with an increase in intake valve size. Most factory heads and aftermarket replacements are close to being maxed out on intake size already so there is not much room to work with, especially on small-bore engines. Shallower fast-burn chambers and some open chambers are less affected by shrouding, as are most two-valve pentroof designs.

The combustion chamber has a tough job, and its contribution to optimizing airflow is not often given its due. Regardless of the engine and chamber type, you must consider valve shrouding as a common barrier to effective flow.

An important point to remember is that air has weight so it follows the rules of inertia. It requires energy to turn it, especially when it gains weight combined with a fuel mass. This makes it easier to visualize and predict where it wants to go and then decide how best to coax it into the cylinder with initial flow followed by intake ramming. The end result must be optimum pressure recovery and the ability to achieve high VE via intake ramming. It is almost always beneficial to map it out on graph paper and carefully consider the existing geometry and the effect it has on engine airflow.

CHAPTER 6
PRACTICAL ENGINE AIRFLOW

CHAPTER 7

EXHAUST SYSTEM

In many racing and performance applications the engine exhaust cycle is not always given the attention it requires to fully support the engine's power potential. Most builders and racers are well aware of the exhaust system's amazing potential for boosting power levels, but for a multitude of reasons this potential is rarely explored. Pressure wave tuning and the ability to adequately service the increasing exhaust volume generated by the engine at high engine speeds is critically important.

Optimizing the tube dimensions holds enormous potential for adding power. It involves determining the most desirable cross section and length and the proper manipulation of pressure waves within the exhaust primaries. This is especially true for naturally aspirated applications in which effective wave tuning has been implemented to provide a natural supercharging effect, and more so on power adder applications where boost pressure or chemical supercharging create a significant amount of additional exhaust volume. The exhaust also represents a primary thermal loss path that can impact power if thermal energy is pulled from the cylinder too early.

Pressure Wave Tuning

Designing and constructing a proper exhaust system is largely a matter of doing the math and selecting the optimum length and cross section for the exhaust components. This is made easy with the use of PipeMax software (less than $50), which makes all the calculations and tells you the optimum dimensions. If you can locate a suitable header that fits the criteria, that's great; but on most performance cars a custom set of headers is required. You are building to suit the airflow dynamic of your particular engine as defined by its displacement, bore size, compression ratio, valve sizes,

The exhaust system offers very significant gains when properly configured for the application. A good exhaust system clears the chamber of residual exhaust particles and encourages the flow of the next inlet charge without contamination during overlap.

EXHAUST SYSTEM

This hemi exhaust port shows the throat area with a finished valveseat and the desired blending on the port exit. (Photo Courtesy Smithberg Racing)

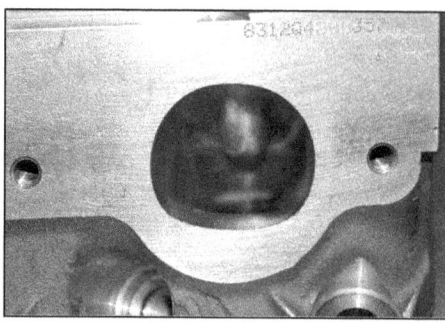

Some porters prefer a semi-D shape on some heads and they widen the ports to increase flow, depending on the application.

and camshaft timing. Any exhaust system that follows the dimensional rules of exhaust tuning will perform well. This applies to street vehicles as well, although a good portion of it is compromised by full-length exhaust systems with mufflers. In that case alway err slightly to the larger size. Most street/strip engines that run through the mufflers work well with a minimum 2.5- to 3.0-inch exhaust system incorporating street mufflers with performance intent.

The three major components of the exhaust event were described in Chapter 1: the high-pressure blowdown at EVO, followed by the exhaust pumping event as the piston chases residual exhaust pressure out of the cylinder, and pressure wave tuning, which affects the overall efficiency of the process.

The blow-down cycle initiates at EVO. In a naturally aspirated engine functioning at high BMEP, the residual gas pressure behind the valve may exceed 100 psi while the downstream pressure in the exhaust port is closer to atmospheric. When the valve opens a pressure spike occurs in the exhaust port.

Exhaust gases residing in the cylinder achieve instantaneous velocity governed by the pressure gradient between the cylinder and the exhaust port, the efficiency of the valveseat, and the cross section at the throat opening. The wave tuning effect in the exhaust is more pronounced than in the intake because of the much larger pressure gradient and broader temperature change, which affects the local speed of sound. The initial high-pressure spike and temperature at EVO causes the pressure wave in the port to travel at a much higher speed and then dissipate to some degree as the pressure and temperature diminish.

Port and Header Dimensions

For most applications, the port and header dimensions fall within the calculated ranges predicted by advanced software programs, such as Larry Meaux's PipeMax. It takes into account that you are not only trying to evacuate the cylinder as quickly and efficiently as possible, but also prep it for the incoming charge to ensure minimal charge contamination on overlap and indeed a slight assisting tug by briefly presenting a lower pressure than the intake ramming effect.

The appropriate dimensions are quite important. Smaller tube diameters tend to increase velocity and enhance the effect of pressure wave tuning, but there are diminishing returns. If the tube diameter is too

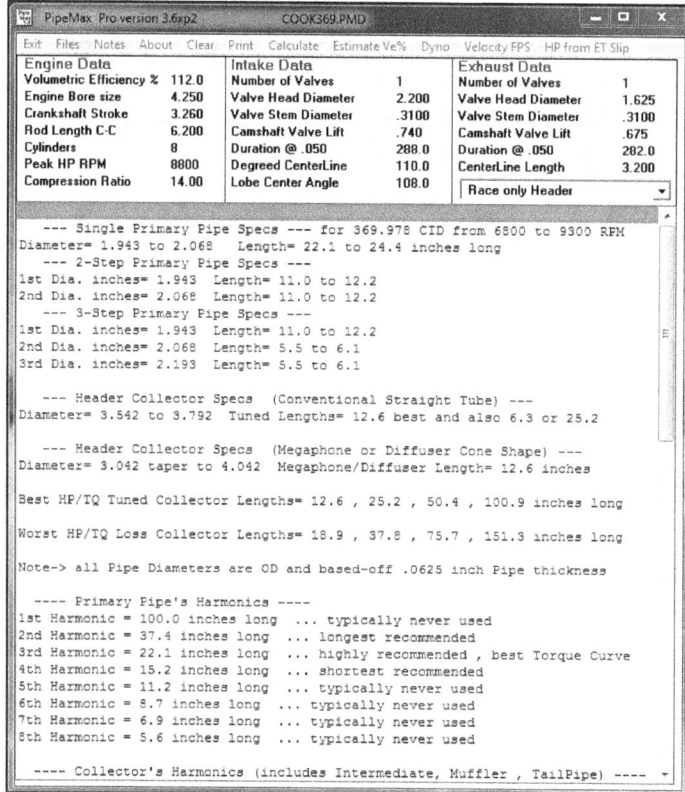

Note that the Exhaust Data column (far right) in the PipeMax software calls for the centerline length of the exhaust port, which is required to calculate the ideal length of the primary tube for the most effective harmonic wave. The third reflected wave typically provides the best torque curve.

small, flow losses occur and the pressure gradient rises to cause restriction and disruption in the pressure wave tuning.

Many applications do not adequately address the first component interface at the exhaust gasket. In most cases the exhaust primary tube is larger than the exhaust port exit and shaped differently. It represents the first area change in the flow path after the positive pressure (compression) wave exits the valve and thus the first opportunity to reflect a negative pressure (expansion) wave back to the valve. That's why modeling programs such as PipeMax need to know the centerline length of the exhaust port to accurately calculate the tuned lengths.

Pulse Timing and Amplitude

For optimal results you need the reflected negative wave to arrive at the back side of the valve at EVO so that its lower pressure influence toward the end of the exhaust cycle will further encourage the remaining gases in the cylinder to exit. If timed correctly it lowers the cylinder pressure enough so that the fresh incoming charge meets little resistance and the next cycle of cylinder filling is enhanced.

The cross-sectional area of the local flow path controls the amplitude (strength or intensity) of the wave. The frequency is controlled by engine speed and the length of the reflecting flow paths between area changes. This is how engine designers, particularly cam designers, determine the ideal combination of timed valve events according to practical flow path dimensions and the speed of pressure waves and gas particles within the known or projected range of exhaust gas temperatures.

Flow Path Disruptions

One thing to keep in mind when contemplating wave action is the state of the signal source at either end of the flow path. The exhaust end (primaries and collector) is fixed and unchanging, but the local signal source on the other end is either the back of the valve when it is closed or the piston top, both of which are constantly changing their position and causing variations in the tuned length.

The flow path is further complicated by obstructions such as the chamber roof, valve head, valvestem, valveguide, and any other disruptions in the path that resist or otherwise affect the flow of exhaust gases and pressure wave reflections.

The temperature also changes along the path, thus altering the local speed of sound at which the waves travel. The same occurs on the intake side. It all becomes quite complicated, but if you can choose the tubes that have the correct cross sections and lengths, you can usually derive 80 percent or more of the available tuning value.

The fixed dimensions of the flow paths are also at odds with broadly varying engine speeds; thus they tend to go in and out of tune at various points in the RPM range. Engine speed, the local speed of sound in the hot primary pipe, and the length of the pipe govern this tuning component. This is very closely controlled in dedicated racing engines.

Exhaust Flow Tuning

Designers identify the engine's ideal operating range and try to optimize the wave tuning component across the desired power band; say, between the torque peak and the power peak. This tuning is mostly accomplished by manipulating flow path cross sections and lengths and the subsequent effects on wave generation. They can also be influenced by valve and throat size, restrictive exhaust bends, and further influences beyond the header, such as collector size and shape and even the positioning of the tubes entering the collector and the way each one affects wave generation in its neighbors.

Primary Tube Area

Small area increases along the primary tubes, as found in stepped-header applications, can generate multiple weaker waves. Each step provides a small but abrupt increase in area that generates a reflection. Because the area change increases, the reflected wave changes accordingly; for example, positive to negative. When the area change decreases, such as when encountering a closed valve, the sense is not inverted and the wave reflects with the same value; for example, positive to positive.

Because the area changes in a stepped primary are minimal these waves are not as powerful, but they are still effective and they tend to broaden the tuning range. The final exit into the collector provides the greatest area change and the strongest opportunity to reflect a powerful wave.

Collector Configuration

Collector configuration offers yet another opportunity to influence exhaust flow and use it to improve the engine's performance. For example, the popular 4-into-1 system typically incorporates four equal-length

Primary tube cross section and length influence the torque peak location and the torque bias above or below the torque peak. A smaller cross section equals a lower torque peak and vice versa. Longer primaries tend to boost torque production below the torque; shorter ones bias torque above the torque peak. (Photo Courtesy Meaux Racing Heads)

These drag race headers incorporate a merge collector to accelerate the flow just before the discharge into the atmosphere. Note the sweeping, gentle bends on the primary tubes and the single-step header configuration approximately 10 inches from the exhaust flange. The step provides a reflection point to influence wave tuning at the valve. (Photo Courtesy Meaux Racing Heads)

primary tubes exiting abruptly into a larger collector tube with approximately three or four times greater area to generate a strong reflection. Up to a point a larger collector reflects a wave of greater amplitude. This is controlled and enhanced by the combined area of the collector itself, plus the area of the inactive primary tubes compared to the area of the currently active primary.

The primary lengths are often adjusted to bias torque production around the peak so that the torque curve is broadened above or below the peak according to the needs of the application. Longer tubes tend to boost torque below the torque peak; shorter tubes broaden the curve above the torque peak. A standard straight collector with equal-length primaries generates a pronounced torque peak when the torque is shifted in the desired direction.

Another approach that has been widely explored in oval track and road racing is to further skew torque production by using alternate-length or -diameter primary pipes or both on, say, every other cylinder in the firing order to produce multiple torque peaks at different engine speeds. Results vary, but in some cases it can help an engine pull stronger out of tight corners without sacrificing torque at or above the torque peak.

One of the best ways to test this beforehand is to model it in a software program. PipeMax, for example, not only calculates results, it also calculates the ideal lengths and diameters for the associated reflections and recommends the best one according to the application's requirements. In addition, it also models collector dimensions and predicts results so you can judge the effects at various engine speeds.

Recent collector science has developed a device called a merge collector. Here the primaries exit into a tapered or nozzle-shaped area resembling a vena contracta. The throat of the nozzle is larger than any individual primary area, but still smaller than the final exit collector

Wherever possible, the exhaust primary tube should exit straight out from the exhaust port for several inches before encountering the first bend. (Photo Courtesy Meaux Racing Heads)

behind the restriction. This configuration maintains gas velocity for a longer period and tends to help scavenge other nearby pipes.

After the merge restriction the collector tapers to its final diameter, decelerating the flow smoothly to enhance the pressure recovery to atmospheric. Merge collectors are tunable in the sense that different shapes, tapers, and areas can be used to further optimize torque via manipulation of the reflected waves. Manufacturers now offer a broad variety of merge collectors with varying nozzle areas, diameters, lengths, and tapers to help manipulate the torque curve to suit the application.

Firing Order

Another less frequently considered aspect of exhaust flow is the general engine architecture and the effects of firing order and crank plane configuration. You are mostly dealing with 90-degree V-8 engines with two-plane crankshafts. That means the firing pulses are unevenly spaced along each bank of the engine.

If you examine a typical first-generation Chevy small-block V-8, you can make several observations. First, the cylinders are numbered 1-3-5-7 on the left bank and 2-4-6-8 on the right bank. The standard firing order is 1-8-4-3-6-5-7-2. So in terms of exhaust event spacing in crankshaft degrees, the exhaust pulses on the left side are at 270-180-90-180 degrees; those on the right side are at 90-180-270-180 degrees. This is a considerable mismatch and far from even.

This means that although much of the flow path tuning described above works well on a one-cylinder engine, it makes effective exhaust tuning seriously more complicated on a V-8 with unevenly spaced firing pulses. For the most part, considerable compromise applies, except in applications unbridled by packaging and layout constraints. In other words, space and rules.

Designers have faced this problem for many years, and it originally led to a hybrid type of exhaust header called the Tri-Y, or 4-into-2-into-1 configuration. This design attempts to minimize the effect of uneven pulses by pairing appropriate cylinders to maximize separation of the power pulses.

In the example above the primary tubes of cylinders 1/5 and 3/7 would be merged into slightly larger secondary pipes, which, at the appropriate length, would then merge into the collector. On the opposite side the primary tubes of cylinders 2/4 and 6/8 are paired, yielding 450-270 degrees of separation between the pulses in each secondary tube.

According to Larry Meaux, the Tri-Y is configured to catch the negative pressure wave at the branching/joining of the two paired cylinders to increase scavenging and velocity. That's why the primary lengths are so critical in a Tri-Y versus a 4-into-1 configuration.

The Tri-Y has a negative pressure wave at the branch, again at the collector, and again at the collector exit. Each branch and the final collector exit provide a significant area change to generate a reflection. The design keeps exhaust velocity elevated throughout the system and pipe surface area is relatively small to radiate less heat and keep the velocity higher.

The 4-into-1 can have smaller negative wave reflections with two- or three-step header designs, but they cool gases better. They basically have two major negative waves coming from primaries dumping into collectors and again with collectors dumping into the atmosphere.

The Tri-Y has three major negative waves. The exhaust wave speed is directly proportional to temperature and the Tri-Y has less primary pipe surface area and shorter tube distances for heat rejection.

Power Adders

Superchargers, nitrous oxide injection, and turbochargers are examples of power adders. They all increase the volume of exhaust you have to deal with in high-performance applications. That makes it doubly

Turbocharged applications also benefit from well thought-out exhaust plumbing that directs exhaust volume and heat flow through the turbocharger. Compact size helps retain heat to drive the turbocharger.

important to configure and tune the exhaust side to effectively deal with the increased exhaust flow.

Superchargers and nitrous oxide, which generate increased volume, may require slightly more primary tube cross section and a larger collector, at least in high-boost high-power applications. But they aren't subject to the issues of flow resistance and back pressure that turbochargers create.

Each power adder application has its subtle differences in the way it feeds the engine. To ensure the most effective use of any power adder you have to examine the differences and configure the exhaust side accordingly.

Superchargers

Superchargers increase airflow by amplifying available air pressure above atmospheric. In that sense pressure recovery within the cylinder is somewhat less critical because you do not have to coax the airflow path into using all the available atmospheric pressure plus ramming pressure to fill the cylinders. In this case, the supercharger provides as much

Siamese exhaust ports, as found on small-block Chevys, concentrate heat from adjacent exhaust valves. In some cases, this alters the local speed of sound and affects the wave tuning and optimal primary length of the center cylinders.

Raised exhaust ports, as on this Dart head, minimize the turn exiting the valve and provide a freer flowing path for the exhaust discharge.

air as you want so you configure the exhaust to deal with the increased output via larger flow paths.

Nitrous Oxide Injection

Nitrous oxide injection also appreciates a well-designed intake port that moves a lot of air, but in this case the additional oxygen is provided chemically. Nitrous oxide is an oxidizing compound that contains 36-percent oxygen by weight. It is a great power adder because it cools the incoming charge to increase density and it doesn't separate until after it enters the combustion chamber and achieves a temperature of 565 to 575 degrees F.

The oxygen separates and combines with additional fuel to further increase density at the ignition point. So whereas supercharging is a pressure-driven process, nitrous oxide injection is chemically induced and thermally activated to achieve the same thing, i.e., a denser charge in the cylinder at the combustion point.

Turbochargers

Supercharging and nitrous oxide injection deal with the increased exhaust volume in a conventional manner. Turbocharging requires a different approach because the exhaust

Supercharged engines also generate high exhaust volume that must be served by adequate flow capacity in the exhaust system. Larger primary tubes and collectors are typically required to optimize performance.

must travel through a mechanical device on its way out of the engine. Although turbocharging increases intake-side pressure and power production like a supercharger, it applies losses via restrictions instead of friction and a supercharger belt.

A turbocharged header has much different requirements than a supercharged header, and frequently has better materials because it must accommodate greater heat loads. With turbocharging you are challenged to not only evacuate the cylinder with equal effectiveness, but to also optimize the recovery of exhaust pulse energy and the increased expansion ratio driven by temperature and load.

This represents a significant challenge on most domestic performance engines with two-plane crankshafts, which by nature generate uneven firing intervals. For maximum efficiency you desire evenly spaced exhaust pulses approaching the exhaust turbine. If you jerk the turbine with unevenly spaced hits to the turbine wheel, you also apply uneven bites of air on the compressor side of the turbocharger.

For best results you need smooth operation. You can't just whack it hard and let it spin a few revolutions before hitting it again. Exhaust pressure against the turbine needs to be smooth and even if the compressor side is to deliver smooth, consistent pressure to the inlet side of the engine. With even firing intervals you can make the header primary tubes equal length. Without that you have to consider alternate unequal dimensions that require some higher-order math to calculate. And at best it leads to a compromise that is never ideal.

With even firing intervals designers often use a split-scroll, or dual-inlet, turbine housing to maximize the recovery of exhaust pulse energy. The primaries feeding each scroll are grouped to take maximum advantage of the ideal pulse separation, which most designers agree is 240 degrees. In this case turbine efficiency approaching 100 percent can often be achieved.

Engines with uneven firing intervals, such as American V-8s with two-plane crankshafts, present a greater challenge. The most common approach is to use two smaller turbos, one serving each cylinder bank with shorter 2-into-1 primaries supplying a split scroll and achieving some energy recovery based on the resulting 450-270 degree pulse intervals. Or a large turbine is configured with equal-length primaries that are split to achieve 180-degree separation. Neither setup is perfect, but both take advantage of the best achievable pulse separation given the available combination.

Another approach is to use a large turbine configured with equal-length primaries that are split to achieve a 180-degree separation. Neither setup is perfect, but both take advantage of the best achievable pulse separation for the combination. I should also note that superchargers achieve their boost regulation via speed and a pressure relief valve where positioning is less critical. Turbochargers using a wastegate are best served if the wastegate is positioned so that it receives direct flow pressure as opposed to static pressure.

Mounting the wastegate 90 degrees to the flow only sees static pressure. For best results the wastegate should be positioned inline with the flow, such as at the beginning of a bend where the full force of exhaust flow is applied.

To maintain maximum energy, heat loss prior to the turbine must be minimized via primary tube coatings, thermal wrapping, or double-walled tubing. The heat must be contained so it is available to expand through the turbine for maximum efficiency.

Exhaust Port Surface Texture

A fundamental difference exists between the flow path surfaces in the intake port and those in the exhaust port. In the absence of inlet pressure via supercharging, you are constantly striving to coax air into the cylinder by manipulating the flow path for optimal flow efficiency based purely on atmospheric pressure and whatever degree of intake ramming you can generate from optimizing the path. As part of that effort, various surface textures are often employed to help keep the fuel mixture in suspension and encourage a homogeneous mixture with evenly sized fuel droplets.

In some cases, texture (roughness) is intensified in selected areas to further energize the boundary layer and increase or alter flow characteristics. It works on the intake side because the texture peaks are tall enough to interrupt boundary flow. Due to stiction (static friction and/or wetting action), the closest fuel molecules adhere to the surface with no movement. From there flow increases along a gradient as you move away from the wall. Texturing keeps this layer active so that excessive fuel dropout does not occur. (For more details, see Chapter 5.)

This treatment is unnecessary on the exhaust side because you have high cylinder pressure initially forcing the spent gases out and there is

Like the intake port, the exhaust port benefits from the careful tapering of material around the valveguide. (Photo Courtesy Smithberg Racing)

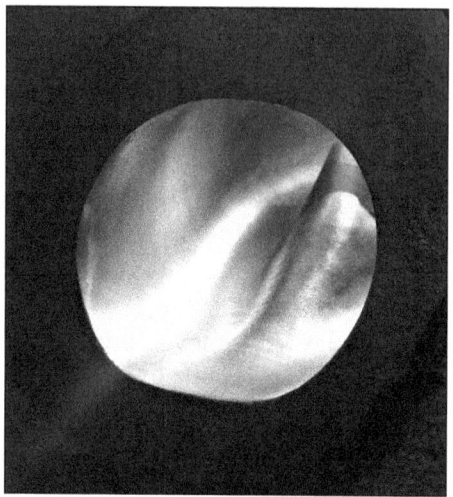

Exhaust ports can be smoothed or polished, as there is no texture requirement to keep the fuel in suspension. (Photo Courtesy Smithberg Racing)

no need to maintain anything in suspension because you essentially have dry flow at high temperature. A mirror-like finish is often employed here, more for appearance and sales appeal than actual necessity. A smooth surface is all that is required in the exhaust port.

High blowdown pressure, aggressive exhaust pumping, and wave tuning combine to ensure a vigorous departure of hot exhaust gases. Most experienced head porters finish the exhaust ports with a 300- to 400-grit finish paper and a light polish.

Valve Shape and Angle

Most exhaust valves are shaped differently than intake valves. One reason is that the exhaust valve operates in a more severe environment even though it functions right next to the intake valve. Throughout most of the exhaust valve's cycle a closed intake valve enjoys the ability to quickly transfer combustion heat to the cooling system via the valveseat and the head. An intake valve is larger in diameter so heat is concentrated over a greater area.

The exhaust valve is smaller, and a major portion of it, including the valvestem, is exposed to the hottest exhaust gases as they exit. It has to be tougher and thus it is heavier and shaped differently. The exhaust valve head is much more robust and has a thicker margin (perimeter height). Unlike the intake valve, the bottom of the exhaust valve margin usually incorporates a significant radius to encourage exiting exhaust gases to flow smoothly around it with minimal disruption.

Most exhaust valves are tulip shaped to encourage exit flow, but some very experienced people argue that a tulip-shaped valve actually inhibits flow because the back side of the valve blocks available flow space. Interestingly, one prominent cylinder head manufacturer uses standard tulip-shaped valves in all his performance heads, most likely because of cost.

Exhaust valve angles typically mimic intake angles with a 60-degree cut in the port throat area to establish a transition to the 45-degree sealing angle that contacts the valve. Above that, a top cut of 15 to 35 degrees typically completes the transition into the combustion chamber. Contemporary high-performance valve jobs incorporate up to five angles, in some cases a 70- to 75-degree throat cut, depending on the port angle and flow characteristics. Generally, inlet flow or exhaust flow does not lose velocity or incur turbulence as long as the valveseat or valve angle transitions do not exceed 15 degrees.

The standard-seat angle on an exhaust valve is 45 degrees, but many short-cycle racing applications (1/4-mile), such as Pro Stock drag racing, use up to a 55-degree angle on the valve and the seat. This has been found to increase flow with more vertical port angles, but it is less durable and is not suitable for supercharged or turbocharged applications because it can't live with the higher temperatures. Exhaust valves generally require the same angles, but use a narrower seat to help the valve cut through carbon buildup and maintain a positive seal.

The bottom line is that all the effort you put into cramming more air into your engine must be matched with equally effective efforts to get it out. If it goes in and struggles to get out you're leaving power on the table. Just as with the intake side, port shape, size, and throat diameter are the most important parameters. Exhaust flow tuning and component configuration is as important as any other tuning component of your overall engine plan.

CHAPTER 8

FLOW-BENCH TESTING

The flow bench is both praised and maligned depending on a person's viewpoint, but there is really no denying its value when it comes to evaluating airflow components. It is the most effective tool for checking flow potential and flow quality. To derive optimal results you have to be willing to accept what it tells you while recognizing its limitations.

In the overall scheme of things, flow-bench work almost always improves airflow. The caveat is that you must always be willing to recognize when a given head presents too many problems. It's always better to walk away and select a different head from the many choices available.

Flow-bench testing is the universal standard by which we evaluate cylinder heads, intake manifolds, carburetors, and other components that are part of the overall engine airflow path. Over the years, flow-bench testing has achieved a high degree of sophistication and popularity so it's fitting that I examine how it's done and what it can and can't tell you about your various test components.

What Is a Flow Bench?

The flow bench is a steady-state device that measures and records the airflow rate through a given flow passage at a particular pressure drop (differential), which simulates the cylinder depression created by the descending piston. It can tell you the airflow rate in CFM, and it can help you discover problem areas in the flow path, such as turbulence, velocity changes, and "dead" areas where the flow is relatively stagnant. It's able to accomplish these tasks

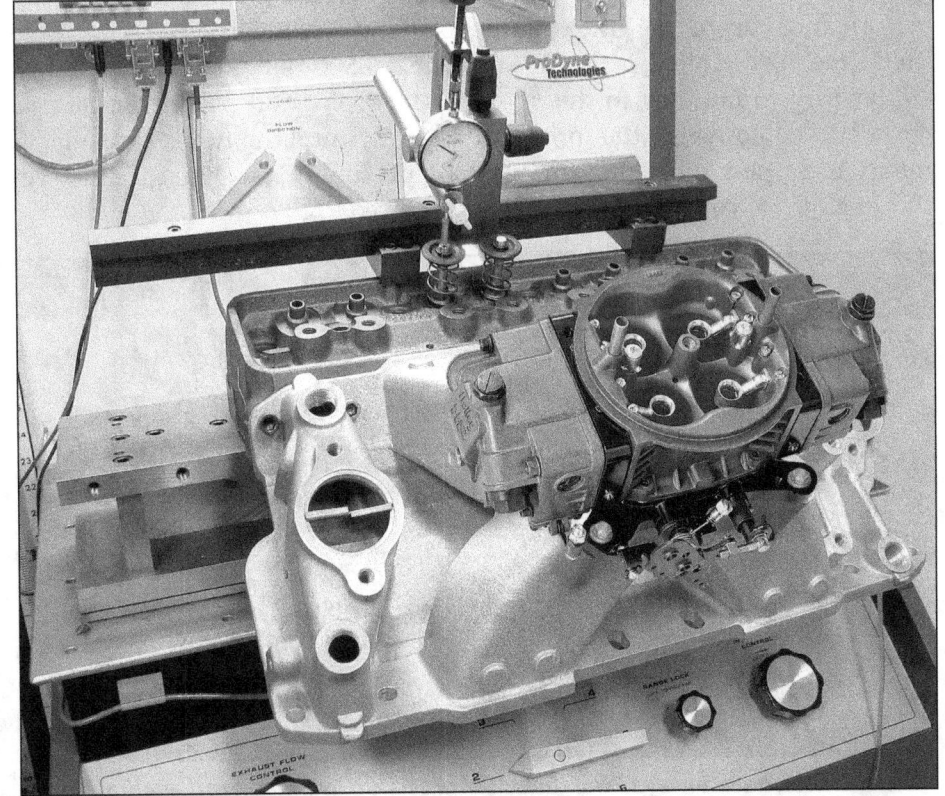

Despite its limitations, the flow bench is still one of the best devices available for evaluating airflow through engine components. Long tedious hours of flow-bench work have helped produce more victories and more records than can ever be counted.

PRACTICAL ENGINE AIRFLOW

by using an assortment of flow tools and testing accessories, such as pitot tubes.

The flow bench is also a comparative device that is most useful for determining gains and losses and judging the quality of flow at various points in the flow path. This leads to multiple uses depending on your intent. You can compare 10 different small-block cylinder heads from 10 different manufacturers that yield comparative flow numbers and determine a flow winner, but it won't necessarily tell you which one will perform best for the specific requirements of a given application. When dyno tested on a specified engine combination, the big-flow winner may work out very well.

However, it might also be peaky and get outperformed by a head with lesser flow that delivers better average power across the desired operating range (RPM). It might accomplish this on several levels, including superior ramming characteristics due to port shape and size, a more efficient valveseat and throat area, and a more effective combustion chamber shape. Many factors that may influence flow numbers can't necessarily be identified on a flow bench.

A common approach to uncover these influences is the steady development of a particular head as the head porter and/or engine builder attempts to groom the head for best performance. Comparative testing means that you are looking for flow gains across the board at every valve lift value without losing anything within the requirements of the application.

Savvy builders calculate the required flow demand based on engine speed and internal dimensions, which determine the piston's CFM demand at maximum velocity. Once the head is capable of servicing this demand, builders must be very careful not to oversize the port or lose airspeed. If this happens, they ruin the port's ramming ability, which is critical to exceeding demand and achieving 100 percent VE in a naturally aspirated engine.

Consider Application Differences

Because the most commonly tested performance components are cylinder heads, they create the most widespread problem associated with the flow bench. The inevitable question is: How much does it flow? After decades of development and unparalleled performance gains, most racers and many engine builders still believe that you can distill engine performance down to little more than a big flow number.

It's easy to fall prey to this misconception. However, the primary intent is to pass more air through the engine so you can burn more fuel and make more power. Why wouldn't you want the maximum airflow possible? Of course you do, but relative to what? Although airflow is the central influence in the final power equation, you have to be mindful of the different elements of that equation. Again, you find yourself confronted by the bottom-line question: What is the application and how do you best support it?

Optimum cylinder filling and evacuation within the required operating range of the engine application dictates your approach. If you simply bolt a set of 10,000-rpm cylinder heads (such as big, rectangular-port big-block heads) onto a 6,500-rpm bracket engine, it won't produce the expected power and the guy in the other lane will smoke you with his iron-headed big-block that's set up better. Likewise, if you bolt those same 6,500-rpm iron heads onto a 10,000-rpm short-block, it never gets there because the heads choke it off well before that engine speed is ever achieved.

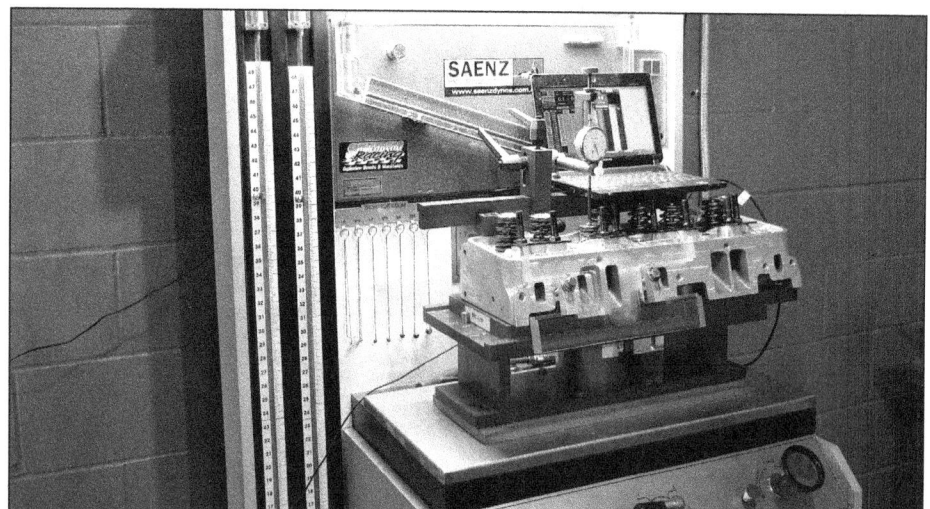

Flow benches have always been used for precision cylinder head evaluations. In the hands of an experienced operator, the bench does more than just record airflow. It can reveal flow patterns, port inconsistencies, turbulence, velocity, areas of little or no flow, and much more. The magic is in interpreting what it shows you. (Photo Courtesy Smithberg Racing)

CHAPTER 8

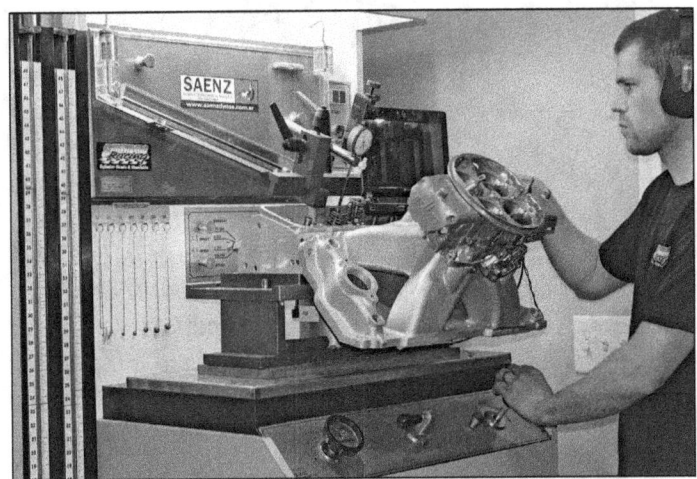

Manifold development is also conducted on the flow bench. It is tedious and time consuming, because you have to block off all other runners during testing to get a true picture of any individual port's flow capacity. (Photo Courtesy Smithberg Racing)

Cubic Feet per Minute

Air movement through an engine is measured in cubic feet per minute. This is also the standard for measuring air movement through any component of the airflow path, carburetor, cylinder head port, or whatever. A cubic foot equals 1,728 cubic inches, so you can imagine the kind of airflow and wind it can generate through typical inlet passages. An average engine produces about 1.5 hp per CFM, but that can increase considerably in an optimized racing package.

Note that any reference to CFM must be accompanied by a reference test pressure (flow depression) to provide a meaningful comparison. Flow-bench work is typically read in CFM, but in a strict sense that may not be entirely accurate without temperature and other references of relatively minor influence. Hence you can call it CFM but technically it may simply be units of flow, which is accurate for our purposes.

As discussed in previous chapters, every engine has a power band at which it achieves maximum efficiency. Once the power band has been determined for the application, builders figure out the most suitable components, flow path dimensions, and timing events that will optimize performance within that range. Simple enough, right?

Well yes, except that the intake port where everyone does all the work is not the most critical part of the flow path. The valveseat and throat are the most critical, and there are many more key elements that determine not just overall static flow (on a bench), but how well the air/fuel mixture is introduced into the cylinder. The flow bench can't fully account for the pressure recovery characteristics of a given chamber, how far the valve head is from the chamber wall and the cylinder wall, the ratio of valve size to bore diameter, and all the seemingly small details that affect the entire process. If you're not flowing the head on the exact same bore size as the engine, it's a crapshoot because you're not accurately simulating real-world conditions.

The most common flow-bench depression is 28 inches of water on a manometer. That's about the best an affordable flow bench can generate and it is adequate to a point. In the real world, the port sees double that depression or more, and it is pulsating with rapidly opening and closing valves, which generate chaotic pressure changes that include rapidly cycling finite amplitude waves. So what you observe on the bench is not nearly as strong or as robust as on the engine. The flow varies with the square root of the delta P, but it may exhibit entirely different characteristics at the much higher depression created by the running engine, not to mention the influence of other cylinders connected by a common plenum.

Flow-Bench Information

So what good is a flow bench if it can't actually simulate real-world conditions? Although it can't directly simulate the pulsing airflow caused by valve action or the wave action and pressure changes that occur, it can still tell you many important things about the components you test.

Flow development takes many forms; this motorcycle head is flowed with the carburetor and intake attached. It is critical that cylinder heads be flowed on the same bore size as the engine for which they are intended. Note the bore size (3.750) on the flow fixture. (Photo Courtesy Smithberg Racing)

FLOW-BENCH TESTING

For example, many builders have spent countless hours flow testing and developing a set of cylinder heads and matching them to the intake and carburetor and then put them on an off-road engine without ever flow testing the overall intake and air filter assembly. You can look bad if you find 20 verifiable hp in a set of heads on the dyno and end up with a 50-hp loss in the vehicle due to inadequate air supply through the inlet and filter.

The most frequent use of a flow bench is for testing cylinder heads. A flow bench consistently delivers repeatable measurements of the same port or flow path. With different modifications, the builder determines the port's initial state and what the port needs to perform better. Modifications typically include grinding or filling with epoxy to change the shape or size of the port. They may also include various forms of port wall texturing with heavy-grit sandpaper or blasting media.

Total Airflow

Airflow is measured at the common constant test pressure of 28 inches of water. The pressure drop is measured across the port being tested and compared to the pressure across a calibrated orifice with a known pressure drop. A typical flow bench uses a bank of vacuum motors to create a depression or (pressure drop) across the port being tested. Air at atmospheric pressure rushes in to fill the depression and the pressure drop is measured by comparing atmospheric pressure to the pressure immediately below the simulated cylinder. Most commercial flow benches automatically self-adjust to accurately maintain the desired test pressure.

Airflow through the port is measured by a second manometer that compares the pressure loss across a calibrated "sharp edge orifice," which yields very accurate results. Pressure is measured immediately above and below the orifice. The difference is indicated on a smaller inclined manometer, which permits a longer and more accurate scale.

Flow Velocity

Velocity is the highest airspeed in the flow path at or close to the minimum cross section. Port flow velocity (in feet per minute) is calculated with this equation:

Port Flow Velocity = $1{,}096.7 \times (\sqrt{H} \div d)$

Where:
$1{,}096.7$ = mathematical constant
H = pressure drop in inches of water as measured by the manometer
d = density of air in pounds per cubic foot (0.075 pound per cubic foot at standard conditions)

High-capacity professional flow-bench equipment is costly, quite sophisticated, and capable of gathering a great deal of data. The Superflow 1,020-cfm bench is a popular choice. (Photo Courtesy SuperFlow Dynamometers & Flowbenches)

Flow-Bench Data

When properly calibrated and operated, a modern flow bench can provide the following information:

- Total airflow in CFM through a port at any specified valve opening (lift)
- Airflow velocity at any given point in the port (via a pitot tube probe)
- A pressure and velocity map that identifies active and stagnant areas of port flow
- Location and intensity of flow as indicated by an accessory flow wand, smoke, or other visual aid
- Identification and evaluation of turbulent areas
- Indication of inefficient non-linear flow (via sound)

Once the velocity has been determined, flow volume can be calculated using this formula:

Flow Volume = port flow velocity x orifice area x published flow coefficient

High-end flow benches, such as SuperFlow units, automatically calculate this for you.

Port Mapping

A pitot tube is used to create a port map (see sidebar "Pitot Tube" on page 133) to measure the port flow velocity at various locations. The port is measured at the floor, the roof, and all points in between. The result is a color-coded representation of the port cross section with velocity gradients indicated in different shades. A thorough mapping job incorporates the same lift values used in measuring total flow volume.

By studying how the map changes at different lift values a head porter can make informed decisions about the areas to concentrate on. Depending on port shape, port size, manifold runner entry angle, valve throat area, and seat efficiency, ports on the same head usually move air differently. A porter tries to equalize the flow biased toward the best-flowing port. This often becomes complicated because the ports are influenced by the different entry angles and runner characteristics of various intake manifolds. Moreover, it requires considerable time to make the modifications (grinding, welding, or claying) and then reflow to quantify the results.

Location and Intensity of Flow

Some head porters work exclusively with the measured and calculated numbers provided by automated equipment. Others prefer visual aids to help them judge the results independent of quantified data. These methods include flow wands with little tufts on the end of a slim probe, bits of thread, colored dye, and even homemade smoke wands. All are used in an attempt to visualize exactly what the air is doing and how it is affected on its journey through the port.

Because it is such a great comparison device, a flow bench can be used to evaluate temporary changes before any metal is ground. Following Darin Morgan's advice, a porter might use the ratio between the valve throat diameter and the valve diameter to determine the head's suitability for further modification (see Chapter 5). If it passes, savvy head porters also consider making the port smaller or significantly reshaping it without increasing volume before grinding. Good examples of this are seen in the Engine Master's challenge where cylinder head ports and manifold runners are routinely epoxied and filled to change their shape or cross section based on the requirements of the application.

Armed with the calculated piston CFM demand numbers, porters can study out-of-the-box flow numbers and characteristics to determine how best to modify the head to meet that demand. In some cases, they may determine that the short-turn radius is too abrupt and needs to be smoothed. Or perhaps, they note that adding material increases velocity and improves flow and ramming potential. In many cases hours on the bench with modeling clay in the ports help identify the best path before any grinding takes place.

Most modern flow benches feature automated data collection, but their output is only as good as the user-provided input. The software makes the appropriate calculations based on the input of recorded measurements. To ensure proper results, the flow bench must be properly calibrated. A good operator always verifies calibration and conducts a leakage test prior to flow testing.

Leakage at the head gasket interface can skew the results and must be accounted for in the final analysis. If it cannot be corrected, the amount of leakage must be subtracted from the flow data. Modern equipment, such as SuperFlow's digital FlowCom, measure the leakage and compensate for it automatically.

Identification and Evaluation of Turbulent Areas

The first indication of turbulent areas and non-linear flow is typically the sound of the airflow. The port howls or roars if these conditions are present. Further investigation is required and that is usually performed by probing the port with a pitot tube, flow wand, or flow balls to locate the troubled area by disrupting the flow and altering the sound or the manometer reading. Fixing the problem is not always easy and may actually include making a modification elsewhere in the port. Flow tools help identify the location, which can often be addressed by adding material or altering the shape or texture. This is generally trial and error to see what works, and sometimes nothing works.

Temporarily altering the port's shape with clay helps you evaluate various shape changes to find the sweet spot. When you do, the sound usually diminishes and flow numbers increase. Often only a small amount of material is required to help the air remain attached. Typical areas where these problems occur include the pushrod pinch where an area change occurs over the pushrod bump, the port floor and short-side radius that should not turn too abruptly, and the overall bowl area where air is tripped up by the valvestem and valveguide and fails to maintain smooth flow approaching the throat area.

Flow-Bench Limitations

Although a flow bench is the best tool for testing and evaluating components of the engine airflow path, it does present some drawbacks in terms of its ability to simulate real-world conditions in a running engine. It provides a measurement of total flow at various valve lifts, hence you are able to judge maximum flow potential relatively accurately. But the pulsating dynamic conditions generated by a running engine are far different and must be accounted for, particularly in the following areas: steady-state flow versus dynamic flow, air-only flow versus wet flow (variable air/fuel mixture), mechanical effects, total flow versus flow velocity, and exhaust port conditions.

Steady-State Flow versus Dynamic Flow

The steady-state flow conditions generated on a flow bench are useful for determining total flow potential and pinpointing where flow deficiencies occur. It does not, however, simulate the dynamic (pulsating) flow that occurs in a running engine in which pressure changes and flow are far greater than what you can simulate at 28 inches of water. Depending on the type of engine and operating conditions, it can create a depression as much as six times that or more, and even higher for an exhaust port. That being said, you can still develop a port and groom it for best flow characteristics at 28 inches; some porters with modified equipment flow at 36 inches or higher.

As a rule, if you increase steady-state flow and it remains non-turbulent you are moving in the right direction and dynamic flow will follow. Still you can only put so much air through a given port and the port indicates that on the bench by refusing to flow any more air at a given depression; in most cases the sound pitch increases as well.

Air-Only Flow versus Wet Flow

A flow bench tests with essentially dry air, meaning that the air is not mixed with fuel of any kind although it likely contains some water vapor. Air exhibits different characteristics when mixed with fuel droplets; these characteristics depend on the size and density of the droplets. To accommodate this, wet-flow benches have been developed primarily through the efforts of Joe Mondello and Lloyd Creek and further pioneered by major companies, such as Dart Machinery and Reher-Morrison.

In wet-flow testing, the port is pressurized and liquid is added via an atomizer to simulate the fuel mixture. A clear-plastic cylinder permits observation of the flow characteristics. The liquid is drawn off at the bottom and recirculated.

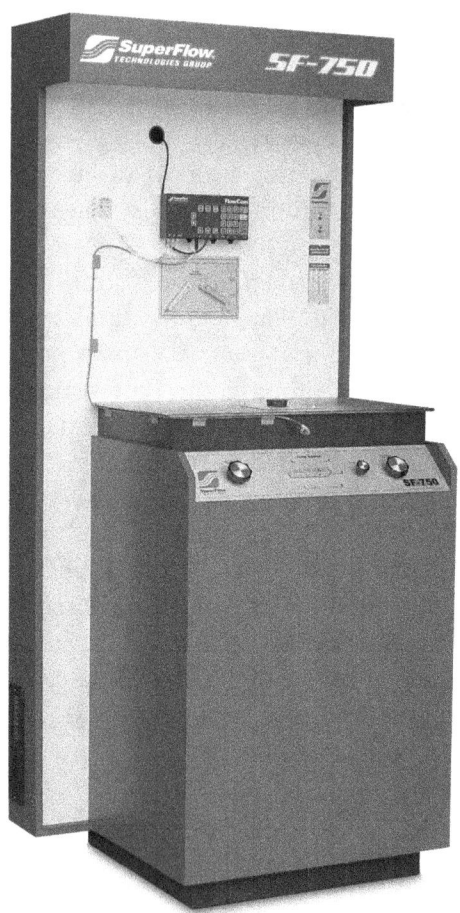

Most shops have a SF600 flow bench, but Superflow recently added capacity and now offers an SF750 version to accommodate higher flow requirements. (Photo Courtesy SuperFlow Dynamometers & Flowbenches)

Superflow's smaller desktop-style flow benches have lower capacity, but results can be mathematically converted to higher depressions with good accuracy for comparison purposes. (Photo Courtesy SuperFlow Dynamometers & Flowbenches)

CHAPTER 8

In early efforts it was difficult to observe the flow through the chaotic mist that developed. Then, designers hit on the idea of adding a fluorescent dye to the liquid and observing the flow with a black light. The change was dramatic, and they were able to observe flow characteristics never before visible.

Wet-flow testing completely reversed contemporary thinking about various aspects, such as fuel wash. Previously, it was believed that the shiny surfaces on the top of pistons indicated areas of fuel wash and no combustion. It was then determined that there was minimal local combustion because the lean mixture

Wet-Flow Testing

Like steady-state airflow testing, wet-flow testing cannot entirely simulate the dynamic conditions that occur during actual engine operating conditions, but it does provide enough simulation to allow designers a good look at flow and distribution trends inside the manifold, ports, and cylinders.

Because the air/fuel mixture is heavier and behaves much differently than dry air, a way was needed to flow heads with a simulated fuel mixture that would help designers observe how fuel behaves when entering the chamber and the cylinders. Port designers are well aware that simply increasing flow without accounting for the fuel mass can actually lead to a power loss due to poor mixture quality and varying air/fuel ratios caused by uneven combustion. Wet-flow testing helps port designers visualize port-flow characteristics in real time close to the actual flow depression that occurs in an operational engine.

In the 1990s, Dart Machinery constructed an elaborate computer-controlled wet-flow bench capable of flowing 800 cfm at a maximum flow depression of 55 inches of water (almost exactly double the industry standard of 28 inches). The bench used a nonflammable liquid with the same specific gravity as gasoline and was configurable to simulate any desired air/fuel ratio.

Wet Flow Air/Fuel Ratio

Most testing is performed at 13:1 air/fuel ratio to simulate common racing engine tuning conditions. The liquid is treated with a fluorescent dye that glows in ultraviolet light, allowing technicians to easily view flow patterns as the air moves through the port, across the valveseat, and into the chamber and cylinder. This quickly became a valuable tool in helping designers construct and evaluate optimized port and chamber designs.

As previously noted, mixture quality holds nearly the same performance value as overall airflow. Designers seek to increase airflow *and* improve combustion efficiency by encouraging the most homogeneous mixture possible. The object is to maintain a uniform (reliable) air/fuel ratio by delivering all of the fuel in equally sized and evenly dispersed fuel droplets. As flow increases, the fuel ratio must follow consistently.

A wet-flow bench measures the actual airflow in cubic feet per minute and the fuel flow in parts per hour. Technicians can physically observe flow characteristics and compare the recorded flow numbers of both the air and the fuel supply to learn if they track well together. Although more complicated than a standard dry-flow bench, the wet-flow bench offers opportunities to observe fuel mixture movement, either directly or by recording video of the observed motion.

With modern fuel systems it is not much of a problem to maintain an adequate fuel supply. It is, however, more important than ever to deliver the desired airflow and serve it adequately with finely atomized fuel capable of providing the best burn characteristics possible (smooth, even combustion) at the desired air/fuel ratio throughout the power range.

Consistent fuel ratios across the engine's operating range are always desirable. In very precise testing it might be determined that you want the air/fuel ratio to richen under certain conditions. Although "lean is mean," as they often say, it is also dangerous. As cylinder temperatures rise near the end of a run, it may be desirable to slightly richen the fuel mixture to help avoid detonation. This is not as easily accomplished with carburetors, but it is possible and certainly achievable with electronically controlled fuel injection that is monitoring everything and reacting accordingly. To some degree, wet-flow testing can help predict this, especially if the fuel curve tends to waver as RPM increases.

When the air/fuel ratio is inconsistent it is also uneven. Pockets of larger droplets burn more slowly than the smaller droplets around them. (A similar anomaly interferes with smooth combustion.) Although the burning happens very quickly, it is important to remember that you don't want an explosion; you want a very smooth combustion and expansion of the burning gases. Uneven mixture quality discourages this and reduces power while inviting detonation.

Dart's Tony McAfee has witnessed the entire evolution of Dart's performance and racing cylinder heads based on burned quickly and completely; hence no soot or combustion residue on the piston top. Further, areas actually experiencing fuel dropout could be seen in the darker, wetter portions of the burn pattern and related to the vortices observed in wet-flow testing.

Wet-flow testing provided a major revelation. Designers observed how the vortices spin in one direction or another depending on port orientation and the direction of the airflow entering the cylinder. The vortices started small and increased in size and speed as they rotated clockwise or counterclockwise around the combustion chamber. From these observations designers were able to revise wet-flow development. He reiterates that the short-turn radius, bowl, and combustion chamber are still critical to superior performance and says that the wet-flow bench has made it possible to learn how to keep more fuel in suspension. Raised ports, line-of-sight to the valve, and port dimensions are all important, but in certain areas fuel still stumbles and sticks to the walls. It's unavoidable. How you address it and attempt to remedy it are lessons the wet-flow bench offers.

Swirl and Tumble

Swirl is the term applied to airflow entering a cylinder and moving down the cylinder in a circular path as dictated by velocity and the initial entry angle. It is a long-recognized method of mixture conditioning via high-charge motion and subsequent mixing action. It is most effective in engines running at slower speeds. Fast-burn heads are a common application of swirl.

By providing a more homogeneous mixture, swirl allows the engine tuner to run less initial timing, which reduces cylinder pressure and negative force against the piston prior to TDC. The burn after TDC is completed more quickly and applies greater cylinder pressure to the piston top. Swirl can be used to improve burn quality and generate more cylinder pressure from the same charge density. It can also contribute to better control of cylinder temperatures on long, full-throttle pulls and prevent the onset of detonation.

Depending on the application, many head porters forgo the use of a swirl meter, especially for very high-speed racing engines that don't produce enough time for swirl to be effective. Some applications generate too much swirl and some engines actually perform well with minimal swirl. The amount is very much dependent on the burn characteristics of the particular combustion chamber, the rising piston top, and engine speed.

Rotating flow (swirl) combined with the squishing action between the piston top and the quench pad provides turbulence beneficial to mixture quality just prior to ignition. Designers continue to investigate the effects of swirl, and the use of wet-flow testing has helped them visualize the actual conditions and charge motion that occur within the cylinder. A related condition called *tumble* refers to the motion that some cylinder heads impart to the charge entering the cylinder. Instead of swirling radially into the cylinder, the mixture "tumbles" over itself vertically. This is thought to help fill the cylinder more efficiently on slower-speed engines, but the evidence is inconclusive.

Swirl and tumble each interact differently with valve action and piston motion depending on engine speed and flow path dynamics that influence charge velocity, density, and inertia. Many designers feel that a combination of swirl and tumble may provide the optimum combination to take maximum advantage of mean flow velocities and turbulences that promote the best possible mixture condition.

Swirl and tumble have distinctive characteristics and can interact differently with piston motion and squish. The optimum rotating flow field may be a combination of the two kinds of rotational motion. Researchers do not yet fully understand the steps that can be taken to optimize swirl and tumble, nor have they fully determined which one is best for high-speed racing applications. Fast-burn combustion chambers have paved the way and further wet-flow investigation is certain to help gain greater perspective on these phenomena. ■

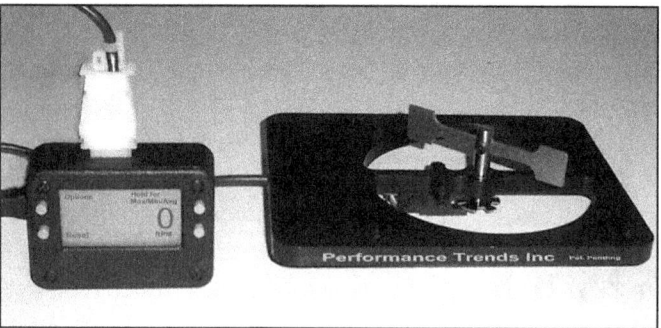

Performance Trends offers a swirl meter for use on any flow bench. Data is ported to the computer to show the amount of swirl generated in each cylinder. (Photo Courtesy Performance Trends)

CHAPTER 8

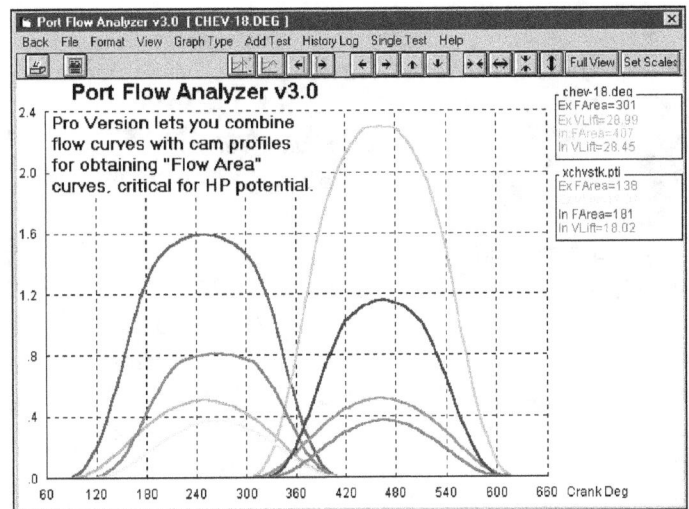

The Pro version of Performance Trends Port Flow Analyzer software allows you to compare flow curves with cam profiles to analyze performance potential. (Photo Courtesy Performance Trends)

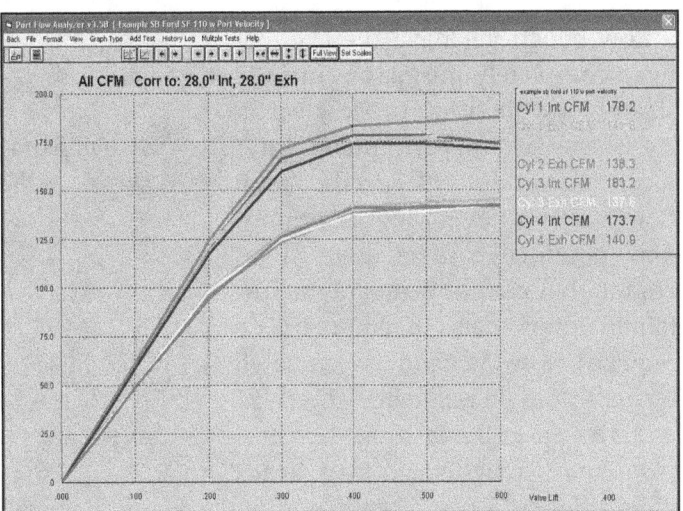

Each port's flow curve is recorded for an overlay comparison of flow values. Here is an exceptionally good port that the head porter will try to match with adjustments to the other ports. (Photo Courtesy Performance Trends)

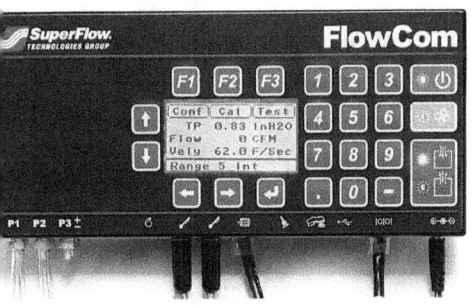

SuperFlow's FlowCom unit permits a myriad of automated tests; all of the information is ported to the computer for analysis. As a fully digital unit, it can be used with or without physical manometers. (Photo Courtesy SuperFlow Dynamometers & Flowbenches)

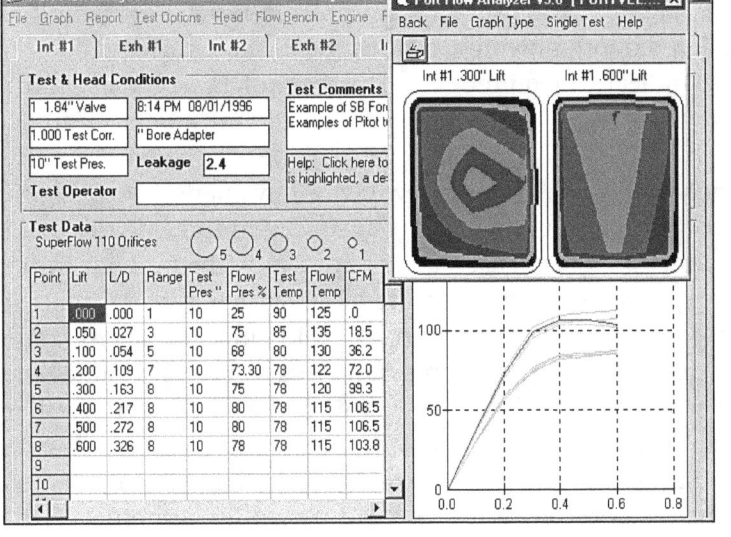

The Port Flow Analyzer software displays a port flow map for each measurement point along with flow data on the same screen for easy analysis. (Photo Courtesy Performance Trends)

spark plug placement, valve location, and port configurations to improve the flow on existing cylinder heads.

Mechanical Effects

The rapid movement of the piston in the bore and the motion of the valves create a fluid dynamic that is not duplicated on either type of flow bench (air-only or wet-flow). Pressure changes and flow dynamics are affected by rapid valve motion and the high-speed start/stop influence on the incoming charge. It is important to remember that the start and stop motions affect not only airflow, but also the airborne fuel mass. Variable-size fuel droplets starting, stopping, and stalling unevenly (due to their weight) creates flow potential from rapidly fluctuating air/fuel ratios that complicate combustion and reduce power.

As the piston rises ahead of TDC, its motion provides some resistance to initial airflow that cannot be duplicated on the flow bench (except during overlap). Also, the rapid depression created after TDC is much stronger than a flow bench can create, particularly at peak demand around 75 degrees after TDC. To more effectively simulate this, the Dart wet-flow bench was configured to flow at a higher depression of about 55 inches of water.

Total Flow versus Flow Velocity

It is possible to observe high flow rates with large ports and valves on a flow bench yet have the cylinder head completely mismatched to the short-block application. Flow velocity is the key to performance, and racers should not fall into the "total flow" trap, believing that enormous flow potential can be used on an engine that cannot generate the sustained flow demand to require it. The required flow demand is generated by increased RPM; hence the head and the short-block must be complementary. Higher flowing heads offer higher RPM potential that takes advantage of the higher flow potential.

It is far better to match the flow potential to the engine's calculated piston CFM demand within the projected power band. This usually means smaller, smooth-flowing ports; it may also indicate a requirement for smaller valves.

Exhaust Port Simulation

A flow bench cannot accurately mimic flow in a functioning exhaust port. The best it can do is measure maximum flow potential and indicate whether it can adequately service the exhaust requirements of the engine. That said, it is very important (if not more important) to fully develop the exhaust port on any racing or high-performance engine to take maximum advantage of inlet-side modifications. This is particularly true of supercharged, turbocharged, and nitrous-oxide-assisted engines that generate much greater exhaust volume than naturally aspirated engines.

The pressures and temperatures within the port are too high and wide ranging to permit any real-world representation other than potential flow capacity. Mean exhaust port pressure easily exceeds 2 bars (atmospheres) and typically about 6 bars or more at EVO. These conditions easily create sonic flow that is choked for a short period of time, or crankshaft degrees.

This cannot be simulated on a flow bench and must be determined on an engine dyno. Nonetheless, flow-bench evaluation can verify port adequacy to indicate the port's ability to deal with the high initial burst of exhaust pressure when the exhaust valve initially opens. High pressure occurs at low lift values and decreases as the valve opens farther. Hence the event commences with the high-pressure blowdown followed by exhaust pumping as the piston rises on the exhaust stroke.

Calculating Lift-to-Diameter Ratios

The recommended procedure for establishing lift-point values for a flow-bench test is to calculate the lift-to-diameter (L/D) ratio for a series of seven or more lift points. This is accomplished automatically on some flow benches that allow you to input the basic values. Otherwise you have to calculate it and input the numbers yourself. Here's the equation to find the net valve area:

$$\text{Net Valve Area} = 0.785 \times (\text{valve diameter}^2 - \text{stem diameter}^2)$$

Where:
0.785 = mathematical constant

SuperFlow pioneered a method for evaluating different valve diameters based on lift settings that are in direct ratio to their diameter. The L/D ratio provides ideal valve-lift test settings that permit valve-diameter flow comparisons based on common ratios. These ratios are 0.05, 0.10, 0.15, 0.20, 0.25, and 0.30:1. Ideal test valve-lift settings are derived by multiplying the valve diameter by the desired L/D ratio. (See the chart "Lift-to-Diameter Ratio.")

To compare different-size valves accurately, you first must select a common L/D ratio. A good choice is one that yields a test valve lift that is about 65 percent of the total valve lift because that is the point where the most flow occurs relative to valve open time.

As an example, say you want to compare a 1.94-inch valve to a

Lift-to-Diameter Ratio

	Intake Valves					Exhaust Valves		
L/D	1.94	2.02	2.05	2.08	2.10	1.50	1.60	1.625
Test Valve Lifts								
0.05	0.097	0.101	0.102	0.104	0.105	0.075	0.080	0.081
0.10	0.194	0.202	0.205	0.208	0.210	0.150	0.160	0.162
0.15	0.291	0.303	0.307	0.312	0.315	0.225	0.240	0.244
0.20	0.388	0.404	0.410	0.416	0.420	0.300	0.320	0.325
0.25	0.485	0.505	0.512	0.520	0.525	0.375	0.400	0.406
0.30	0.582	0.606	0.615	0.624	0.630	0.450	0.480	0.487

Courtesy SuperFlow Corporation

CHAPTER 8

2.02-inch valve, and you know that the total net lift is 0.450 inch. The lift at 65 percent is 0.2925 inch (0.45 x 0.65).

On the chart under "1.94-inch intake valve" you find an L/D ratio of 0.15:1 that recommends a test lift setting of 0.291 inch (1.94-inch valve diameter x 0.15 L/D ratio). For the 2.02-inch valve, the same L/D ratio indicates a 0.303-inch lift (2.02 x 0.15).

Why more lift for the bigger valve? Because the flow increase is proportional. That means testing the 2.02-inch valve at the same lift as the 1.94–inch valve shows a flow increase, but not as much as the 2.02-inch valve is actually capable of delivering.

That might lead you to think that it is not worth switching valves. The flow technician can make the flow comparison using the appropriate L/D ratio to get an accurate picture of any valve's performance in proportion to the smaller valve. Then you know the true flow value of the larger valve and can make a more informed decision.

Calculating Valve Curtain Area

When evaluating engine combinations and camshafts in particular, it is often useful to calculate the valve curtain area for a given valve lift and compare it to proposed changes by percentage. The valve curtain area is the area of the flow window that opens when the valve is lifted off its seat. For example, say you have a 2.02-inch intake valve that opens to 0.500-inch lift. You need to know the valve curtain area measurement and the amount it increases if you open the valve to 0.535 inch.

You can't go by the valve diameter itself when performing the calculation. You have to use the flow diameter where the actual valveseat begins, which is typically about 0.040 inch smaller than the valve diameter. Here's the formula to find the total available flow area for a valve's flow diameter at any given valve lift:

Valve Curtain Area = valve diameter x 0.98 x 3.14 x valve lift

Where:
0.98 = mathematical constant
3.14 = the measurement of pi

The example above works out to a valve curtain area of 3.107 square inches (2.02 x 0.98 x 3.14 x 0.500). If you open the valve to 0.535-inch lift, it works out to 3.325 (2.02 x 0.98 x 3.14 x 0.535).

To find the percentage of change you divide the new measurement by the current measurement. You can use either valve-lift numbers or valve curtain area numbers. Using the examples, you get a 7-percent increase:

- Percent of Change = 0.535 new valve lift ÷ 0.500 current valve lift = 1.07
- Percent of Change = 3.325 new valve curtain area ÷ 3.107 current valve curtain = 1.07

At some point the throat area becomes the final restricting factor. Lifting the valve farther does not increase the flow (see "Port Saturation Point" section).

This does not represent a 7-percent increase in flow, but rather a 7-percent increase in potential flow area. Flow gains are still dictated by the combination of available flow area, port velocity, cross-sectional area, valve job, opening rate, and other factors influencing the induction system. The additional flow area relative to valve-opening rate and duration offers increased potential for overall cylinder filling.

Increasing the example valve lift to 0.550 yields an approximate 10-percent increase in valve lift (0.535 ÷ 0.550 = 0.972 inch) and available flow area (3.107 ÷ 3.418 = 0.909 square inch). Again, it does not mean a 10-percent increase in airflow, but simply a 10-percent increase in flow area and, thus, flow potential. Any actual airflow increase must be verified on a flow bench.

Port Saturation Point

Another important thing to consider is the port saturation point

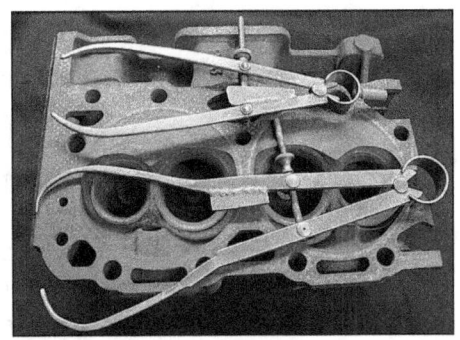

You can build your own calipers for measuring port wall thickness. Larry Meaux at Meaux Racing Heads makes these hand-built tools. (Photo Courtesy Meaux Racing Heads)

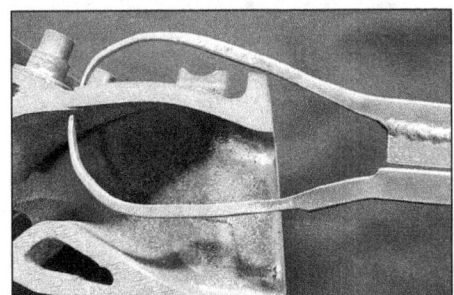

Here's an example of how Larry Meaux uses his hand-built tools to make certain the wall isn't too thin at any point in the port. (Photo Courtesy Meaux Racing Heads)

FLOW-BENCH TESTING

Meaux's specialty tools are particularly useful to prevent breaking into the water jacket or valvespring pockets while grinding. (Photo Courtesy Meaux Racing Heads)

Make certain that your dial indicator spindle is mounted parallel with the valve travel to eliminate valve lift error during testing. (Photo Courtesy Meaux Racing Heads)

Pitot Tube

Among the tools used to develop a port profile the pitot tube is one of the most familiar. It allows porters to examine how air moves through a particular portion of a flow path and it measures the pressure and velocity at any given point. Because air and fuel molecules are affected by turbulence, port texture, area changes, and other influences, they exhibit different characteristics on their journey to the valve. Some areas of the port are quite active; others are relatively dead because the air takes the best path to the valve.

As part of the effort to influence the air a head porter first uses the pitot tube to map and understand these areas to determine how best to correct them. He or she is looking for the weakest areas and the sections of the port that are most inefficient. It's a delicate process and takes time to learn because the pitot tube itself interrupts the airstream and the porter has to account for that. If you thought a head porter was just a mad grinder in a ski mask you might be surprised to learn that many of the good ones approach the job scientifically.

A J-shaped pitot tube is used for mapping local airstream velocities in the intake ports; a straight tube is used for exhaust ports. A pitot is actually two tubes: one inside the other. The inner tube is left open and faces the oncoming air to measure the dynamic (flow) pressure combined with static pressure measured within the secondary tube. The outer tube is sealed at the tip and measures the static pressure in the tube. A series of small holes around the periphery of the outer tube take this measurement.

A differential pressure sensor connecting the inner and outer tubes compares the pressures and calculates the air speed based on air density. The pitot tube can also be connected to a manometer so the technician can read the pressure and make judgments based strictly on observed pressure.

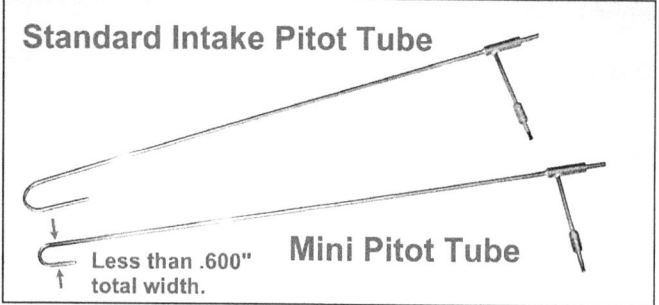

These Performance Trends pitot tubes are used to determine pressure and velocity in a port being flowed on a flow bench. They connect to the flow-bench manometer and are positioned at different points within the port to record pressures, which are then converted to velocity and flow. (Photo Courtesy Performance Trends)

When probing a location in the port, the pitot tube is positioned to obtain the highest reading. This indicates that the air is flowing directly into the inner tube. The tip is moved around in the port looking for fast-moving air and stagnant areas of relatively dead air. Readings are recorded in a logical sequence to construct a port map. If the probe is supported by commercial software available through specialty companies, such as Performance Trends and Audie Technologies, the readings are recorded and mapped automatically by depressing a foot switch.

Typical readings are taken at the top, center, and bottom of each port along the centerline and both sides to develop a picture of the flow at any given point. A complete set of readings is taken through as many cross-section points as the technician deems necessary to map the port. The results are then studied to determine the best way to correct port anomalies and improve airflow. ■

PRACTICAL ENGINE AIRFLOW

CHAPTER 8

Larry Meaux's setup with the PTS system is seen here. He prints the previous test and keeps it handy next to the screen for quick review during the current test. (Photo Courtesy Meaux Racing Heads)

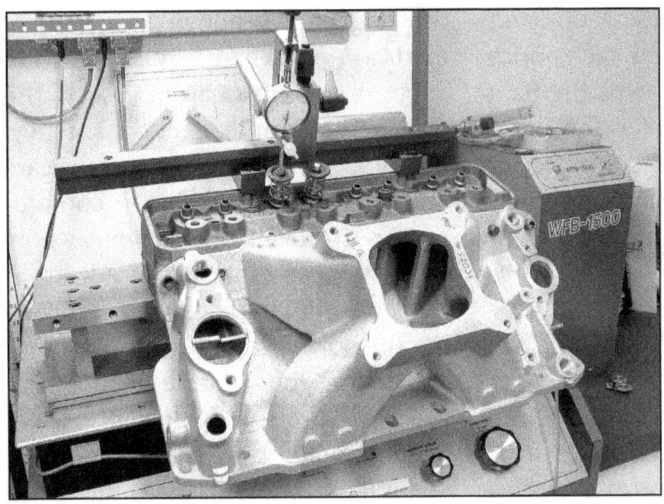

Repeatable flow work requires consistent valve openings. Lightweight valve checking springs are typically used with good results. The valve actuator must be solidly mounted to ensure accuracy.

with regard to valve curtain area versus port cross-sectional area. It's typically somewhere in the mid-lift range (roughly 0.300 to 0.400 inch) for most applications. Beyond this point, the valve curtain area becomes larger than the minimum port cross-sectional area (throat) and the port (throat) itself becomes the restriction. You can determine this point with the following formula:

Port Saturation Lift Point = L x T ÷ C

Where:
L = valve lift
T = cross-sectional area (throat)
C = valve curtain area

Here's an example: a 2.02-inch valve at 0.400-inch lift and a port cross-sectional area of 2.15 square inches measured at the throat immediately above the valve.

If the valve curtain area is 2.486 square inches (2.02 x 0.98 x 3.14 x 0.400) and the port cross-section area is 2.15 square inches (1.87 x 1.15), the saturation point is at 0.346-inch lift [(0.400 x 2.15) ÷ 2.486].

So 0.346-inch lift is the point where the valve curtain area exactly equals the port cross-sectional area. Above this valve lift the port cross section becomes the controlling factor in flow capacity.

Flow-Bench Tools

Flow-bench work is much easier and more accurate if you employ the proper tools. Some of these tools are basic fixtures for mounting cylinder heads or other components on the flow bench. Others measure or demonstrate the flow characteristics or influence the flow in some meaningful way that relates to the work or research being performed.

Flow Test Stand

Usually made of aluminum or Lexan a flow test stand is designed to mount a cylinder head above the flow test orifice on a flow bench. Some stands have a fixed bore that provides two different bore sizes depending on which side is up. More sophisticated stands are made of anodized aluminum plate and feature interchangeable bore sleeves so the technician can flow with the proper bore size for the anticipated engine.

An important component of any good flow-bench fixture is the ability to accurately position the combustion chamber over the proper-size cylinder bore. Some fixtures do not have this feature and thus require a calibrated eyeball and corresponding coefficient of accuracy. Others have sliders with positioning pegs to ensure perfect positioning every time.

Bore Simulator

This indispensable test component promotes flow accuracy by simulating the cylinder head's actual bore size. It is typically part of a larger flow test fixture that supports the entire cylinder head on the flow-bench test surface while positioning it over the calibrated flow orifice. Simple bore fixtures have a fixed size; others, such as those offered by Brzezinski Racing Products, have interchangeable bore sleeves that come in different sizes.

Bore simulators are installed beneath a sliding surface plate so the head can easily be moved from one chamber to the next with pinpoint accuracy. This provides a consistent bore reference for testing each port in a cylinder head and helps the technician equalize cylinder-to-cylinder flow performance to account for differences in manifold runner length and entry angle.

Radius Inlet Guide

The "edge effect" of air rushing into an inlet port skews the results, affecting accuracy and possibly altering flow characteristics within the port that may not exist with a manifold in place. Whenever flowing without a manifold, a radius inlet guide should be positioned to smooth air entry into the port. These are available for standard-size ports, but almost always require minor smoothing with modeling clay to accommodate casting inaccuracies.

The flow radius is typically 1/2 to 3/4 inch with rounded corners to promote smooth entry. Radius inlet guides often increase flow by 5 to 10 percent, but the flow increase is not the important factor. The desired effect is to increase the flow velocity more like a real engine with smoother air entry so you can evaluate stable conditions in the port without the influence of edge-effect "shear" and subsequent turbulence.

In the absence of a readily available guide, some machinists mill a custom guide or simply fashion a crude replica out of clay. This works, but may not always provide the smoothest air entry due to inconsistent shape as you move from port to port.

Exhaust Flow Tube

An exhaust flow tube, or stub pipe, is often used to simulate the desired exhaust exit to get the highest flow velocity just like a real engine. This avoids the exit "edge effect" and the large area change immediately exiting the exhaust port. On the exhaust side, this can also skew the flow numbers and affect consistency.

Flow tubes are easy to fabricate and most sizes and flange configurations are available. A typical flow pipe uses the same-size header tubing and simulates a gentle bend exiting the port. They are typically about 10 inches long. Some technicians leave the bolts out and clock them to more closely simulate the exit angle of the headers they intend to use. When doing so, it is important to ensure accurate positioning over each exhaust port to minimize possible blockage.

Port Mold Rubber

Experienced head porters often use port mold rubber to make accurate models of the ports they design. Once the port designer achieves a great working port, he or she makes an exact copy to help duplicate it. This is doubly important because many ports are reversed, but not quite mirror images of themselves. Hence dimensional comparison is necessary.

The rubber mold is a full-size positive model of the port. It can be accurately measured for cross section at any point. It allows detailed visualization of critical areas, such as the short-side radius, bowl details, and pushrod pinch area. The molds are easily made from silicone RTV (room-temperature vulcanizing) mold kits available at any hobby shop or from some cylinder head shops.

Many porters purchase their molding materials from U.S. Composites. They typically use 74-30 RTV Liquid Urethane Mold Rubber and the No. 2300 Mold Release spray. The rubber is inexpensive, and quick to mix and pour. Curing time is 18 to 24 hours at room temperature and the molds push right out with minimal pressure. The molds remain fairly soft, but firm enough to hold their shape for measurement and evaluation. Firmer material is also available. (You can use these same materials to make combustion chamber molds.)

The process is straightforward: The port is prepped with a releasing agent to help prevent the RTV from

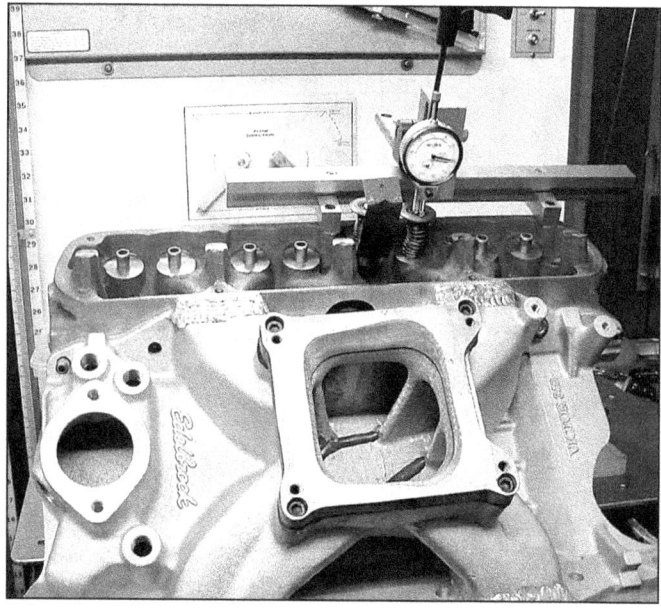

Flow testing helps you find problems and develop solutions. Here, Larry Meaux is evaluating port flow with a Quadrajet carburetor that has very large secondaries compared to the primaries. He uses small strips of clay on the plenum floor to help ensure equal flow capacity. (Photo Courtesy Meaux Racing Heads)

sticking. With the valve in place, the RTV is mixed according to the instructions and slowly poured into the intake or exhaust port. The curing time is usually 24 hours at room temperature. When the mold is cured, the valve can be removed and the mold can be pushed and pulled out of the port. This often requires some cutting to accommodate the valve-guide, but it is generally pretty easy to remove the mold from the port.

Modeling Clay

Clay is often used to temporarily alter a port shape for quick evaluation. Used as a filler or to build up selected areas for quick flow testing, it can help pinpoint areas that require more permanent filling or significant alteration. This is very typical for use on port floors. It is also very useful for blending in and smoothing areas where the transition is mismatched. As a rule, a good head porter does a little clay work before grinding.

Successful clay testing is followed by adding epoxy and smoothing with the grinder once a good shape is identified. This is frequently repeated and combined with port molding and careful measurements to ensure equal-performing ports.

Clay is also used to form quick-and-dirty radius entries when a pre-fashioned one is not available. It can be rolled into a rope shape and strung around a port entrance. Then it is carefully blended in by hand until it forms a reasonably even radius entry all around the port.

Flow Wand

Flow wands are used to observe flow direction inside a port. Head porters fashion their own by gluing small 3/4- to 1-inch pieces of nylon thread to the end of a length of welding rod. When inserted into a flowing port, the thread follows the flow direction and provides visual indication of smoothness. This simple method is remarkably effective in many cases. No pitot tube port mapping going on here just yet, but it is certainly a quick visual confirmation of flow activity and a handy starting point.

The flow wand helps identify the best places to begin velocity probing with the pitot tube because it points out areas of stable and turbulent flow along with direction and, to some degree, intensity. It takes a little experience to learn the subtleties of the flow wand but as a rule, you are looking for the thread to remain straight and stable indicating smooth flow. If it begins to whip and fan out you have encountered unstable flow and must figure out what is causing it and how to correct it.

Further checking with the pitot tube is required to verify results. You can generally identify smooth flow near the center of the port and move the wand slowly outward in each direction until the thread just begins to flutter, marking the onset of unstable flow. It is important to remember that slow-velocity air follows most turns and contours, but high velocity is the goal and it has a much greater tendency to detach from the port walls and do what it wants. When flow leaves the port wall, turbulence ensues and is directly related to velocity and the severity of the turn, or obstruction, that may also influence it.

We all strive for total flow stability throughout the port, but that is rarely achieved. Experience counts, but so does patience. It takes time to analyze a port and identify exactly what needs to be done.

A flow wand indicates areas of laminar flow, areas of turbulent flow, areas of flow separation, airflow direction, and mixture motion.

As previously mentioned, you want the flow to remain attached and never become turbulent. If it separates and becomes turbulent the flow wand shows you where it separates. It also indicates the intensity of turbulence and airflow direction at that point.

Flow Balls

Different-size flow balls attached

Meaux retests with the Quadrajet in place to assess flow balance. Note the welded runners where the port roof has been raised. (Photo Courtesy Meaux Racing Heads)

FLOW-BENCH TESTING

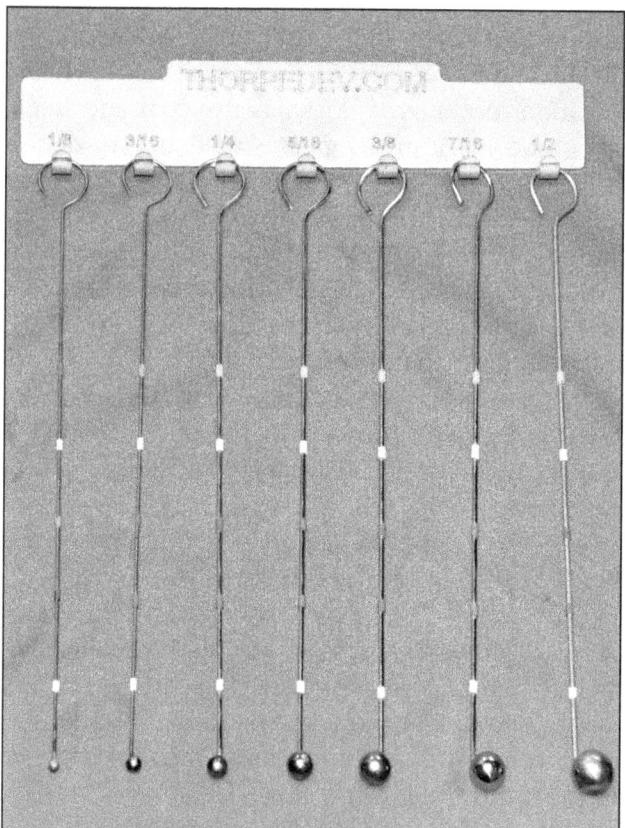

Thorpe Development flow balls are essential tools for flow-bench development work. They help you hone in on the location of the boundary layer and solve air-speed problems in intake ports. (Photo Courtesy Thorpe Development)

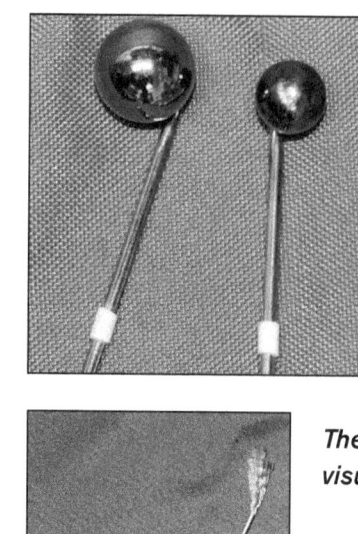

Flow balls come in sizes ranging from 1/8- to 1/2-inch diameter. Each provides a different level of flow disruption. The flow ball disrupts the airflow and helps you pinpoint when and where the airflow becomes active.

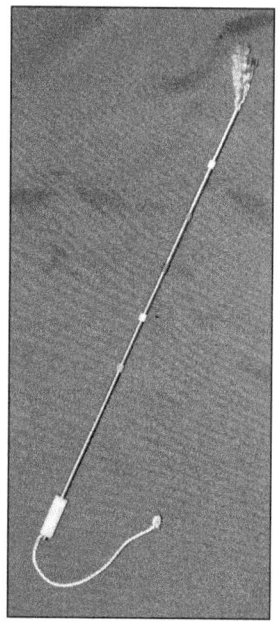

The flow wand is used to help you visualize the direction of flow in a port.

to a length of rod are used to increase and decrease flow in a port during the evaluation process. Their presence at any point in a port positively or negatively affects flow. You can interpret the observed results and decide if the port requires modification at that point to improve flow.

Flow balls indicate areas of dead flow, location of turbulence, and location of flow separation.

Carefully move the balls around in the port. You can check suspect areas to see if the ball causes the flow to increase or diminish as indicated by a change in the test pressure on the manometer. By locating the dead areas and points of separation and turbulence, you can pinpoint the problems and determine the best way to make the flow remain attached to the wall.

Depending on the port shape, the ball can be used to induce separation during tests and to cure separation. Based on the ball's effect on flow you can determine whether to remove or add material in selected locations to smooth the flow.

Evaluation with flow balls, flow wands, and pitot tubes is always the first step before you pick up a grinder.

This large flow ball is in a port adjacent to the pushrod pinch area. This area is known to accelerate the airflow and the flow ball helps you determine exactly where by observing the real-time pressure activity on the manometer.

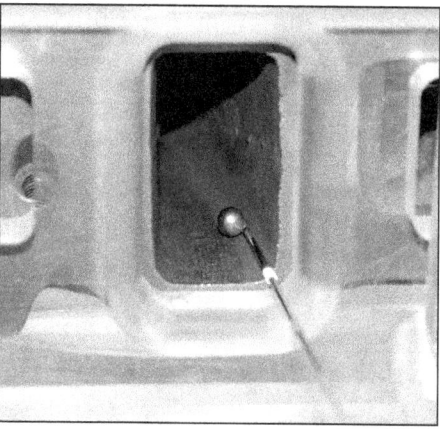

Corner areas are often inactive and the flow ball can tell you where airflow may increase within the ports. Move the ball slowly into the port until you see the manometer indicate a pressure change. As flow increases, the dynamic pressure decreases.

PRACTICAL ENGINE AIRFLOW

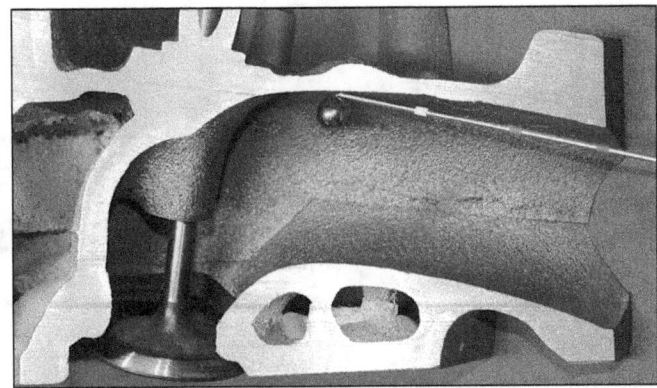

A flow ball is used to check the roof activity where the flow wants to detach and follow the most direct path to the valve. The flow ball can help you determine the path and evaluate changes to improve the flow.

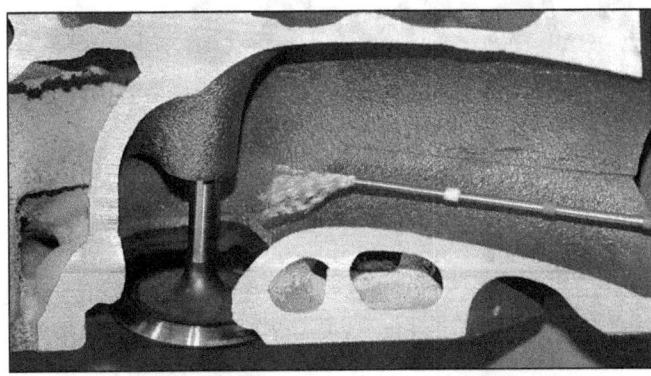

A small flow ball is used to see how the air moving into a carburetor venturi is affected.

This flow wand is indicating high-speed flow approaching the valve.

As indicated, the flow makes the turn over the short-side radius directly toward the valve throat. Careful observation of the wand activity can indicate the smoothness of the turn over the radius and the degree of disruption around the valvestem.

Ideally, you're looking for similar flow characteristics around the entire circumference of the venturi opening.

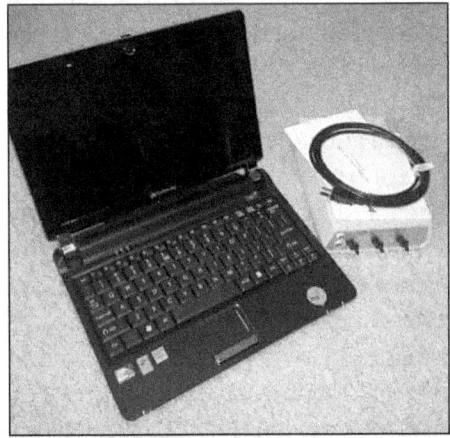

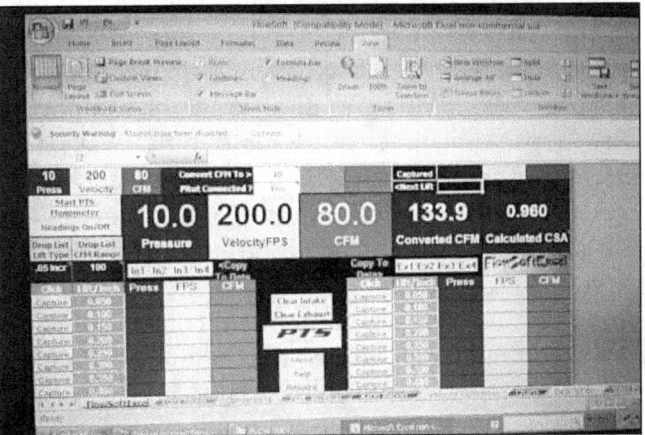

The Flowsoft program displays pressure, velocity, CFM, corrections, calculated cross section, and more to give a complete picture of port activity. (Photo Courtesy Smithberg Racing)

Nick Smithberg uses a PTS digital manometer with his Saenz flow bench. It ports data directly to his laptop in a special Excel file. (Photo Courtesy Smithberg Racing)

CHAPTER 9

PRACTICAL APPLICATIONS

The information discussed in the preceding chapters applies across the board to all performance engines. Air doesn't change its behavior, so your best bet is to understand thoroughly how it responds when passing through an engine and apply that knowledge to prepping the flow path for optimal results.

You've learned that increasing velocity and transferred air mass are, for the most part, more important than swirl and tumble as the air mass enters the cylinder. This is particularly true in a high-speed race engine for which increasing RPM leaves less and less cylinder-filling time per cycle. You discovered that air hates to change direction and is highly sensitive to changes in area and volume. I have covered the role of pressure waves within the flow path and you understand how they influence the performance and efficiency of both the filling and emptying cycles. I have discussed how airflow is influenced by the boundary layer and how it responds to textured surfaces. And I have examined the seven engine cycles and noted the importance of intake ramming, exhaust pumping, and overlap.

Your task now is to apply this knowledge to planning, designing, and constructing effective airflow paths that are best suited to specific applications based on engine speed and the distribution of torque and power within the required power band. It can be a difficult process because most builders use off-the-shelf parts that are essentially a compromise for packaging and marketing purposes. The bulk of these early planning efforts entails determining the optimum dimensions for each section of the flow path and then selecting or fabricating suitable components.

Many of you have the talent and wherewithal to fabricate some of these pieces yourselves, at least when it comes to headers and maybe intake manifolds for specific applications. For those who can't, hundreds of talented fabricators and machinists around the country can fashion one-off pieces to your exact dimensions or modify existing manifolds as required.

And of course, specialty shops can build sheet-metal intakes and other components to your specifications. Many of these shops are also head specialists that can port your heads and properly match components. If you require a specialized application, such as a one-off individual runner EFI intake for an early Hemi or Buick V-8, for example, dedicated specialty fabricators, such as Smithberg Racing in Nebraska, can get the job done. An increasing number of street and drag racing projects require custom manifolds and it has become a rapidly growing specialty industry.

Begin with a Software Program

One of the most intuitive ways to plan your engine is to use one of the many available engine-modeling programs, such as Engine Pro, Dynomation, Engine Analyzer, or PipeMax. These are, for the most part, PC-based engine simulation programs designed to predict a power curve and the associated parameters based on user input of specific components and dimensions.

Some, such as PipeMax, provide the ideal range of component dimensions for optimal wave tuning and they are remarkably accurate for minimal cost. They predict trends based on known factors and their desktop utility allows you to try unlimited combinations to determine the optimal combination digitally. Thus you avoid the considerable expense of purchasing

CHAPTER 9

Engine Masters Challenge Hemi Intake

All photos courtesy Smithberg Racing

This intake system for a 385-ci early Chrysler Hemi was built by Nick Smithberg for the 2012 Engine Masters Challenge. An inspired team of very competent competitors including well-known names such as John Beck, Gene Adams, Bob Holmes, Bob Walker, Ron Pratt, Scott Clark, Nick Smithberg, and Elaine Miller contributed to complete the engine and enter it as a tribute to their friend Dan Miller who died from a heart attack while the engine was being planned.

The rules of the competition presented special conditions that required dyno pulls from 3,500 to 7,500 rpm. To win the competition the engine has to produce max torque everywhere in the RPM range. While the others handled the basic engine package Smithberg took on the challenge of making the engine perform like a champ across the required range.

A Hot Heads intake manifold was joined with a Hilborn four-port injector unit converted for use with electronic fuel injection. Considerable time was spent determining the proper injector angle to match the mechanical layout of the system. In a massive undertaking of brainstorming and machine work Smithberg essentially created a complete individual runner setup inside the Hot Heads manifold. The plenum was epoxied and topped with a plate that separated the induction path for each cylinder. The Hilborn unit was modified with tediously created throttle plates that blend into a plate that bisects the four-port unit along the axis of the throttle shaft.

This unit was topped with a superb set of airhorn stacks with the divider wall extending into the four-port unit on the bottom and the stacks on the top with the throttle plates in the

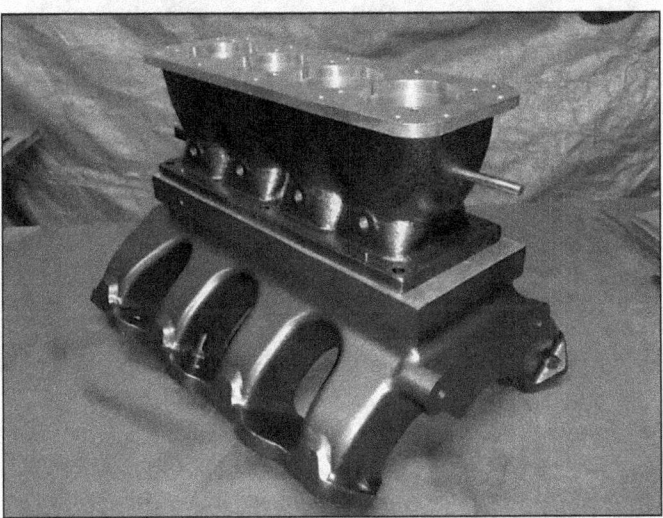

The Hot Heads intake manifold had a Hilborn four-port throttle body on top. It conceals the high degree of internal modification to convert the system to individual runners.

The 385-ci Hemi engine that stunned the competition at the 2012 Engine Masters Challenge incorporated this complex induction system to take maximum advantage of inlet wave tuning.

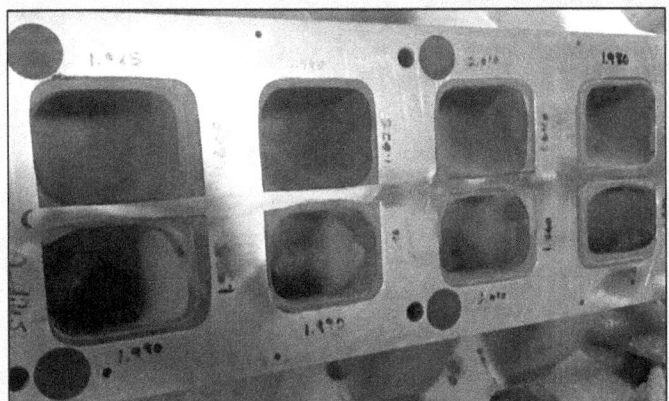

Smithberg epoxied the plenum and ported it to achieve individual runners that matched up to the machined plate attached to the top. The new runners effectively created eight individual flow paths, one for each cylinder. Runner lengths and cross sections were sized to optimize wave tuning.

middle. Lest we forget, this whole exercise is about optimizing airflow into the engine by overcoming existing obstacles. Cross talk between the runners seriously affected the tune so the IR setup was conceived to correct it and it is reinforced by the EFI system that can tune individual cylinders for best performance.

All this effort generated a close second-place finish with 2,456.1 points in the 2012 EMC Street Division. The engine delivered a strong 689 hp at 7,200 rpm with a maximum of 572 ft-lbs of torque at 5,500 rpm. It had 414 ft-lbs at 3,500 rpm, leaping past 500 at 4,500 rpm, and carrying well above that all the way up. This performance reinforces the utility and benefit of constructing a proper IR system designed to take maximum advantage of wave tuning via runner length, cross section and separation of interference pulses in the inlet tract.

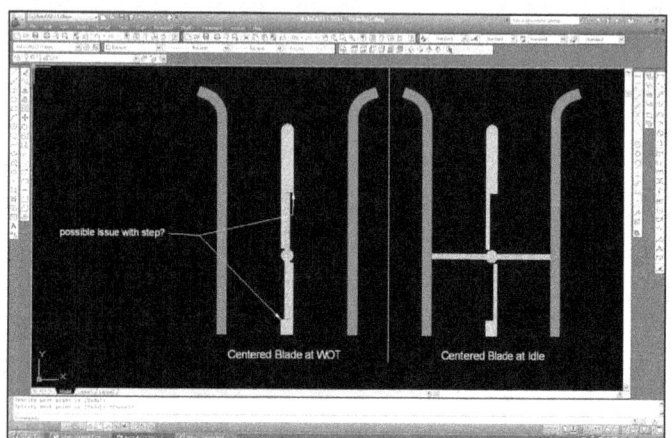

Initial design elements displayed the working mechanism inside the four-port injector housing. Red indicates the throttle bores, teal the divider plates and green the throttle plates. The right side shows the throttle plate position at idle and the left side shows how the throttle plate merges into the divider plate when fully open to create a completely divided system individually serving each cylinder bank.

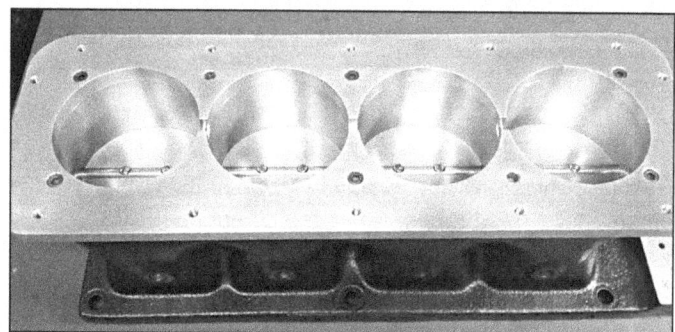

This top view of the Hilborn four-port injector unit reveals the central location of the four large throttle plates fitted to a common throttle shaft.

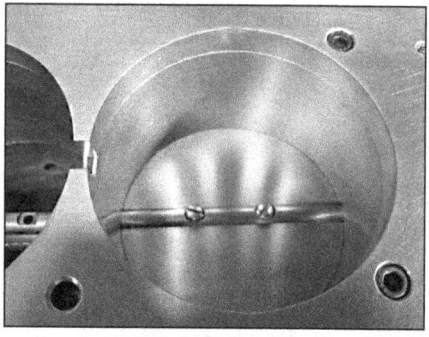

The notch on the left helped center and anchor the center divider plate.

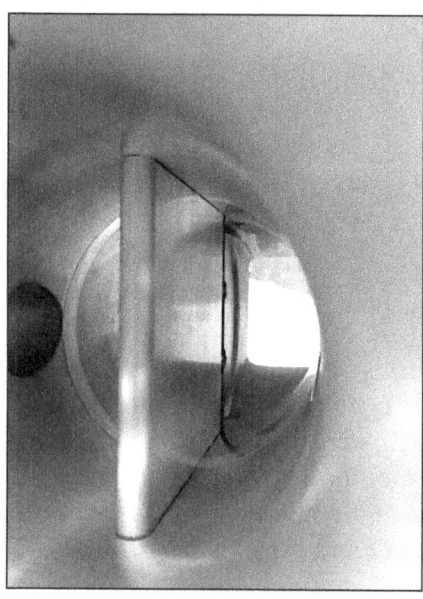

Looking down the injector stack and through the bottom of the Hilborn unit you can see the top and bottom dividers with the open throttle blade captured between them to provide a smooth airway.

Smithberg made the individual injector stack from solid billet, which required careful machining to make them all the same.

CHAPTER 9

Engine Masters Challenge Hemi Intake CONTINUED

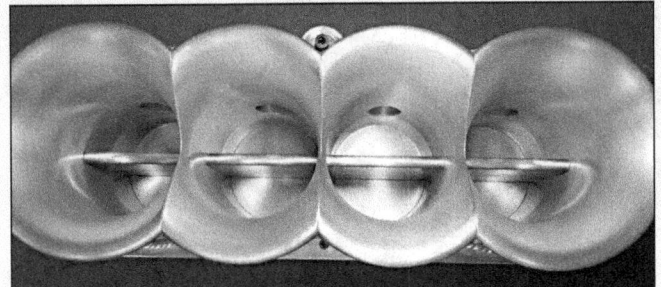

This view with the stacks installed shows the central divider wall. Holes in the sides of the stack were incorporated while evaluating the best possible injector location.

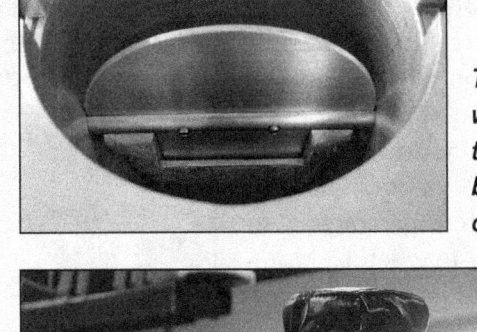

The split divider walls captured the throttle blades when open.

An early test fit. Note that both the Hilborn unit and the stacks have provisions for mechanical injectors. EFI via port injection was subsequently determined to be the best approach.

This view shows the EFI injector angle in the intake runner as it was modified after the competition so the engine could see street duty in Bob Walker's street rod. The competition version placed the electronic injectors in the tall injector stacks to take advantage of the cooling effect of the high-speed air.

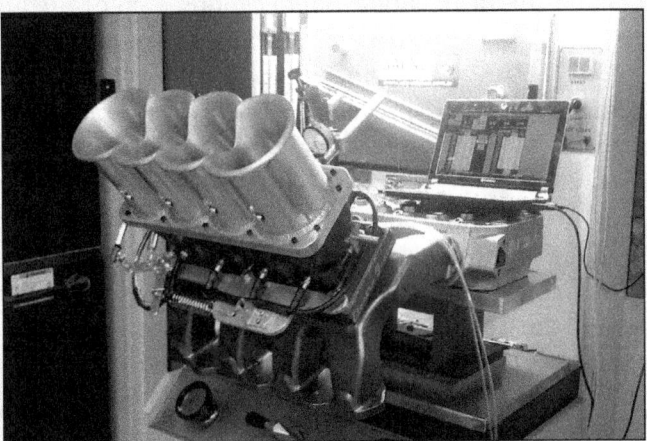

Extensive flow testing was conducted with the complete assembly attached to the head with the goal of balanced flow in each cylinder.

Here is the final version as run at the Engine Masters Challenge competition.

142   PRACTICAL ENGINE AIRFLOW

components that may or may not work to your advantage.

Based on mathematical models and known science, these programs calculate the piston air demand and simulate engine performance with remarkable accuracy. You can model an infinite number of combinations and mix-and-match parameters to find the best possible setup. Moreover, the process is intuitive and easy to perform with only moderate computer skills. Once you have determined the airflow requirements based on engine size, RPM range, and application, you can begin to consider specific components.

Piston tops and camshaft events also contribute to airflow with regard to how they affect air movement with the overall trend moving strongly toward flat-top pistons, fast-burn chambers, and ever higher valve-lift specs. But most modifications to the airflow path center primarily on entry and exit components such as carburetors, intake manifolds, heads, and exhaust headers.

The information in this chapter concentrates on some of the most common application-driven mods, which are largely dictated by intake manifold requirements and the ability to feed more air to the engine.

Software Sources and Products

Audie Technlogies Engine Expert
Motion Software DeskTop Dyno 5, DynoSim 5, Dynomation 5
Performance Trends, Inc. Engine Analyzer, Engine Analyzer Plus, Engine Analyzer Pro, Compression Ratio, Fuel Injector Calculator, Rotating Inertia Calculator, Engine Build Log
Pipe Max PipeMax
Meaux Racing Heads Exhaust Simulation
ProRacing Sim Desktop Dyno 5, DynoSim 5, Dynomation 5, DragSim 5
Racing Systems Analysis Engine Pro, Quarter, Quarter Jr., Bonneville Pro, Density

Air Filters

The air filter is almost always a significant restriction so it is one of the first things you have to consider. If you're a drag racer, you are likely not running a filter, but rather a scoop that tends to pressurize the intake as speed increases; a useful quality. Most other applications require a filter and it is essential to provide enough flow area to move the necessary amount of air.

Street cars can use the traditional 14 x 3–inch filter offered by most manufacturers because they spend most of their time at lower engine speeds and the typical high-performance filter does pretty well up to 6,000 rpm or so. On engines that have a higher air demand, racers often stack filters to increase the area. And manufacturers such as K&N make larger filters to accommodate these requirements.

For most applications, you definitely want to run a filter with adequate clearance between the top of the air cleaner and the top of the carburetor vent tubes. One added benefit of running a filter is its tendency to straighten the airflow and reduce turbulence prior to making the turn into the carburetor.

Carburetors and Throttle Bodies

Once electronic fuel injection became the predominant fueling strategy in production cars and slowly began penetrating the aftermarket, carburetor science suddenly surged. We noticed a renaissance of performance upgrades not previously deemed necessary in mainstream production carburetors. As the main engine throttling devices, carburetors and throttle bodies are chosen primarily for their airflow ratings. To ensure optimum performance, carburetors (and throttle bodies) are typically selected to provide sufficient airflow at max power and engine speed with the smallest possible throttle bores to ensure good airspeed, crisp throttle response, and effective fuel atomization.

Throttle bodies are also sized according to predicted engine air demands, but they are typically larger with only a single butterfly because they are only moving air (for EFI applications); the injectors provide fuel atomization. It can become complicated because many versions are available depending on the individual EFI or carburetion requirements. Some applications might require extra-sharp throttle response at lower engine speeds while others forgo it because they leave the starting line at 7,000 rpm and run wide open through a narrow range of engine speed. Several decades ago this bred a cottage industry of carburetor modifiers that eventually evolved into a strong and vibrant industry.

Although carburetor specialists have their tricks and favorite mods to improve airflow in a particular carburetor, most of them now concentrate on circuit and booster modifications to alter fuel delivery according to the performance requirements of specific applications. Many modifications first implemented by carb tuners have now been integrated into production carburetors from Holley, and the Demon Carburetor line was an early contributor to increasing carburetor sophistication.

Although circuit modifications are critically important to proper carburetor function, here you are more interested in airflow characteristics and modifications. To increase performance you have to flow more air and supply it with fuel to burn. So what kind of modifications do carb tuners perform to get the most efficient airflow out of any particular carburetor? Typically, they work with different boosters, air horn and air-entry mods, butterflies, and in some cases additional modifications to the throttle bores.

You can use a larger carburetor, but that might sacrifice essential airspeed and response. Hence larger venturis and throttle bores do not always guarantee a performance gain. Adding a second carburetor may help. As seen on many higher-performance engines with tunnel ram manifolds, increasing airflow and relocating the carburetors directly over the manifold runners can add 20 to 30 hp. That's not always possible and you are mostly concerned with modifications made to a single Holley carburetor to increase airflow.

Because of the wide range of available carburetor configurations in the aftermarket it has become easier to achieve the required airflow to match engine demand. As such, performance carburetors that already incorporate the necessary mods have replaced most typical airflow mods. So, most modifications tend to focus on matching the fuel curve to the engine's demand as sensed by the pressure drop in the boosters.

The most desirable trait is to maintain airspeed even as the current trend is toward larger carburetors. Although circuit modifications can accomplish a lot in matching the fuel curve to the engine's requirements, other areas need to be addressed to ensure maximum airflow and good pressure recovery exiting the throttle bores. One of them is post-carburetor effect, accomplished by adjusting plenum volume, carb spacer configuration, and discharge angles.

With throttle bodies, you are not concerned with creating a pressure drop in a booster to establish fuel flow. With electronics, it is considerably simpler to maintain a proper fuel curve under almost any conditions.

Still, throttle bodies do benefit from smooth entry gradients. When the big butterfly snaps open you essentially have full atmospheric pressure in the plenum and the runners. In a sense, the throttle body still emulates a venturi as pressure drops while passing through it, but it is nothing like the pressure change in a carburetor venturi and booster.

Race applications can accept the large throttle opening because they operate at elevated engine speeds. Street systems still incorporate smaller throttle bodies and most aftermarket EFI systems still emulate a 4-barrel throttle body arrangement that helps ensure high vacuum and good velocity at lower speeds.

Intake Manifolds

Of all the components that make up the airflow path, the intake manifold represents the broadest variable in terms of type, shape, size, and overall configuration. Not surprisingly, intake manifolds are the one component constantly subject to modification and change. Variations have been made to accept two, four, six, and even eight carburetors in some cases and that's without mentioning the different types of EFI manifolds and assorted manifolds designed to accommodate superchargers and individual runner setups.

The point was simply to add more carburetors to increase airflow. So intakes were designed to accept multiple carburetors without much thought to the size, shape, and configuration of plenums and runner lengths. Although the dynamic principles were already well known to the aircraft industry, it wasn't until the 1960s that manifold designers began to display obvious concern for equalizing flow path dimensions, incorporating proper plenum sizing, and creating a more direct approach to the cylinder head ports.

As discussed in Chapter 4, the primary focus of intake modifications is to equalize flow through properly dimensioned runners that are well matched to the cylinder head ports. Most applications deal with three

---

Typical Airflow Mods

These modifications are typical for most carburetor builders striving for more airflow:

- Remove choke horn on choke-equipped carburetors
- Reshape the air horn and venturi entries
- Reshape the venturis
- Reshape the boosters for optimal flow and jet sensitivity
- Streamline the throttle shafts
- Minimize butterfly screw interference
- Align the throttle plates for optimal flow

basic manifold types: dual-plane intakes, single-plane intakes, and variations of a tunnel ram. In many cases a better mousetrap is available for those who wish to pursue building or commissioning a custom manifold. This is particularly true for vintage engines where the benefit of modern science can add more muscle.

Performance Influences

As previously described, manifold configuration and sizing has a profound influence on performance. One venue where this is particularly apparent is the annual Engine Masters Challenge. Here, purpose-built dyno engines are pitted against each other under difficult rules and performance requirements. Although not necessarily representative of real-world applications, these engines are forced to build as much torque as possible over an exceptionally broad power band. They typically run 6,500 to 7,000 rpm and they have to start their dyno pull as low as 2,000 rpm. So it is difficult to build for a typical performance application where the low end is so tough to accommodate.

Builders try to run optimal compression ratios dictated by pump gas, and the engines tend to detonate severely when loaded at such a low engine speed. To address this, manifold ports are often reduced in size with epoxy to help maintain airspeed and good mixture quality to resist detonation under high load and low RPM.

Specialty manifold manufacturers offer purpose-built sheet-metal racing manifolds and detailed modifications. Sheet-metal intakes are built and sized specifically for each application. Commercial manifolds are tweaked for more performance by altering plenum shapes and sizes, modifying and realigning runner entry and port entry angles, port matching, and modifying to incorporate nitrous oxide injection or port fuel injection.

Custom Manifold Projects

Another area of interest is the demand for custom manifolds to fit vintage and muscle car engines that are stepping up their game. Many of these adaptations require considerable work and expertise to realize a functional component that performs better than anything else available. One popular application is to adapt a contemporary 4-barrel single-plane intake to an early Hemi.

The following projects incorporate considerable cutting, welding, porting, and other modifications to suit very specific applications. They illustrate the broad variety of modifications currently being applied to intake manifolds and include a look at the ever-growing trend of building custom manifolds from scratch and/or modifying existing manifolds to fit different engines where no current version exists. Among the projects is an IR port injection setup for a 409-based engine and a conversion of a Mopar 440 aluminum 4-barrel intake manifold, also to fit a 409.

Edelbrock makes a great dual-plane for these applications and as you know, a dual-plane is hard to beat for max torque on the street. GM W-engines have enjoyed a robust resurgence in recent years and with more of them being raced on the dragstrip, racers have clamored for a single-plane intake that revs higher and makes more power upstairs without sacrificing too much mid-range torque.

Bruneau Performance in Alberta, Canada, recently released two single-plane 4-barrel intake manifolds for the 348/409-based GM W-engines. They have proved to work very well, but racers are never satisfied, hence another project is Smithberg Racing's conversion of a Mopar 440 single-plane intake to accommodate a larger displacement drag engine. You will also see some home-built mods by other Canadian racers who built their own high-port 409 heads with tunnel ram intake.

Also included are a single 4-barrel, single-plane manifold being converted for duty on a Chrysler Hemi and a special one-off four-port inline conversion for a Chrysler Hemi used in the Engine Masters Shootout. Nick Smithberg points out that when making these one-off conversions, it's important to accomplish more than just making a different manifold fit the engine. You can do that and make the engine run tolerably well for a cruiser. But for a racing or high-performance engine the core ingredients of runner cross section and length, plenum size, and a direct flow path must still serve the application with the necessary science. So these adaptations are carefully thought out on paper to ensure that the difficult and labor-intensive efforts will realize a final component that indeed improves performance.

Cylinder Heads

Many racers are satisfied with purchasing off-the-shelf hardware for their performance needs, and a broad range of these cylinder heads is currently available. This approach works well for many people. Still, head porters continue to enjoy a brisk business by wringing that last bit of performance out of whatever cylinder heads you might bring them.

CHAPTER 9

Defining the Performance Package

You may have wondered, "Why do the technicians always want to know my tire size, gear ratio, transmission ratios, and all that other stuff when I am just trying to order a cam or heads and a manifold? Why don't they just give me what I ask for?"

They usually will if you insist, but it makes them look bad if the final mix doesn't perform well because it is improperly matched. The math will never support the results if you get the wrong stuff.

The overriding concern is to keep the engine in its power band at all times. It all boils down to combination, combination, and combination. The techs seek to optimize your combination and in some cases provide a crutch for a bad combination that you may have described.

For example, if any of the gear ratios in your transmission cause the engine to drop out of its power band on a shift, the engine momentarily struggles to get back on its game and you lose the race. So they're looking at the percentage drops with each ratio and what that does to your engine speed and the known power band. They may recommend a smaller or longer primary tube and a smaller collector on the headers. Their experience helps them determine whether the intake or the exhaust side can best carry the car through a bad spot and whether there is a happy medium that optimizes for existing hardware even though it might not be the ideal combination.

Although it doesn't always translate perfectly, it's a big help if you have existing dyno numbers and data acquisition from the car for them to study. It helps them understand the positioning and range of your power curve and how the torque is positioned around the peak. So, rather than being annoyed by those questions, strive to give them every last bit of information possible.

Cam techs and the like are well schooled and have a lot of experience. If they don't agree with the cam or the header specs you're asking for, there's likely a good reason. Instead, what they offer will almost always serve you better by moving your combination closer to the ideal and minimizing any drawbacks within the system. ∎

Many high-end race shops, including Reher-Morrison, offer signature-series cylinder heads designed for specific applications. When you are dealing with them you are assured of a top-quality head with generally superior performance. Advancements in cylinder head technology have incorporated most of the major performance features known to improve power.

Some racers follow a common path with intake manifolds by adapting cylinder heads to suit their needs. This practice is seen in motorcycle racing, drag racing, and frequently at Bonneville. The most common modifications include adapting better flowing late-model heads to an engine for which the cylinder bore spacing closely approximates that of the engine block and the proposed head swap. Quite frequently, the upgrade is done to adapt newer four-valve-per-cylinder heads to earlier engines originally equipped with two-valve heads. The intent, as always, is to gain performance by improving the airflow path on engines for which no suitable component is available.

The Exhaust Side

There are many ways to select, build, and tune an exhaust system for your performance engine. Likewise, there are a lot of talented header fabricators and suppliers who can help ensure that your exhaust system fully supports the extensive efforts you have made to move air through the engine. Most specialty header builders have the experience to cut and fit tubing with reasonable precision. For those who don't, a recently introduced method from icengineworks allows you to model the headers in position. You can make sure that they clear all obstacles and provide the precision performance you require.

This header modeling system is extraordinarily useful for applications where spec headers don't easily fill the bill. The 1-inch segmented pieces snap together and swivel to let you form even the most difficult shapes. Their utility for specialty applications is unmatched and they help you ensure equal length by using the same number of segments on each primary. The curved radius pieces are also 1 inch long at the centerline.

Once you know the necessary length and tube diameter, you can model and remodel until you get it just right for the optimum fitment of the engine in your particular chassis. Accompanying components then allow you to mark and disassemble the model for easy transfer to metal tubing.

Some header fabricators have not been quick to embrace this method because they view it as extra work. Those who have largely relate that it has improved their designs.

PRACTICAL APPLICATIONS

Cal Automotive Customs 409 Hybrid Intake Manifold

All photos courtesy Smithberg Racing

Smithberg Racing loves to tackle challenging projects. Here's another one for a 1961 Impala going together at Cal Automotive Creations in Bennington, Nebraska. This car features a 509-ci 409-based engine. The shop was looking for a unique induction system to fit under the hood and still deliver eye-popping power on demand. Nick Smithberg was up for the gig.

The engine sits high in the car and hood clearance is an issue. Bob Thrash at Cal Automotive did the initial sketch to set the parameters. Following that it was up to Nick Smithberg to make it all work. He is still striving to achieve the ideal length and cross section for this performance application while accommodating the unique requirements of a show car setup.

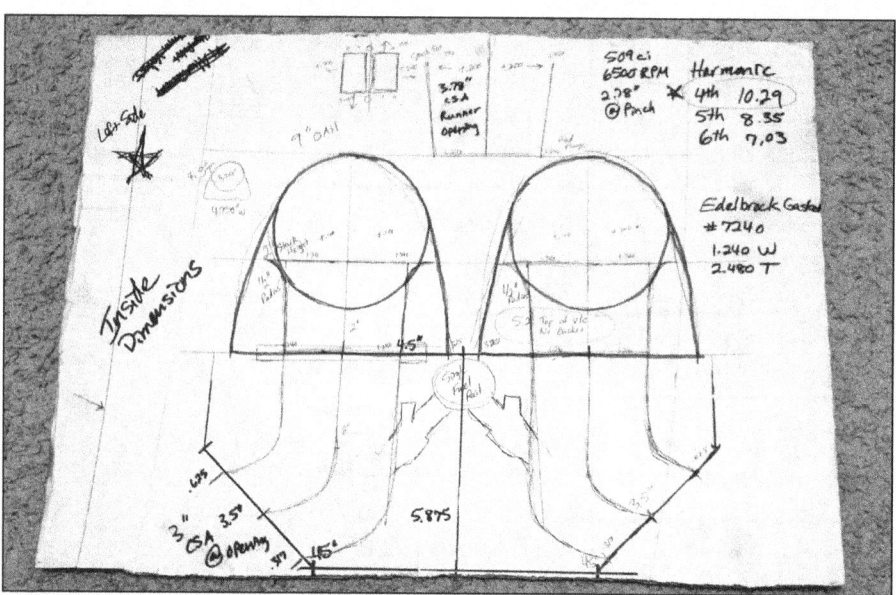

After careful measurements this sketch was used as the basis for developing the custom intake system. Note that it calls for a 9-inch overall height and includes all pertinent dimensions along with the calculated harmonics. Due to the packaging restraints Smithberg had to target the fourth wave, which is slightly less ideal than the third wave, but still in the ball park.

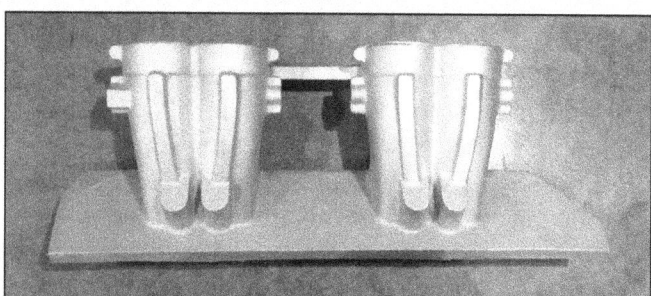

Hilborn raw injector castings for a big-block Chevy served as the base runners for this build.

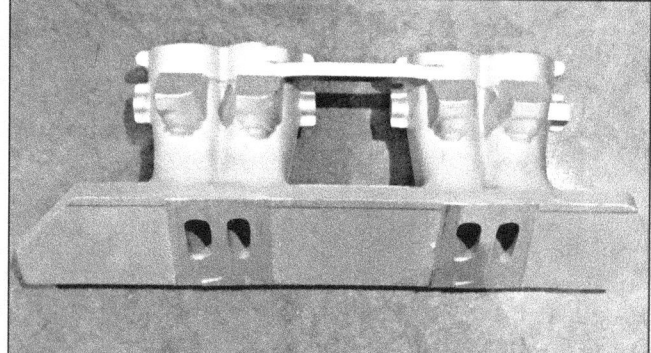

The Hilborn castings were selected for their shape and similarity in bore spacing to the 409-base engine. It was also important because the unported casting left plenty of meat for custom port placement.

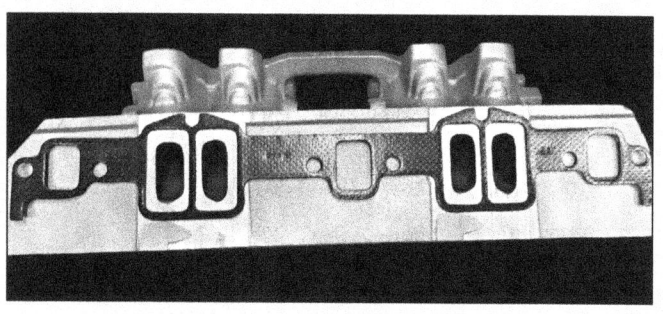

With an intake gasket in position, note the amount of material left for porting. This allowed Smithberg to target the ideal runner cross section and the taper from the large openings on the top.

PRACTICAL ENGINE AIRFLOW

Cal Automotive Customs 409 Hybrid Intake Manifold *CONTINUED*

The initial trial fit on the engine gave assurances that this system could provide the desired dimensions and finished characteristics for the project.

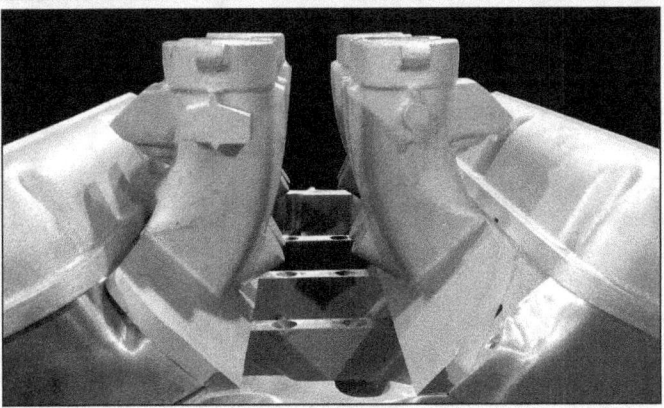

It is easy to see that the big-block injector manifolds are nearly ideal for this application. The fit is precise and there is room for a central fuel rail.

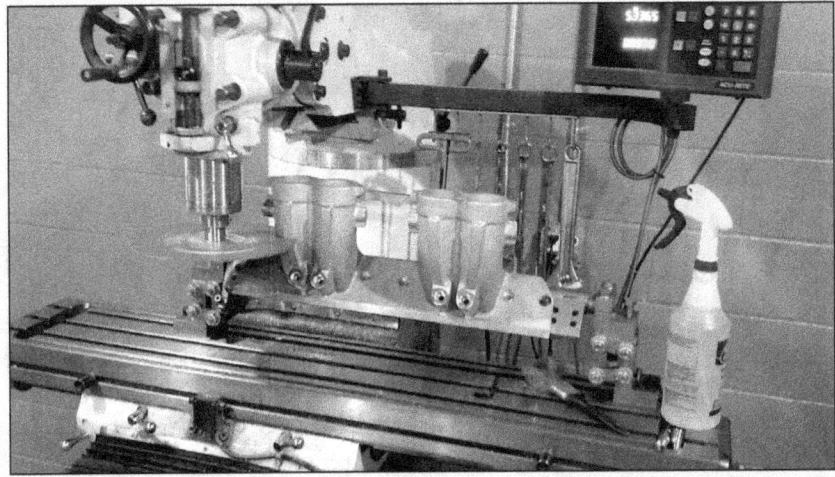

After determining the correct height, Nick cut off the housing tops to make room for the plenum base plate.

Next to the ported cylinder head you can see how the manifold runners can be positioned to accommodate the common wall between the ports. From there it is a matter of basic port matching while maintaining the calculated cross section.

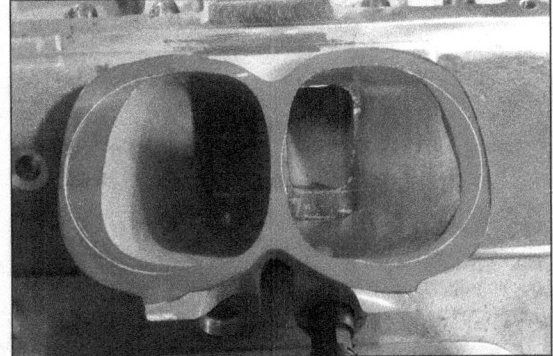

It's not so pretty on the upper end. Filling and judicious porting are required to turn this mismatch into one continuous port with the correct taper and cross section.

A central fuel rail was also desired to add to the clean functionality of this high end hot rod.

PRACTICAL APPLICATIONS

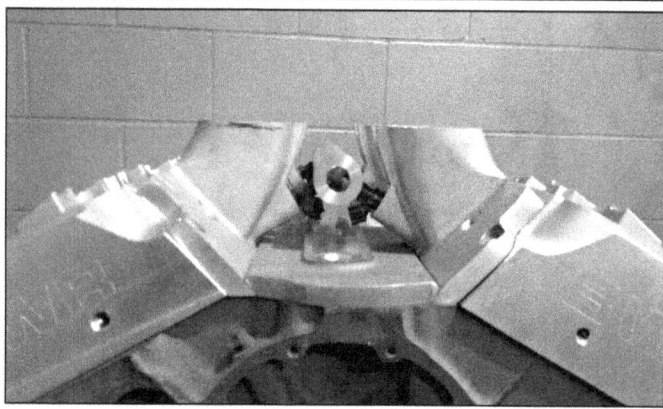

Some initial cuts were made to align the manifolds with the top of the block and prepare them to accept the valley plate.

The valley plate locks under one side to help align the distributor. The plate was adjusted fore and aft and sideways for best alignment, then all the ends were machined to pretty it up.

The distributor hole was remachined to accept and align the modern distributor.

The injector flanges were sport faced and fuel injector holes were drilled into each boss on the correct port centerline.

Injectors were installed at the precise location to intersect the central fuel rail.

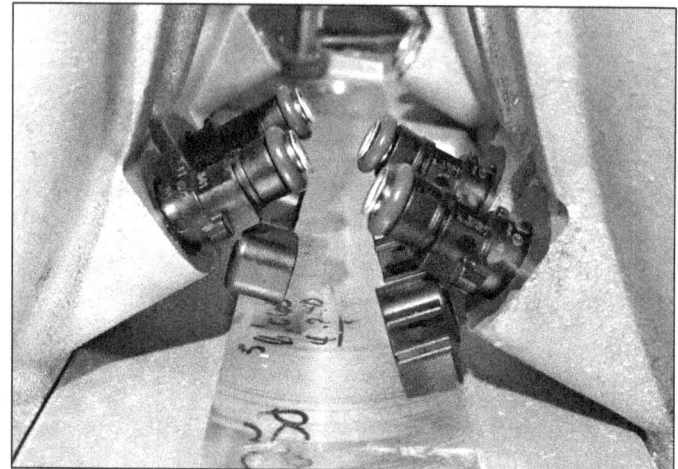

Precise measurements were required to match the feed holes in the fuel rail to the injector tips in place on the manifold.

Cal Automotive Customs 409 Hybrid Intake Manifold CONTINUED

The completed system incorporated internal stacks to add runner length.

The base of the plenum air box accepted the four custom pairs of runner stacks to complete the tuned length. They bolted through the air box and attached to the runner beneath.

Nick machined these custom radius tops to complete the stacks. The radius helped to smooth airflow into the runners.

A custom air bonnet will top this setup with provisions for air entry and throttling. The fuel rail and injectors are completely hidden underneath.

CONCLUSION

As reiterated time and again throughout this book, the fundamentals of engine airflow science must be followed to ensure the best possible results and subsequent on-track performance. The most efficient high-velocity path to the cylinder is your goal, along with the most efficient exit. I have covered much of the fundamental principles here and shown you many examples, but it's important to always keep the final application in sight.

Consult only with knowledgeable people. If a fellow racer tells you that a particular component or modification is the baddest thing ever and he can't explain how or why, it may only be the baddest thing *he's* ever seen.

Most of all think hard about how well your component recipe matches your requirements. If you need more RPM, you need a bigger flow path, but only to the extent that it fills the need without sacrificing velocity. Strive to ensure the best possible intake ramming cycle and consider how carb size and placement as well as plenum size affect what you're doing. And make sure your exhaust system is fully complementary.

You begin and end with atmospheric pressure and there are many pressure changes in between that have to be appropriately managed. It's been described as "breathe, squeeze, pop, exhale," but there's a massive amount of science going on in there and, for the most part, it is not difficult to grasp. You can accomplish a great deal without knowing or applying a boatload of math. If you can work a tape measure and calculate areas and volumes you're 90 percent there already. Plus, software can help with the rest so you can talk intelligently with machinists about what you need.

You can't go wrong when working with any of the top manufacturers and head porters. But keep in mind that there are lots of local people including head porters, engine builders, and fabricators who are very capable. If they're in business you can be pretty sure that they know airflow. In today's results-driven business, the old grind-and-shine approach just doesn't do it anymore. If they

No air cleaner here, but a sizeable air hat to feed the blown beast. For best performance blown applications require plenty of filter airflow capacity, or none at all as shown here. Although the study of engine airflow is primarily concerned with naturally aspirated applications, supercharged engines can take advantage of most of the mods used to improve airflow because it typically makes the blower's job easier.

CONCLUSION

can communicate what they propose and it seems compatible with your newfound core knowledge, they can probably serve you well. So don't be afraid to work with those local shops. Many of them are surprisingly savvy.

One cautionary word about Internet forums: There are very knowledgeable people on some of them and they genuinely intend to answer questions and be of help. I think the forum at Speedtalk.com is the best source of good information, and you're also in good hands at maxracesoftwares.com.

But some forums are quagmires of bad information. They are packed with keyboard commandos intent on showing everyone how smart they are about the subject without really participating in a useful discussion that raises everyone's knowledge base. Just be careful, and don't take everything at face value.

SOURCE GUIDE

Air Flow Research
28611 W. Industry Dr.
Valencia, CA, 91355
877-892-8844

Audie Technologies
23 N. Trooper Rd.
Norristown, PA 19403
610-630-5895
audietech.com

Brodix Cylinder Heads
301 Maple Ave.
Mena, AR 71953
479-394-1075
brodix.com

Dart Machinery
353 Oliver Dr.
Troy, MI 48084
248-362-1188
dartheads.com

Darrin Morgan Cylinder Heads
1120 Enterprise Pl.
Arlington, TX 76001
817-467-7171
rehermorrison.com

Edelbrock
2700 California St.
Torrance, CA 90503
310-781-2222
edelbrock.com

Jamison Equipment
1908 11th St.
Emmetsburg, IA 50536
800-841-5405
jamisonequipment.com

Meaux Racing Heads
9827 Hwy. 343
Abbeville, LA 70510
337/652-6220
maxracesoftware.com

Performance Trends
P.O. Box 530164
Livonia, MI 48153
248-473-9230
performancetrends.com

Pro-Filer Performance Products
P.O. Box 217
New Carlisle, OH 45344
937-846-1333
profilerperformance.com

ProRacing Sim
535 W. Lambert, Bldg. E
Brea, CA 92821
901-259-2355
proracingsim.com

PTS Flowbench Technology
260 N. Line Rd.
Stevens, PA 17578
717-951-6558
flowbenchtech.com

Racing Head Service
3416 Democrat Rd.
Memphis, TN 38118
901-259-1134
racingheadsercicce.com

Racing Systems Analysis
racingsecrets.com

Reher-Morrison Racing Engines
1120 Enterprise Pl.
Arlington, TX 76001
817-467-7171
rehermorrison.com

Smithberg Racing
1901 Clay St.
Fort Calhoun, NE 68023
402-616-7643
smithber.ipower.com

Saenz
1908 11th St.
Emmetsburg, IA 50536
800-841-5405
flowbench-saenz.com

SuperFlow Corporation
4747 Centennial Blvd.
Colorado Springs, CO 80919
719-471-1746
superflow.com

TAP Plastics
800-246-5055
tapplastics.com

Thorpe Engine Development
1110 Crow Bench Rd.
Orofino, ID 83544-5155
208-476-7572
thorpedev.com

Trick Flow Specialties
285 West Ave.
Tallmadge, OH 44278
330-630-1555
trickflow.com

U.S. Composites
6670 White Dr.
West Palm Beach, FL 33407
561-588-1001
uscomposites.com

Wilson Manifolds
4700 N.E. 11 Ave.
Ft. Lauderdale, FL 33334
954-771-6216
wilsonmanifolds.com

Additional books that may interest you...

MODERN ENGINE BLUEPRINTING TECHNIQUES: A Practical Guide To Precision Engine Building by Mike Mavrigian Expert engine builder and veteran author Mike Mavrigian includes engine building techniques and detailed procedures so the engine is perfectly balanced, matched, and optimized. Balancing and blueprinting is a time-consuming and exacting process, but the investment in time pays off with superior performance. Through the process, you carefully measure, adjust, machine, and fit each part together with precision tolerances, optimizing the design and maximizing performance. This book covers the block, crankshaft, connecting rods, pistons, cylinder heads, intake manifolds, camshaft, measuring tools, and final assembly techniques. Softbound, 8.5 x 11 inches, 176 pages, 500 color photos. *Item # SA251*

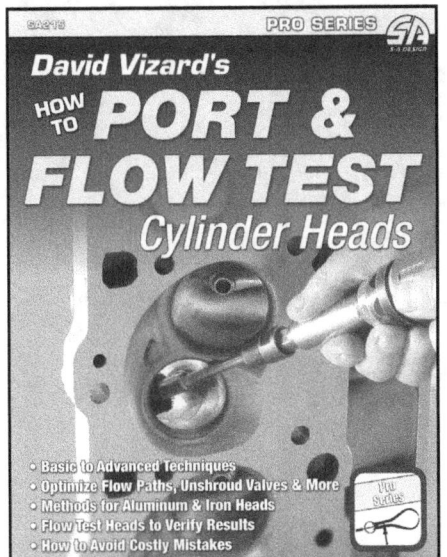

DAVID VIZARD'S HOW TO PORT & FLOW TEST CYLINDER HEADS by David Vizard This is the only book ever published covering the specific techniques of head building and porting. It provides insight and instruction for maximizing performance of engine heads. All the aspects of porting stock as well as aftermarket heads in aluminum and cast-iron constructions are covered. David Vizard goes into great depth and detail on porting aftermarket heads. Starting with the basic techniques up to more advanced techniques, you are shown how to port iron and aluminum heads, plus the benefits of hand and CNC porting. Crucial instruction is provided to help prevent major mistakes that could ruin the heads. Softbound, 8.5 x 11 inches, 160 pages, 400 color photos. *Item # SA215*

PERFORMANCE AUTOMOTIVE ENGINE MATH by John Baechtel When designing or building an automotive engine for improved performance, it's all about the math. From measuring the engine's internal capacities to determine compression ratio to developing the optimal camshaft lift, duration, and overlap specifications, the use of proven math is the only way to design an effective high-performance automotive powerplant. Author John Baechtel reviews the proper tools and measurement techniques, and carefully defines the procedures and equations used in engineering high-efficiency and high-RPM engines. This book goes into great detail on the subject and how to use the data acquired to make more power and improve engine durability and reliability. Softbound, 8.5 x 11 inches, 160 pages, 350 color photos. *Item # SA204*

DAVID VIZARD'S HOW TO BUILD HORSEPOWER by David Vizard Extracting maximum torque and horsepower from engines is an art as well as a science. David Vizard is an engineer and, more aptly, an engine building artist who guides you through all the aspects of power production and high-performance engine building. The book explains how to optimize all the components in between, such as selecting heads for maximum flow or porting heads for superior power output, ideal valvetrain components, realizing the ideal rocker arm ratios for a particular application, secrets for selecting the best cam, and giving unique insight into all facets of cam performance. His proven high-performance engine building methods and techniques are revealed. Softbound, 8.5 x 11 inches, 144 pages, 350 color photos. *Item # SA24*

www.cartechbooks.com or 1-800-551-4754

www.ingramcontent.com/pod-product-compliance
Lightning Source LLC
Chambersburg PA
CBHW081449070526
44586CB00019B/2284